Understanding the

BIBLE

Before Reading It

UNDERSTANDING THE
BIBLE
BEFORE READING IT

ALAN W. HAYDEN

SOUL WINNER
Ministry

First Edition

Understanding the Bible Before Reading It

Copyright © 2023 Alan W. Hayden

Published by Soul Winner Ministry
For Worldwide Distribution
Paperback ISBN: 978-1-956203-26-4
eBook ISBN: 978-1-956203-27-1
Library of Congress Control Number: 2023935741

Printed in the United States of America.

Book designed by Multimedia Publishing Project
PO Box 50553
Mesa, Arizona 85208
480.939.9689 | MultimediaPublishingProject.com

DEDICATION

THIS BOOK IS DEDICATED TO THE MANY MILLIONS OF PEOPLE WHO HAVE attempted, but failed many times, to read and understand the one and only book God has ever communicated to mankind, the Holy Bible. It is also true many people are sincerely searching for answers to life's meaning. I would wager just about everyone is interested in knowing what is going to happen to them and their loved ones after death, and what will happen to the future of the planet. The Bible not only answers these questions, but does so in a detailed way. The Bible provides answers unknowable from any other source, because the words come from God himself.

People have a sense there is something out there that can help them get answers to their deepest questions, but whatever it is, it continues to escape them. They yearn for a higher purpose for their life, but are stifled as to how they can go about finding it. Most people know about God, but are unable to reconcile their understanding of Christian religious beliefs with reason and science. From their standpoint, faith seems to make no sense.

These same people, whether they realize it or not, are attempting to get closer to the God who created them, and to understand themselves and the world in which they live. A good parallel is to think of them as we would a crying child attempting to get back into the loving arms of its mother. Likewise, they too, whether they realize it or not, yearn to be in the protective love of the One who created them, and protects them.

As you read this book, you will notice the further away from God people get, the more fear, anxiety and worries they experience. On the other hand, the closer to God they get, their fears, anxieties and worries are soon replaced with a quiet, inward, confidence in knowing everything will work out for their good in the end, when they allow God to direct their minds and hearts. This is a promise God has made to all of us, irrespective of the sins we have committed in the past. All sins, past, present, and future, can be forgiven for those who believe. Why? Because the Bible, at its heart, is a redemptive story of love and forgiveness. So, please put aside any preconceived ideas you may have about this great, holy book, and make your best effort to gain the knowledge and wisdom we all need in order to make sense out of the purpose for our lives.

Please don't make the mistake of planning for a physical, dignified retirement, without planning for your eternal retirement!

CONTENTS

FOREWORD

THE BIBLE CAN BE CONFUSING AND INTIMIDATING TO MANY PEOPLE, so they simply just don't bother to read or study it. Some claim it is too long, too confusing, and not relevant to our modern society. Consequently, they go through life without ever understanding the spiritual principles that could protect them from harm, provide real meaning for their life, and show them a way forward that God has already planned for them. This book, which is not intended as a substitute for the Bible itself, acts as a primer by reducing the number of Bible words down to less than ten-percent, for a more manageable read. This is accomplished by focusing on the main points of God's story of redemption. In this way, the reader can obtain many valuable pearls of wisdom in less than fifteen hours of reading. So, for those people who are always on the run, who are too busy to grasp the purpose of why they were born, this book will create a course correction in their life, which will be everlasting. If you are searching for meaning in your life, or confused by what the future will bring, I highly recommend this book for your library. Read it, study it, apply its principles, and then, with the knowledge you gain, you should then study the Bible for yourself as a daily endeavor. Master the principles of the Bible until it masters you!

Pastor Charles Dubbs
East Mesa Christian Church, Mesa, Arizona

THIS BOOK IS A LABOR OF LOVE. IT IS WRITTEN SPECIFICALLY TO HELP THOSE WHO struggle to find time to read and study the Bible, and who find it difficult to understand. They are not sure why it was written and why it should be read. Alan loves the Bible, and he knows how hard it is for some people to understand it. For this reason, he has diligently researched its historical and literary background, in order to make it relevant to modern readers, and because he wants everyone to love and trust Jesus as he does. It shows on every page. I have known Alan for many years, and as his former pastor in Arizona, I can vouch for his love for Jesus Christ. I have read this book and I encourage you to read it also. Maybe you've read the Bible, and maybe you haven't. Either way, this book will help you in understanding the Bible much better. It will also clarify, in a meaningful way, God's plan for the world, and for your special life in it. Maybe you believe in God and maybe you don't. Once again, this book is for you, because its store of knowledge will expand your thinking on the most important subject of all – your life beyond the present one.

Alan is a gifted writer, and he sincerely wants you to know who God is. This book is written to glorify and honor the Lord Jesus Christ (who is God) as our Savior. So, if you don't know Jesus, I pray this book helps you to find him. If you do know Jesus, I pray this book helps you to know him better so you can spend the next eternal life with him.

Senior Pastor Steven R. Speichinger
First Community Church, Hebron, Nebraska

INTRODUCTION

Y EARS AGO, I RECALL A MAN FROM THE "BIBLE BELT" OF THE SOUTH who once said his family always had a beautiful Bible located on the coffee table right in the middle of the living room. Its purpose was to remind the family, in a symbolic way, that their family life centered around the principles of this wonderful, God-created book. Unfortunately for the family, it was never read. They simply had the Bible sit there, year after year, only opening the pages to record a family event such as a wedding, a funeral service, or some other special occasion. Consequently, this man grew up learning about the Bible by listening to Sunday morning Bible classes and then later pulpit sermons, which often bored him. He never actually read and studied the Bible for himself in order to gain the wisdom he needed to understand himself better and to navigate his way in the world that God had created.

As a result, his Christian faith was "paper-thin," and he went on to live his life not really knowing what God wanted to teach him in developing the spiritual side of his own nature. Subsequently, he went on to make many mistakes that might have been avoided, including a marriage turned sour; children not respecting him, and a bumpy road of uncertain finances. He later admitted to never having gained the spiritual growth that would have led him to greater wisdom and understanding of what this very short life is all about. He later came to realize the answers he was seeking were right in front of him all the time he was growing up, tucked away, and captured inside the pages of that beautiful book sitting on his parent's coffee table. How sad!

Today in America, you will find between 600,000 and 1,000,000 new book titles published in any given year. These books cover all types of genres, fiction, and non-fiction, with subjects running the gamut from A to Z. If someone were to read one book per week for the next 50 years, they would read about 2,500 books. The questions then to be asked are, what did they learn, and how much was implemented to improve the quality of their lives? Statistics tell us we lose 50% of our reading retention within one hour of reading; we lose about 70% in the next 24 hours and, in some cases, up to 90% within seven days! This happens because we "read it," but did we really "study it?" The Bible is no different in the sense that it can provide enormous amounts of practical wisdom, offering solutions to everyday problems, but it too must be both read and studied frequently throughout our lives, in order for us to gain from its many benefits. So, over the next 50 years, do we read 2500 books, or do we grasp and master the one divinely inspired book written by God Himself?

Is education upside down?

Today, our "educated" citizens are learning more and more about less and less. They study deep into a narrow subject, such as computer science, for example, but are deficient in knowing about many other subjects that are vital to being a well-rounded individual. Contrast our current educational system with that of the Middle Ages, when to become *liberi*, or freemen, it was necessary for students at universities to master the *trivium*, consisting of grammar, rhetoric, and logic, with the *quadrivium* requiring arithmetic, geometry, astronomy, and music. Later, as universities began forming in America, the emphasis was placed on students mastering the doctrines of Christianity, and this meant spending a great deal of time studying the Bible.

From 1620, when the Pilgrims landed, until about 1837, all education in America was both private and Christian. In the 1636 Harvard University student handbook, for instance, it read: "Let every student be plainly instructed and earnestly pressed to consider well: the main end of his life as a student is to know God, and Jesus Christ, which is eternal life." (John 17:3). Compare the Harvard of 1636 with the Harvard of the 21st century where Christianity is mocked and de-emphasized. It should be noted that the first 100-plus American colleges and universities devoted their education system to ensuring students took the principles of the Bible seriously. They believed in a simple truth: Civil law without a moral compass grounded in biblical concepts is really no law at all!

Interestingly, as you walk around Washington D.C. today, visiting many of its famous sites, you will still find plenty of evidence supporting a belief in God. The Washington Monument, for instance, has a capstone with the Latin phrase, *Laus Deo*, which means "Praise be to God," and many more could be cited. Unfortunately, these inscriptions have become words with little application to the way our government is managed today. Much of this sorry state of affairs can be attributed to a famous U.S. Supreme Court (SCOTUS) case in 1962, when the president of the American Atheists, Madalyn Murray O'Hair, was successful in getting SCOTUS to effectively ban the practice of Bible study in public schools across America. Since then, we have experienced a number of generations of Americans who have been raised without gaining the wisdom of the Bible. Consequently, our country has become metaphorically like a ship without a rudder, tossing around in deep water without any specific plan to get to a safe harbor. We have clearly "lost our moorings."

Increase in ignorance

Mark Twain once said, "We are all ignorant, but about different things." Getting the best university education money can buy will only provide half of an education without an understanding of the Bible. For instance, how many men have lost the woman of their dreams because they did not realize she was a Christian, who held tight to certain Christian values they could not relate to? How many sales and marketing people have lost a big sale due to some off-colored joke the Christian buyer did not appreciate? An understanding of earthly rules, without an understanding of spiritual rules, can be detrimental in both the short and the long run of life. You see, ignorance of Bible knowledge and wisdom can be very costly if a person does not realize how its contents can have such a significant impact on their life. It is also important to recognize that just a few major decisions we make about our lives can have an enormous effect on our future.

Wrong decisions can be very costly. For example, choosing the right education path can have a huge difference on future income, as can our choice of occupation or profession. Let us also not forget the importance of marrying the right person, deciding where to live, and the decision to bring children into the world. Yes, these few life-altering decisions can have long-lasting implications for our future, which stresses the importance of discussing them with God first, who knows our future better than we do. It seems obvious that the more wisdom we gain, and the quicker, the more successful our life becomes.

Inside the Bible

Entering the world of the Bible provides a whole new dimension on how we perceive ourselves and the world in which we live because we open ourselves up to a greater understanding of the spiritual side of our nature. It is essential for us to realize we grow physically automatically through nourishment and love. We grow intellectually automatically as we evolve from a child to an adult, as we benefit from education and experience. However, the third part of our nature, our spiritual part, does not necessarily grow automatically. This explains why we see older men and women committing sins and acting like infants. The spiritual side of our nature must be nourished and developed through biblical education and prayer. We all have the responsibility of lifting our spirit from a lowercase "s" to an uppercase "S" as we grow closer to God. Our five senses allow us to operate in this physical world, but we must also seek God, who is latent within all of us until we deepen that connection.

As we mature in our faith, we begin to identify and use certain spiritual gifts made available to us. The Fruit of the Spirit, for instance, provides a greater capacity for expressing love, joy, and more peace. We experience more patience, kindness, gentleness, goodness, self-control, and faithfulness. Stop and meditate for a moment on what I have just said. Do you have these qualities in your life now? Believe it or not, they are all available and free just for the asking! They are free gifts from God for all those who accept Jesus Christ as their Lord and Savior. Seriously, it doesn't get any better.

Most people know Heaven and Hell exist, and they have a choice as to which of two permanent addresses they wish to reside in after this short life ends. So, imagine, for a moment, a horizontal line with one end representing the beginning of time, (as we know it) and the other end running off into eternity. Then place a small dot on the line. The dot represents your life and your world. Now imagine inside the dot is a bubble, which represents your worldview, which in turn is the result of the parents you were given, the geographical location where you were born, your upbringing, the culture, language, and religion you are exposed to, coupled to your education level, and the overall experiences you gained during your formative years of development. Education and experience are instrumental in allowing us all to think "outside the box," or the "bubble," so to speak, which provides us with a much larger picture of our lives and the world in which we live. It makes us realize we are all part of the cosmos, and there is a future life, either in Heaven or Hell, for those who respect and love their Creator.

Information, knowledge, wisdom

It is true today we are suffering from busy lives and information overload. We have untold access to obtain answers to any questions by simply turning on our smartphone, tablet, or computer and asking. Would you believe on any given day, we send out 500 million tweets and four million hours of content uploaded to YouTube? There are some 4.3 billion Facebook messages posted each day, along with about six billion Google searches and 205 billion emails being sent. This is just online information. This does not account for bumper stickers, billboards, web pages, pop-ups, banner ads, T.V. shows, songs, movies, and much more, all competing for our attention. Is it any wonder we are confused and frustrated?

Turning this easily accessible information into something coherent and relevant that can be used in our lives is called knowledge, which requires practice, repetition, and implementation. Knowledge is taking facts, information, and skills acquired through experience or education, which helps us create mastery over some skill or subject. It is also the theoretical or practical understanding of a subject. Turning knowledge into wisdom, however, is another matter entirely, as wisdom, we have found, is much rarer and, in many ways, more valuable. The Bible is the main source for gaining true wisdom because it represents the written words of our Creator, God Almighty.

Living in a world of disarray

Our world today is in a state of confusion and uncertainty about the future. People who don't know their Bible are worried about the world coming to an end. They look into the future and see blackness and gloom. They fail to understand the end of the story is all played out in the Bible, and all those astute Bible readers enjoy a quiet confidence non-believers fail to grasp.

So, when the World Economic Forum (W.E.F.) says in their 2016 video, America will no longer be the number one nation in the world by 2030, and a Great Reset is being planned, which will drastically change our way of life, people worry and shudder. Millions of people do not realize it is God who triggers the Great Resets, and not wealthy men and women from powerful, international organizations, such as The World Economic Forum, The Trilateral Commission, The Council on Foreign Relations, The Bilderbergers, The Chatham House (aka The Royal Institute), The Club of Rome, or the Bohemian Club, et al. These organizations may think they are planning future earth-shattering changes to the world population's way of life. Still, they are ignorant of what the Bible has to say. They don't seem to realize it is God who implements the Great Resets, and he has already triggered a number of Great Resets in the past, known in the Bible as divine covenants, which significantly altered man's way of life. God is also pledged to create another Great Reset in the future. These Great Resets will all be discussed in later chapters.

Meanwhile, *Understanding the Bible Before Reading It* is designed to encourage everyone to take a fresh look at the many values and benefits the Bible has to offer. Yes, the Bible's 2,700-plus pages, including notes (ESV version), spread out over many books, might appear intimidating and time-consuming, but it is well worth the effort to discover what God wants to tell us.

Quick book summary

The main takeaways from reading this book are as follows:

1.   Although the Bible has two parts, we need to understand both the Old Testament as well as the New Testament. Watching the second act of a play without understanding the first act and the players involved would be to ruin the experience. Besides, the Old Testament contains more than 70% of all the words in the Bible.

2.   Part of the "spine" holding the body of the Bible together are its covenants. Old Testament people placed great emphasis on covenants, especially the covenants created by God. An understanding of these covenants will not only help us understand the past but also learn what the future has in store for us. The importance of God's covenants will be addressed in later chapters.

3.   The Bible tells us this world will come to an end one day, so it is very important for all of us to know the end of the story in order to secure our place in the eternal kingdom. We all need to understand the Kingdom of God is a spiritual kingdom, which can only be entered into while here on earth by being born again (John 3:3). God gave us the Bible to provide us with the knowledge we need to gain our future life with Jesus Christ. B.I.B.L.E., is an acronym for Believers Instructions Before Leaving Earth!

4.   The good news is that God has a plan for each and every one of our lives if we are willing to allow him to unfold it for us. All we have to do is seek Jesus Christ and ask him to become our Lord and Savior.

5.   G. K. Chesterton once said, "The huge modern heresy is to alter the human soul to fit modern social conditions, instead of altering modern social conditions to fit the human soul!" What

Chesterton is saying is we can either allow society to shape our culture (and you can readily see what a mess we have made by doing that), or we can shape our culture by applying God's Law to the way we conduct our everyday life. When citizens know their Bible, the proof is evident that society improves morally in a dramatic way.

6.   In reading this book, you will be distilling the time it takes to read the whole Bible down to a fraction of the time. By reducing the word count of the Bible down to about 100,000 words, from more than one million words, including explanations, teachings, and reference material (ESV version), you will hopefully gain a quicker, clearer overview in understanding the Bible story, with the goal of accelerating your wisdom learning of what the Bible teaches. Much of the "heavy lifting" has already been done for you, with more than 900 Bible references for easy navigation, and to simplify your journey. All you need to do now is read and study this book and then use your newfound knowledge to study the Bible for yourself as a life-long learning habit. You need to master the Bible to the point that it masters you!

7.   Finally, please note that the Bible is written in a laconic style, using few words to describe people and situations. This book will add additional non-biblical evidence to expand and hopefully enrich your reading experience.

SECTION ONE

THE HEBREW TESTAMENT

1

OLD TESTAMENT JEWISH HISTORY

"If we were forced to choose just one, there would be no way to deny that Judaism is the most important development in human history." –David Gelernter, Yale University Professor

IN UNDERSTANDING THE BIBLE, IT IS OF GREAT IMPORTANCE TO REALIZE the significant role the Jewish people have played, and continue to play, in the unfolding story of the Bible drama. In the Hebrew or Jewish Testament (The Old Testament), God declared the Jews to be his chosen people. They were selected by God from all the many other people groups that existed at that time in man's history. All the writers of the Old Testament were Jewish. In fact, in the new Christian Testament, we must also keep in mind that Jesus Christ was a Jew, and so were his twelve apostles. Furthermore, all of the 27 books in the New Testament were written by Jews, with the possible exception of Luke, who wrote the Gospel of Luke, and the Book of Acts. We moderns, therefore, owe a great deal of thanks to the Jews for their enormous contribution in introducing Christians to the kingdom of God, through Jesus Christ, even though the Jewish people to this day have not accepted Christ as their Messiah, with the exception of some converted Messianic Jews.

For these and many other reasons we need to learn about the great Jewish contribution to the Christian faith in order to truly understand the Bible.

Before we begin, it is important to mention the words, Hebrew, Israelite, and Jew, because they are often used interchangeably in the Bible. The word, Hebrew, first refers to Abraham (Genesis 14:13), and later, Joseph (Genesis 39:14,17). Hebrew and Israel are also mentioned concerning the other descendants of Abraham (who was the founder of the Jewish people), his son, Isaac, and his son, Jacob (Genesis 35:10-12; 43:32). The name, Jacob, was later changed to Israel (Genesis 32:28), and his descendants became known as Israelites (Exodus 9:7). When the twelve tribes later split, we find ten tribes using the name, Israel, and the other two tribes using the name, Judah, from which we derive the word, Jew. It should be mentioned that all these three terms are also used interchangeably in the New Testament as well (2 Corinthians 11:22; John 4:9).

So, with the above background in mind, it appears appropriate to begin the start of our journey with a closer look at the Jewish people, particularly the Jews of antiquity. We will take a peek into their history, culture, and traditions. In this this way we can gain a clearer understanding of what their life was like living in the Near East, prior to the arrival of Jesus Christ some 2,000 years ago. This knowledge will in turn, assist us in gaining a better perspective as we delve into later chapters, and especially as it applies to the New Testament.

People influenced by the land

A careful look at an ancient map of the Near East, sometimes referred to as the Middle East (see Exhibit "A"), will indicate seas, mountains, and deserts, which help explain how civilizations developed in the plains, valleys, and the mountains. As you look towards the south you see the Nile River of Egypt, where about 3,000 B.C., the Egyptians became an important people, who were governed by the dynasties and Pharaohs (kings). Their power centers were in Memphis in the north, or Thebes, in the south. Looking north on the map towards the plains of Asia Minor, the powerful Hittites ruled for about 1500 years or so, but appear to have disappeared by biblical times. Looking toward the east, you will find the vast land of Mesopotamia, a Greek name for "Between the rivers," referring to the Tigris and Euphrates. Today, this land area engulfs most of Iraq. The Near East, stretching from modern day Israel, the PLO, Lebanon, Jordan, Syria, and Iraq, is referred to as the Fertile Crescent. With the exception of Egypt, this is the area where the great civilizations came to power, almost side by side, who often fought each other. In southern Mesopotamia there were the civilizations of Sumer, Akkad, and Babylonia, with Assyria residing in the north. Traveling east would have led us to the Medes, who were later followed on the world-stage by the Persians (Iran). Not to get too far ahead of the story, these great civilizations were later conquered by the Greeks, and then the Romans.

As these great nations fought each other, it became necessary to move their troops through the narrow corridor between the Mediterranean and the Arabian Desert. This created a huge problem for the people of Israel, who lived right inside this corridor, causing them to make alliances with these other nations for protection, whenever possible. Acting as a buffer state between two warring armies, Israel served as a forward post for one and then the other, but ultimately Israel got swallowed up in these larger wars.

A people influenced by their surrounding neighbors

Throughout history, Israel was in contact with her neighbors, and therefore became familiar with their cultures and religious practices. As the Israelis looked south, they were impressed by Egypt's great civilization. Egypt was the first territorial kingdom, the first national state. Egypt's timeline dates back to about 7000 B.C., when farmers began settling in the Nile River Valley. Between 3200 B.C. and 3000 B.C., there is evidence of the use of hieroglyphic writing. By 3100 B.C. there were kingdoms in Upper and Lower Egypt, and great pyramids were being built. Because the king (Pharoah), acted as the intermediary between his people and the gods, (the sun god being the greatest of their gods), there was no clear boundary between secular and religious matters. Official worship was conducted in temples, which were the palaces of the resident gods. Egypt's religion had no systematic theology, and many versions of their myths are unknown.

You will find most of ancient Egypt's 2000 plus gods were connected with some aspect of life and nature. Examples would be Ra, the sun god, and Taweret, associated with fertility and pregnancy. Their gods fell into two classes: local gods and universal gods. To foreigners, the most shocking part of Egyptian religion was their worship of animals, with Apis, the sacred bull of Ptah, being one of the most famous. They also venerated cats! The religion often veered off into magic, thus causing many people to wear protective amulets, love charms, and various spells to cure sickness. Note: a visit to the modern-day Cairo Museum yields many examples of various medical concoctions and magic spells, that did more harm to the patient than good. Later, Hippocrates, the Greek writer of the Hippocratic oath, would have been appalled at such medical treatments! At this time, however, Israelites would experience much interaction with the Egyptians, either through war and subjugation, or trade and exchange of ideas. There is no question the Israelites certainly felt the influence of the Egyptian way of life.

While Egyptians tended to be optimistic in their everyday attitudes, the peoples of Mesopotamia were, by contrast, more pessimistic. Many of the people lived in valleys where floods were unpredictable, causing great harm as archaeological digs have verified. The people also suffered with regular invasions by nomadic tribes from the Arabian desert, or from the east. They were also besieged by capricious gods who were constantly fighting among themselves. Mortal man found himself acting in a terrified way, and was constantly seeking refuge from the gods' anger. We will find in a reading of the Gilgamesh epic, for instance, that the gods had given man death for his destiny, and filled him with deceit. The kingdom of the dead is a sorry story, as the joyless dead are reunited for a dark destiny.

We are told in the epic of Atra-Hasis, dating from 1600 B.C., that the gods grew weary of all the chores they had to do, so they transferred the burden on the backs of mankind. They formed man from clay, mixed with the blood of a god whose throat had been cut. Mankind, later grew in numbers, and began making trouble for the gods, who in turn inflicted various spells culminating in the floods.

We also find in the poem of Enūma Eliš, written about 1100 B.C., where it tells of the beginning, involving two sexual principles, Apsu, the sweet water, and Tiamat, representing the salt waters of the sea. These two gods originated all the other gods, but because these god offspring began to annoy Tiamat, she decided to kill them. The other gods are saved when the god, Mardu, overcomes Tiamat, and divides her in half like an oyster. Mardu then makes her into the vault of heaven. Mardu goes on to make man from the blood of a rebel god.

The most famous work of ancient Mesopotamia, however, is the Epic of Gilgamesh. Created in Sumer, it developed over

1000 years in Assyria and Babylon. In the reading, we find Gilgamesh becoming unbearable to the gods due to his pride. So, the gods produce a rival named, Enkidu, a monster living with wild beasts. He is humanized by a woman and becomes a friend of Gilgamesh, and together they enjoy great adventures. Then, one day, Enkidu died, and Gilgamesh discovers the horror of death for the first time, and ends up searching out the secret to immortality. One of the heroes of the flood gives him the secret of the herb of life, which he gets hold of. But then the serpent snatched the herb away from him, and Gilgamesh has to resign himself to death. Many of these Mesopotamian stories and myths were also familiar to the Jewish people, who would later be entangled in accepting some of their gods and rituals.

In discussing some of the Israelites' neighbors, we must also examine the influence the Canaanites had on them. The ancient country of Canaan is equivalent in size to modern-day Israel, the Palestinian territory, and the Gaza Strip. This is the area where Abram, later to become Abraham, migrated from his home city of Ur, in Babylonia. Canaanite thinking has become better known to us since the discovery, in 1929, of the library in the city of Ugarit, which was located in the modern city of Ras Shamra in Syria. The Ugaritic civilization was at its height about 1500 B.C., when the Jewish patriarchs, Abraham, Isaac, and Jacob, lived.

The Canaanite chief god was El, often presented in the form of a bull. Canaanite religion was based on nature, much like many other ancient people groups. Baal was the god of storms and rain, and Anath, his sister, later called Astarte, was the goddess of war, love, and fertility. We find the Israelites were very much influenced by Canaanite religious practices, especially the sex cult offered by the naked goddess. Its chief aim was to obtain fertility for the land and animals.

The degeneration of the Israelites, due to influences by their neighbors, caused them to move further and further away from

God, thus bringing God's wrath down upon them, as we will see in the next section.

A people chosen by a monotheistic God

As we dwell on the immoral, and sacrilegious lifestyles of Israel's neighbors for a moment, it becomes more understandable why God was motivated to intervene in man's life and create a course re-direction. For this purpose, he chose a select group of people, the Hebrews (later Israelites and Jews), to become a special people, a chosen people, who would be guided by God and serve as an example to all other people groups in the proper way for them to conduct their lives to please God.

As mentioned earlier, the founder of the Jewish faith was a man named Abram (later Abraham), born in 1948 B.C., in the City of Ur, Mesopotamia, according to the Jewish Virtual Library. His father was an idol maker, as the citizens of Ur worshiped many gods. Yet, later in chapter 15 of Genesis, we find Abram receiving a call from God to leave his country and travel to the Land of Canaan. God told Abram, "I will make you into a great nation, and I will bless you. I will make your name great, and you will be a blessing. I will bless those who bless you, and whoever curses you I will curse; and all the peoples on earth will be blessed through you." (Genesis 12:2-3).

Later, in chapter fifteen of the same book, God said to Abram, "To your offspring I give this land, from the river in Egypt (Nile) to the great river, Euphrates (modern-day Iraq), the land of the Kenites, Kenizzites, Kadmonites, Hittites, Perizzites, the Rephaim, the Amorites, the Canaanites, the Girgashites, and Jebusites." (Genesis 15:18-20). God mentions Abram's ancestors as being God's chosen people in such Bible verses as Deuteronomy 14:2; Jeremiah 7:23; Genesis 12:1-9, 13:14-18, and again in 15:12-21. Abraham, formerly Abram, along with his son, Isaac, and his son, Jacob, became the patriarchs of the Jewish faith going forward. Jacob's sons later formed the twelve tribes of Israel.

A people blessed with great leadership

As the storyline of the Bible progresses, we find in the Book of Genesis an account of a great famine, causing the Israelites to move to the Land of Goshen in Egypt, where they were protected by one of their own. His name was Joseph, one of the twelve sons of Jacob, and he had become a high official in Pharaoh's court. After the death of Joseph, a later Pharoah enslaved the Israelites for more than 400 years and used them as laborers in building great construction projects to please the Egyptian elite.

The Israelites yearned for a liberator. In the 14th century B.C., another great leader arose by the name of Moses, who later played a crucial role in developing both the Jewish and Christian faith. The Bible tells us Moses was born a Jew, but to avoid the persecution of Pharoah, his mother placed her child in a bed of reeds and sent him down the Nile, where Pharaoh's daughter rescued him. Consequently, he was raised a prince of Egypt, receiving the best education and palace privileges. However, at about the age of forty, Moses killed an Egyptian who was abusing a Jew. Realizing the consequences of his actions, he fled into the wilderness, where he spent the next forty years of his life with his Jewish family. God then called him to rescue his people from their bondage in Egypt, and the Bible provides a compelling account of how this was achieved. He died at Mount Nebo, in modern-day Jordan, at age 120, having never stepped foot on the promised land that God had given to the Israelites. Moses is credited with writing the first five books of the Old Testament: Genesis, Exodus, Leviticus, Numbers, and Deuteronomy, which are referred to as the Pentateuch (from the Greek meaning "five scrolls") or the Torah (in Hebrew meaning "instruction"), and receiving the famous Ten Commandments from God.

Upon the death of Moses, we find Joshua becoming the new leader, successfully taking control of Canaan, and preserving the people's faith in obeying God's commands, for the most part. However, upon his death, we find the people moving further away from God towards religious apostasy. They began embracing the gods of the Canaanites. It was at this time that tribal leaders rose to address the issues of moral decline and to protect the people from their enemies. Over the next 400-plus years, there arose, from time to time, twelve judges or leaders. Beginning with Othniel and ending with Samuel, a judge, priest, and prophet. By the end of the period of the judges, the people had violated its covenant with God in every way imaginable. It states: "In those days there was no king in Israel. Everyone did what was right in his own eyes." The people yearned for a king, similar to other nations around them.

A people yearning for a monarchy

God eventually granted the Israelites their wish by instructing Samuel to seek out a king, who later became King Saul. He started well, but later, he proved himself unsuited for the role of king. He failed to obey the Word of God through Samuel. Finally, God rejected Saul, and he later committed suicide on Mount Gilboa after losing a battle with the Philistines. That day, three of his sons also died. This tragic state of affairs led to David becoming king, whose legacy will be discussed in a later chapter. Meanwhile, David was a very successful king, and before he died, he brought honor and prestige to the monarchy.

It is important to point out that the king was not an absolute ruler. Although there were no longer judges, there were priests, prophets, and tribal leaders, who held considerable power, which affected the king's ability to rule autonomously. The king needed the tribes to provide an army, of which he was powerless without. The king also needed input from the prophets and the priests because their religion was all-inclusive to their way of life and was not separate from how government was managed. King David's successor was his son, Solomon, who became the wisest man in the world before degenerating into apostasy in marrying 700 women from kings of other tribes and keeping 300 concubines who worshiped gods other than God Almighty. This led to a degeneration of Solomon's faith. He successfully built the temple and placed the Ark of the Covenant inside it. This act strengthened the image of Jerusalem as being the Israelites' religious center, as well as its capital.

The people split the twelve tribes

Many people blame Solomon's successor, his son, Rehoboam, for the reason why the twelve tribes broke up. However, it should be pointed out that King Solomon had done much to create animosity among the tribes during his reign. He used tax collections to favor Judah's defense system in the south at the expense of the northern tribes, and he established twelve administrative districts that did not align with the territories of the tribes, thus causing much unnecessary friction. He also introduced the *missim*, a tax not for money but for physical labor. It required each citizen to work for one month each year on various government projects. Considering the people's forefathers had been enslaved people in Egypt, this policy must have been tough to accept.

So, when Rehoboam came to the throne, he was almost immediately asked by the tribal leaders to make certain changes that would be fair and equitable for all the tribes, but Rehoboam refused. This caused the ten tribes to rebel and form the northern kingdom, which they named Israel. The other two tribes, Judah, and Benjamin, remained with their capital in Jerusalem and called themselves Judah (This is when the word, Jew, was first used). The country's political divide created serious problems for Israel's new king in the north, Jeroboam. He could have set up a new country, but Israel and Judah shared a common religion, with the main religious center being in Jerusalem under the control of Judah. Both worshiped the same God; both held beliefs and traditions of the same heritage of the original patriarchs, and they both shared the slavery experience in Egypt, as well as the Mount Sinai revelation with Moses. Eventually, over some time, the two entities evolved quite differently, with Jeroboam setting up new religious centers in the north, along with a number of new holidays, plus the establishment of a new priesthood.

A people under siege

The Northern Kingdom of Israel lasted just over two-hundred years, and during this time, there were 19 kings, beginning with King Jeroboam and King Hoshea being the last. It is noted that none of these kings were found righteous in the eyes of God. The Southern Kingdom of Judah had 20 kings, starting with Rehoboam, and ending with King Zedekiah, and only eight were found to be righteous.

The rivalry between the two kingdoms was soon overshadowed by the mighty nation of Assyria to the north. Israel defended herself by creating alliances with neighboring states, including Judah, but the coalition was later defeated. The main aim of the Assyrians, until the mid-eighth century, was plunder and tribute. Still, after the Assyrian King Tiglath-Pileser III (745 – 727 B.C.) came to power, he began a system of territorial expansion in his attempt to acquire the whole of the Fertile Crescent for himself. After successfully taking Damascus in 732 B.C., the Assyrians soon took Galilee and Gilead. Later, after the new Assyrian King Shalmaneser V took the throne, he was denied tribute by King Hoshea, who had decided to rebel. The capital of Samaria was put under siege that lasted almost three years before they finally surrendered to the Assyrians in 722 B.C. After Shalmaneser died a few months later, there was another Jewish rebellion put down by the new Assyrian King Sargon II, who later took back control of Samaria and renamed it Samerina, a new Assyrian province. The Israelites were sent into exile to places as far east as Media and, in history, became known as the Ten Lost Tribes of Israel.

Prophets, such as Amos, Micah, and Hosea, all deplored the sins of both the northern and southern kingdoms and predicted their future fate if they did not repent from worshiping pagan gods. As mentioned, the northern kingdom did not listen, and their doom became a reality. Judah continued its pagan practices under King Jehoiakim (609 – 598 B.C.), including acceptance of the odious Moloch cult, including child sacrifices at the Moloch shrine in Jerusalem's Valley of Hinnom (this is the valley just out-side Jerusalem, which the Greeks referred to as *Gehenna*, which came to mean *Hell*, along with *Topheth*).

According to the Second Book of Kings, these abominable re-ligious practices would also doom the Kingdom of Judah. Later, after Judah lost its sovereignty to Babylon (597 B.C.), the first ex-ile of some 15 to 20 thousand Jews to Babylon took place in 605 B.C., which fits the timeline of King Cyrus of Persia, who, after having conquered the Medes, then successfully defeated the Bab-ylonians in 539 B.C., and allowed the Babylonian Jews to return to their homeland. This release from captivity after 70 years corre-sponds to Jeremiah 29:10, who predicted a 70-year Jewish exile in Babylon before they were released as part of God's overall plan. Please note there were several Jewish exiles during this turbu-lent time, which happened over a number of years. Also, during this chaotic chapter in Jewish history, the Babylonians burned Je-rusalem to the ground, including Solomon's Temple.

2

THE JEWS DURING THE INTERTESTAMENTAL YEARS

There is a famous story in which the Kaiser asks Bismarck, "Can you prove the existence of God?" Bismarck replied, "The Jews, your majesty. The Jews."

THE LAST BOOK OF THE OLD HEBREW TESTAMENT WAS WRITTEN BY THE prophet, Malachi, which was written in the middle of the 5th century B.C., according to the best estimates of scholars. From that time until the coming of Jesus Christ, we find God and the prophets are silent. For about 400 years there is nothing recorded in the Bible, causing scholars to extract research material from non-biblical sources, including Apocryphal books, Josephus, and many other validated sources that shed light on this period of history. The fact that nothing is mentioned in the Bible about this silent period does not alter the rich history that took place during this time.

In fact, Alexander the Great unified the Greek empire and overpowered the Persians, before going on to conquer the known world. During this period, we also find the Jews gaining independence for about 100 years before being conquered by the Romans, who were in power in Palestine when Jesus Christ was born.

Rise of the Greeks

Hellenism, or Greek culture, had been spreading throughout the known world through Greek trade and colonization. Hellenism was devoted to ancient Greek thought, customs, and styles. It embraced philosophy, art, and science. The Greek language became the *lingua franca* for common trade and diplomatic language by crossing frontiers, which helped to bind people together in a more homogenous way. However, Hellenism was also polytheistic and animistic in the worshiping of a pantheon of Greek gods, which created problems for the Jews. Many of the Jewish elite embraced Hellenism, but it was resisted by the orthodox Hasideans.

When Alexander the Great unified the Greeks, it resulted in him becoming a world conqueror, causing his armies to overpower the number one most powerful civilization in the world at that time, Persia, whom he defeated in three great battles: Granicus (334 B.C.), Issus (333 B.C.), and Arbela (331 B.C.). He also broke the 1000-year maritime rule, and the influence of the Phoenicians, as well as guaranteeing all inland people their positions and rights.

Alexander died at the tender age of 33. His heirs were a young, posthumous son, and a mentally retarded brother, neither of whom were capable of ruling. The regent Perdiccas tried to hold the empire together, but after he was murdered in 321 B.C., Alexander's generals fought one another for power, which became known as the Wars of the Diadochi ("successors"). The wars continued until 301 B.C. and by that time the empire had been divided into five kingdoms under Macedonian dynasties. Macedonia itself fell to Cassander, who murdered both of Alexander's legitimate heirs. Lysimachus took Thrace; Antigonus controlled Anatolia (part of modern Turkey), as well as Greece, Syria and the Levant (modern day Holy Land area). Ptolemy satisfied himself with Egypt, and Seleucus controlled Mesopotamia, Persia and the East. For New Testament purposes, two parts of Alexander's fractured empire are important for historical background, mainly the Ptolemaic Empire in Egypt, with Alexandria as its capital, and the Seleucid Empire in Syria, with Antioch as its capital. Israel lay between these rival powers.

The Ptolemies ruled Egypt until 30 B.C., when the last of their rulers, Cleopatra, committed suicide as the Romans were moving into Egypt. Alexandria was a magnificent city where the famous Alexandrian library was built, causing scholars from all over the known world to move there. Many Jews moved to Alexandria, and it has been estimated that a fifth of the population of the city were Jews. This is also the city where the Bible was translated into Greek. (The Septuagint). The fact that Jewish holy land was located between the two empires of Egypt and Syria, caused it to become a victim of rivalry between the two powers, which wanted to collect taxes from Jewish inhabitants, while also making it a buffer zone to protect themselves from attack. The Ptolemies controlled the holy land (old name for modern Israel, Gaza, Lebanon, and Jordan), for 125 years, from 323 B.C. until 198 B.C. During this time the Jews were allowed to live in peace as long as they paid tribute to the Ptolemies.

The Seleucids in Syria had attempted to gain control of the holy land on a number of occasions, either through marriage alliance, or by invasion, but each time they failed. That is, until 198 B.C. when Antiochus III (the Great), finally defeated the Ptolemies, thus gaining control of this Jewish land, and turning it into a satrap. Under Antiochus, the Jews fared well with a great deal of autonomy granted to the Jewish high priest. However, after the death of Antiochus III, his third son, Antiochus IV Epiphanes became king, and his relationship with the Jews soon went sour.

Jewish resistance

The Jews were divided into two parties: the Orthodox Hasideans (Pious Ones), and a reform party that favored Hellenism. Antiochus naturally sided with the reform party as he was desirous of homogenizing all people groups under his kingdom into the Greek way of life. He built a gymnasium in Jerusalem to educate young Jews on Greek culture, and replaced the high priest, Jason, with Menelaus, another Hellenized Jew, who had offered to collect higher taxes for Antiochus. Jewish priests were supposed to be descended from Aaron, the elder brother of Moses, but Menelaus may not have belonged to a priestly family. In any event, the Jews resented the idea of selling their most sacred office to the highest bidder.

While Antiochus was campaigning in Egypt, the outed high priest, Jason, heard a rumor that Antiochus had been killed. Jason and his followers then decided to rebel, and took over Jerusalem. Upon his return, Antiochus responded with a "scorched earth" policy that resulted in thousands of Jewish men, women and children being put to death. He then forced the Jews to accept his Hellenization policies, and Syrian troops were permanently garrisoned there. His forces then entered the Temple, reinstalled Menelaus as high priest, and stopped regular sacrifices. The Syrians also set-up an altar to the god, Zeus, and offered swine as a sacrifice, which was abhorrent to the Jews. This act is called the "Abomination of Desolation" mentioned in the Book of Daniel, and by Jesus in the New Testament Book of Matthew.

The Maccabean Revolt

The Jews reacted swiftly. In the village of Modein, a royal official of Antiochus tried to compel an elderly priest named Mattathias to set an example for the villagers by making a pagan sacrifice, but Mattathias refused. Another Jew stepped forward to comply with the request, but Mattathias killed him and the Syrian official, before demolishing the altar, and escaping to the mountains with his five sons and other sympathizers. This started the Maccabean revolt, which began in 167 B.C. Mattathias' family were known as the Hasmoneans, after Hasmon, who was the great grandfather of Mattathias, or the Maccabees, which comes from the nickname "Maccabeus," ("the Hammer"), a name given to Judas, one of the sons.

After Mattathias died, his son, Judas, led the Jewish rebels in a very successful guerilla war campaign until they were able to defeat the Syrians in open battle. The Maccabean revolt also created a civil war between the pro-Hellenistic Jews, and the anti-Hellenistic Jews. This civil war continued even after the death of Antiochus Epiphanes in 163 B.C. Eventually, the Maccabees were able to expel Syrian troops from their citadel in Jerusalem, and regain their religious freedom. They rededicated the Temple, and eventually conquered the whole of Palestine.

Judas Maccabeus was killed in battle in 160 B.C., and leadership was turned over to his brothers, Jonathan and then Simon. Jonathan began building the damaged walls of Jerusalem, and named himself as high priest. Simon was able to gain recognition for Judean independence from Demetrius II, who was a contestant to the Seleucid throne. Simon also renewed a treaty with Rome that had originally been accomplished under Judas. Simon was proclaimed the "great high priest and commander and leader of the Jews," and he officially brought together the religious, political, and military factions all under his command as leader of the Jewish state.

Unfortunately, the rest of the history of the Hasmonean dynasty (142 B.C. – 37 B.C.), tells a sad story of internal conflict in a bid for power. The political aims of the Hasmoneans had alienated many of the religious Hasideans, who ended up splitting into the Pharisees and the Essenes. Some of the Essenes produced the Dead Sea Scrolls, which were not discovered until 1946/47 A.D! On the other hand, the aristocratic and politically minded supporters of the Hasmonean priest-kings, became the Sadducees, who lasted until 70 A.D. when the Temple was destroyed. Subsequently, the Jews lost their independence again, when the Roman general, Pompey, took over Palestine in 63 B.C.

Jewish everyday life

During the turbulent and chaotic Intertestamental period, the Jewish people continued to live, as best they could, in the same way they had lived for centuries. Domestic life centered around the home, which was built to accommodate climate and financial limitations. For most of the year the weather was very hot and dry, with rain in both Spring and Autumn. The poor lived in one-room houses, built of mud-brick on a stone foundation, which was later replaced with limestone. The family slept on mats, which were illuminated at night by olive-oil lamps. In sharp contrast, the richer families lived in larger homes, slept in beds, and were waited on by servants who served them quality food and wine, instead of the goat's milk, olives and barley bread, consumed by the poor.

Peasant families had no choice but to work in order to live, with men working either in the fields, or at a village craft, with women and children working at home, and fetching water from the village well in goatskin buckets. Their clothes were conditioned by the weather, and included long flowing robes to stay cool. The wealthy afforded brightly dyed cloth, and they wore short jackets over their tunic. Clothes often determined the profession of the person, with special dress for the priests, and the rabbi's wearing blue-fringed robes. Footwear for the poor, if they could afford it, included a cowhide sole fastened to the ankle by a leather thong between the large and second toe. The Israelites lived mostly as an agricultural community, with corn being the main staple food. Other major crops included grapes, olives, and figs, all mentioned later by Jesus in his sayings and parables during his ministry.

Not conceiving children was considered a calamity, and a woman's happiness was proportionate, (so it was said), by the number of children she conceived, with emphasis on sons. When the firstborn son arrived, his mother became the "mother of?" instead of 'the daughter of?' Daughters were less preferred due to their subordinate position, and became an asset to the family only as a worker. At birth, the parents rubbed salt on their babies to make them firmer, and they were wrapped in swaddling clothes to make their limbs grow stronger. Naming a child was very important, as it was used to indicate some moral or physical property of the child. After eight-days a boy was circumcised, and the firstborn was redeemed by the mother a month later, by making a payment to the high priest. Babies were not weaned until they were at least two-years old.

Traditional Jewish marriage

Jewish marriages were often arranged by parents, and courtships were restricted and watched closely, with very little social mixing between the sexes. Because it was the duty for everyone to marry, the bride had to be paid for as she was a working asset. The wedding ceremony was formal and binding, and gifts were exchanged. On the wedding day, the bridegroom and friends went in the evening to the bride's home, where she and her family waited. The couple were blessed, with the bridegroom then leading the bride through the village over to his own home, with village guests lighting the way with a torchlight procession. Then came a great feast that usually lasted a week! (The spiritual significance and value of this subject, and how it plays out in the New Testament, will be further discussed later).

When a Jew died there was set in motion an elaborate ceremony for mourning, which sometimes included professional mourners. With the climate being so hot, the body had to be buried within 24-hours. Before burial, the body was washed and clothed and then wrapped in grave clothes, with a linen napkin bound around the head. The wealthy were buried in tombs cut out of rocks, and then sealed with a boulder. The poor were buried in common graves or in caves.

Jewish education

With reference to education, in Old Testament times there were no schools for the ordinary man's children. Every day skills were taught to them by their parents, who also explained the law, and all the meaning of the religious festivals. By the time of Jesus, a young girl's education still depended on her mother. However, every boy was now going to the school attached to the synagogue, from age six forward. The Jewish scriptures were a boy's only textbook, where he would learn the history, literature, geography, and the law of the Jews. If a boy was bright enough, he could get sent to Jerusalem to be taught by a top rabbi. Besides gaining knowledge of the law, a boy would need to learn a trade. Teaching a boy a trade, and introducing him to the Jewish festivals, were the responsibility of the father. When a boy reached the age of 13, he became 'Bar Mitzvah,' which means a son of the law. At this point he was considered a man, and he qualified for the Minyan, which is part of the minimum ten male adults required in order to conduct a synagogue service. On the first Sabbath following Bar Mitzvah, the boy, now a man, was able to deliver a portion of the law in Hebrew, and then receive leadership blessing.

Everyday Jewish religious life

The Feast	The Feast The Fulfillment In Christ (New Testament)
PASSOVER (APRIL)	Death of Christ. The Passover Lamb (1 Corinthians 5:7)
UNLEAVENED BREAD (APRIL)	Christ's sinless perfection (1 Corinthians 5:8; 2 Corinthians 5:21)
FIRST FRUITS (APRIL)	Christ's Resurrection (1 Corinthians 15:23)
PENTECOST (JUNE)	Outpouring of the Holy Spirit (Book of Acts 1:5; 2:4)
TRUMPETS (SEPTEMBER)	Israel's Regathering (Matthew (24:31)
ATONEMENT (SEPTEMBER)	Cleansing by Christ (Romans 3:25)
TABERNACLES (SEPTEMBER)	God dwelling with his people (Zechariah 13:1; 14:16-18)

There was no big division between religious and civil law in Israel. It was found that priests, Levites, and elders, all worked together in the dispensation of justice. The gate of the village or city was traditionally the place where grievances were resolved and formally judged. Israel's religious life centered first on the tabernacle, then the temple, and the regulations laid down by the law governing sacrifice, offerings, and the great annual festivals. The great day of the year was the Day of Atonement, the once-a-year event when the high priest entered the innermost shrine of the temple (the Holy of Holies), to atone for his sins and the sins of the people. Today, this event is called Yom Kippur.

The other great festivals included: Passover, Unleavened Bread, which celebrates the escape from Egypt; First Fruits (following unleavened bread, acknowledging the fertility of the land) the Feast of Weeks, held 50 days later, (we call Pentecost), which celebrates the beginning of the harvest; the Feast of Tabernacles (Booths - the Harvest Festival); the Feast of Trumpets (Rosh Hashanah), which represents a spiritual new year. All of these Jewish festivals are mentioned in Leviticus 23, with the Sabbath foundational for solemn rest, the basis for all the feasts.

In the Spring, the festivals include: Passover, Unleavened Bread, First Fruits, and Weeks or Pentecost. In the fall, the festivals include: Trumpets, Day of Atonement, and Tabernacles. Connectivity between the Old and New Testaments can readily be seen when we compare Jewish biblical feasts with New Testament fulfillment in Christ.

So, as you can see, the Bible in Old Testament times is played out in an environmental background of rural and family life, which had not changed much for centuries despite the bloody, internecine warfare carried out by the various regional powers in the Near East, and then finally resulting in the occupation by the Romans.

Readers may find it of great interest to read the Book of Daniel, as he describes, well in advance, the forthcoming panorama of Near East history with one great dynasty defeating another, all of which eventually came about. There were four kings who ruled Judea during Daniel's lifetime: Josiah (640 – 609 B.C.); Jehoahaz (609 B.C.); Jehoiakim (609 – 597 B.C.), and Zedekiah (597 – 586 B.C.). During the time that Daniel was captive in Babylon, he was asked to interpret a dream for King Nebuchadnezzar of Babylon, in which Daniel describes a statue with a head of gold, chest and arms of silver, a middle and thigh of bronze, with legs of iron, and feet partly of iron and partly of clay. We are told the head of gold represented Babylon (626 – 539 B.C.); the chest and arms of silver represent the Medo-Persians (539 – 331 B.C.), with the two arms representing both the Medes and the Persians who had joined forces. The middle and thighs of bronze identified Greece (331 – 66 B.C.) and the legs of iron, represented the Roman Empire. In the 5th century A.D., the Roman Empire split into two-parts: one part remained in Rome, and the other half was established in Constantinople (modern day Istanbul in Turkey). This explains why the legs became iron, thus demonstrating the empire becoming weaker, and eventually failing in the West in 476 A.D. Each of the above-named empires conquered the Israelites at one time or another, and Daniel, through his dream, had accurately prophesied these future events. (Note: The feet of iron and clay, mentioned by Daniel, chapter two, are future events that have not yet come about, but will during the tribulation period (explained in a later chapter). Why? Because the first four metals have already happened).

Over time, some Christians have wondered why it is necessary to study the Old Testament Jews, and you may have asked the same question. Is it possible for us to disregard the Old Testament without diluting our faith in Jesus Christ? Or, is the story of the Jews of Israel necessary for us to understand the life of Jesus Christ? Well, I hope the material you have read so far has put you in good stead, as you later tie what you have learned so far, with the upcoming Christian movement, and the establishment of the New Covenant of Jesus Christ. As we later delve into the details of the ministry of Jesus, the importance of Old Testament knowledge will take on even more importance as the flow of God's story becomes clearer.

Long before criticism of the Old Testament was begun by certain cult groups, we find Jesus treating the complete Old Testament as "the Word of God." I refer you to various biblical passages in the New Testament, such as: Mark 7:13; Matthew 22:31-32, and John 10:35. Jesus may have objected to the religious leaders' misuse of his Father's Words, but he never contradicted or corrected the Old Testament laws and prophecies. Instead, you will find he fulfilled them, and he treated them as part of his Father's will. The early Christian leaders esteemed the Old Testament as God's Word, because their Savior had recognized the words of the Old Testament as God's Word. This explains why churches in the second century A.D., rightly renounced anyone who challenged God's Word. Finally, there is unmistakable continuity between the two testaments, because the same God was fulfilling his promises in both testaments. It has often been said that the Old Testament is the New Testament concealed, and the New Testament is the Old Testament revealed! The two testaments are like a horse and carriage – you can't have one without the other, as the song goes.

3

GOD SPOKE THROUGH HIS PROPHETS

"For prophecy never had its origin in the human will, but prophets, though human, spoke from God as they were carried along by the Holy Spirit." 2 Peter 1:21

NOW THAT WE HAVE COMPLETED AN OVERVIEW OF ANCIENT JEWISH history, which has assisted us in better understanding the great contribution Jews have made to the Bible, we will now address gaining more Bible knowledge by looking through another lens of history. This will provide us with further insight into how God uses certain people to communicate his thinking based on his standard for proper human conduct. Because no one has ever seen God, we find God communicating with certain chosen people who demonstrated great faith in God despite his invisibility. For instance, in the Old Testament, we find Abraham and Moses, being exalted as prophets for the tremendous work they did to carry out God's will, and to convey his covenants. It was Abraham's great faith in God that caused him to uproot his family from Ur, and travel hundreds of miles to an unknown place called Canaan. It was Moses' prophetic vision that encouraged him to face the power of Pharaoh, and then lead his people to create the Kingdom of Israel, all based on a promise from God.

Attempting to learn about the future is very popular with modern readers, and a source of great fascination, and we will discuss the subject in much greater detail in a later chapter. It is also true ancient people were just as enthralled about knowing the future, because they believed only a supernatural being could know what lies ahead, and for them to gain such knowledge required some sort of divine revelation or omen. Most ancient societies had their own particular procedures for discovering the will of their deities regarding coming events. Israel, like many other nations, had a long history of gaining knowledge of the future through a number of means. It should be pointed out, however, that Israel later developed distinctive religious traditions that produced a remarkable type of prophecy that clearly set them apart.

Before God's true prophets came into prominence, we find that the use of divination was the most common type of prophecy in early Israel. By "divination," it means the idea of discovering the direction of future events by manipulating objects, or by attempting to interpret phenomena. Typically, the diviner would usually focus on something that was unusual or random, and beyond the control of humans. The procedure could be as simple as casting lots, but often it meant using specialized techniques of interpretation. Examples would be the location of stars and planets, the way an arrow would fall, or the pattern of birds in flight. Or, it could be the markings and shape of a liver of an animal being sacrificed. Any such methods might provide an omen of things to come. The prophet, Ezekiel, for instance, described the King of Babylon trying to make a decision: "He shakes the arrows, he consults the teraphim, he looks at the liver." Despite the ban imposed on divination in Israel (Deuteronomy 18:10-12), we find divination did not disappear. The Prophet, Isaiah, described his people as: "full of diviners from the East and soothsayers like the Philistines."

Another form of divination in early Israel was the use of the Urim and Thummim, which were small sacred objects of unknown form, that could be cast as a lot to get a "yes" or "no" answer to a question. Under careful control, they were kept in the "breast piece" of the high priest's sacred robe, or "ephod." Joshua, for instance, was found obtaining guidance in leading his people by standing before the high priest: "who shall inquire for him by the judgment of the Urim." Even though the Urim and Thummim fell out of favor during the period of the monarchy, the belief in divine revelation through lots did not cease until much later.

The interpretation of dreams was yet another method whereby the future could be predicted. We find throughout the Bible, dreams are repeatedly mentioned as a form of divine revelation. Abraham, while he was asleep, for instance, learned the future of his descendants, and we are told the patriarch, Jacob, dreamed of a ladder reaching to heaven with the Lord speaking to him from its top. One of his sons, Joseph, was a great dreamer and an interpreter of the dreams of others. Other examples include King Solomon, who was given the gift of wisdom from God while in a dream.

It was in the context of the widespread forms of divination, with its many claims of special dreams, and visions of ecstasy, that the role of God's true prophets eventually emerged. There were various types of prophets. Some, known as seers, maintained religious shrines, and made predictions to visitors. One such prophet was Samuel, who was told by God to anoint Saul as king. Seers often lived and traveled in groups, and they would be found prophesying in the depth of ecstatic trances, and sometimes accompanied by musical instruments. For example, when Saul was on the road to Gibeah, "a band of prophets met him, and the spirit of God possessed him, and he fell into a prophetic frenzy along with them." (1 Samuel 10:10). Another example of many prophets, is to recount the story of Queen Jezebel, who killed scores of prophets, while hundreds more hid in caves.

After Samuel became the selector and anointer of kings, some prophets joined the court as counselors. Samuel advised King Saul, and later we find Nathan advising King David. In later development, the prophets became the guardians of the covenant, and if a king broke the covenant, he would be criticized by the prophets, who also had great influence over the people.

During the classical period, the Jews divided the Hebrew Bible (Old Testament), into former and latter prophets. The former prophets were grouped as: Joshua, Judges, Samuel, and Kings. The latter prophets are grouped as: Isaiah, Jeremiah, Ezekiel, and the Twelve (see below), which contain pronouncements of these prophets as receiving the prophetic call from God, after the kingdom was divided in 931 B.C. It was the latter prophets we think of as the classic era, when Israelite prophecy began, which spanned a period of about 400 years, from the eighth through the fifth centuries B.C. They began prophesying just before the Northern Kingdom fell to the Assyrians. By the time of the Assyrian assault, we find the prophet Hosea complaining, to no avail, that the people had turned from God, and had adopted the gods and worship practices of their Canaanite neighbors. It is also true in Judah, (note: Judah was later Hellenized to Judea, but they are the same place), that the people's worship was corrupted by the influence of the Assyrians, and the Mosaic laws were being forgotten. Each time the people forgot God's covenant, the prophets were always there to remind them, to challenge them, and to plead with them to avoid the coming disaster, if they did not change their behavior.

The latter prophets, to whom the longer books are attributed, are also referred to as the Major Prophets, which include: Isaiah, Jeremiah, and Ezekiel. The prophet, Daniel, was included in the Writings, (Hagiographa). The other Twelve, are referred to as the Minor Prophets, due to the brevity of their books. The Twelve include: Hosea, Joel, Amos, Obadiah, Jonah, Micah, Nahum, Habakkuk, Zephaniah, Haggai, Zechariah, and Malachi, who is the last prophet before the four hundred years of silence, before Christ came.

Coming up, I have listed the 39 books identified by their names in the Hebrew Old Testament canon, compared with their English names for the same books. Also, for convenience I have listed all 66 books of the Bible on Exhibit "C", at the back of the book. In this chapter our focus is on the former and latter prophets of the Old Testament. The Law books will be discussed in a later chapter.

During the days of the monarchy, we find many prophets attempted to make a living by acting as advisors to the royal court. They helped guide the king in executing his plans, and often saying whatever the king wished to hear. The idea of future revelation through visions, dreams, or spirit possession made it perhaps difficult for an observer to distinguish between true and false prophecy. Consequently, the biblical prophets criticized and condemned their prophetic opponents. In Jeremiah, for example, God says, "I have heard what the prophets have said whose prophecy lies in my name, saying, 'I have dreamed, I have dreamed!' How long shall there be lies in the heart of the prophets who prophesy lies, and who prophesy the deceit of their own heart . . ." (Jeremiah 23:25-26).

This conflict between true and false prophets was real, and often the kings would side against the true prophets. Therefore, it is understandable the words of true prophets, which have survived, are usually not those spoken by officials of the royal court. The true prophets' words that became treasured scripture, were not just foretellers of future events, but in actual fact were men who, in God's name, called their whole country into judgment for its immorality, injustice, and lack of faith in the one Almighty God. Time and again, the prophets attempted to reform the religious practices and governmental policies of their nation. Yes, they were just a few voices among many, but they provided Israel's guidance regarding their concerns about the future.

As we continue to explore the Old Testament, we find the Bible is very clear in its theme, which is from first to last, the story of Jesus Christ. The 39 books of the Old Testament are held together by a common thread that focuses on God's promise to redeem mankind, with the thread continuing into the New Testament where we find the promise being fulfilled in the ministry of Jesus Christ. So, although Jesus' name is not mentioned in the Old Testament, we find when we look for him, he is in every chapter. So, if we look for Christ, the books of the Old Testament become more alive to us, and there are many ways in which he is revealed. We find him in his work as the Creator of our world, his role as the sustainer of the creation, the "types" and portraits of institutions, events, ceremonies, and persons that point to him. He is found in his office of prophet, priest, and king, that all point to his future work to come. Jesus also made appearances, which we call "Christophanies," and we see him in God's covenants, that are ultimately fulfilled by him. Some of the key covenants are mentioned in greater detail in later chapters.

The Hebrew Canon of the Old Testament

Most importantly, we find Jesus mentioned in many Messianic prophecies and in the great prophecies decreed some hundreds of years before Jesus' birth. In the Book of Hebrews 1:1-2, it says: "Long ago, at many times and in many ways, God spoke to our fathers by the prophets, but in these last days he has spoken to us by his Son, whom he appointed the heir of all things, through whom also he created the world."

You will find there are numerous prophecies about a future Messiah mentioned in the Old Testament. A number of renowned scholars have concluded there are more than 400 passages where

Book Classification	Hebrew Name	English Name
THE LAW (TORAH)	Bereisheet (beginnings)	Genesis
	Shemot (names)	Exodus
	Vayikra (he called)	Leviticus
	Bamidbar (in the wilderness)	Numbers
	Devarim (Words)	Deuteronomy
PROPHETS	Joshua, Judges, 1 Samuel, 2 Samuel, 1 Kings, 2 Kings	Joshua, Judges, 1 Samuel, 2 Samuel, 1 Kings, 2 Kings
LATTER PROPHETS	Isaiah, Jeremiah, Ezekiel The Book of the Twelve: Hosea, Joel, Amos, Obadiah, Jonah, Micah, Nahum, Habakkuk, Zephaniah, Haggai, Zechariah, Malachi	Isaiah, Jeremiah, Ezekiel, Hosea, Joel, Amos, Obadiah, Jonah, Micah, Nahum, Habakkuk, Zephaniah, Haggai, Zechariah, Malachi
THE WRITINGS (HAGIOGRAPHA)	Praises	Psalms
	Job	Job
	Proverbs	Proverbs
	Ruth	Ruth
	Song of Songs	Song of Songs
	The Preacher	Ecclesiastes
	How!	Lamentations
	Esther	Esther
	Daniel	Daniel
	Ezra	Ezra
	Nehemiah	Nehemiah
	1 The words of the days	1 Chronicles
	2 The words of the days	2 Chronicles

Jewish Rabbis have interpreted the mention of a Messiah. Some claim as many as 456, with many mentioned in the Pentateuch (first five books of the Hebrew Bible), 243 from the Prophets, and 138 from the Writings (Hagiography). They go on to say their Messianic application is supported by more than 558 references to the most ancient Rabbinic writings.

One of many examples of a coming Messiah can be found in the Book of Isaiah 42:1-9. Isaiah, who lived some 700 years before the birth of Jesus, spoke about a servant of God who would become a light for the Gentiles (all non-Jews) and who would bring justice to the nation. The prophecy went on to mention the servant would be gentle and meek (verse 2), and yet he would have a great impact on the people of the world (verses 1, 4, and 6). In many other passages in the 66 chapters of Isaiah and other prophecies mentioned in the Bible, we are told the Messiah would be born in Bethlehem (Micah 5:2) and that he would suffer and die for the sins of others (Isaiah 52:12-15; 53:1-12). Isaiah goes on to say the Messiah would be eternal (2 Samuel 7:16 and Isaiah 9:6, 7). No matter how much additional research a person does, they will find Jesus Christ is the only person in history who is the fulfillment of the many prophecies that are too numerous to mention in this chapter.

I mentioned earlier, the Old Testament is the New Testament concealed, and the New Testament is in the Old Testament revealed. To help tie this together, you will find six major Jewish Feasts fulfilled in New Testament passages. To further press the message home, on page 34 you will find a number of Old Testament prophecies (but by no means all) regarding the future Messiah (Jesus Christ), which have already been fulfilled in the New Testament.

In discussing the subject of Bible prophecy, I offer two reliable sources indicating one-fifth and one-quarter of Bible verses contain prophecy. John MacArthur Jr. states one-fifth of the Bible have prophecy, and one-third of those Bible prophecies relate to the Second Coming of Jesus Christ. He states there are 333 prophecies specifically discussing Christ in the Old Testament, and 109 have already been fulfilled at Christ's First Coming. We can conclude, then, that the other 224 prophecies will be fulfilled at or before his Second Coming. Of the 46 Old Testament prophets, only ten speak of the First Coming, whereas 36 speak of the Second Coming. Also, of the 7959 verses in the New Testament, we find that 330 refer to the Second Coming. Jesus refers to his Second Coming about 25 times, and there are at least 50 verses where he impresses his listeners to be ready for his return. It is obvious to us all that God takes Bible prophecy very seriously![1]

The second source is from J. Barton Payne, who states there are 1239 prophecies mentioned in the Old Testament and 578 in the New Testament for a total of 1817. Considering the 31,124 Bible verses, this would indicate 26.8% is prophecy.[2]

Irrespective of exact numbers of prophetic verses, it is quite obvious God takes the subject of prophecy very seriously, which will be further reinforced in a later chapter.

In summing up this chapter, it is important to understand the New Testament, along with its New Covenant of Jesus Christ (which we will be discussing later), does not supersede the Old Testament, though the New Covenant of Jesus Christ does supersede the Old Testament Covenant. In Jesus's own words, he said: "Do not think that I have come to abolish the Law of the Prophets; I have not come to abolish them but to fulfill them. For truly, I say to you, until heaven and earth pass away, not an iota, not a dot, will pass from the Law until all is accomplished. Therefore, whoever relaxes one of the least of these commandments (The Ten Commandments discussed in a later chapter), and teaches others

---

1   John MacArthur Jr., *The Second Coming of the Lord Jesus Christ* (Panorama City, CA; Word of Grace Communications), p. 1.

2   J. Barton Payne – *Encyclopedia of Biblical Prophecy.*

Prophecy	Old Testament Reference	New Testament Fulfillment
SEED OF THE WOMAN	Genesis 3:15	Galatians 4:4
THROUGH NOAH'S SONS	Genesis 9:26-27; 1 Chron. 1-1	Luke 3:23-28
SEED OF ABRAHAM	Genesis 12:3	Matthew 1:1; Galatians 3:8, 16
BLESSING TO NATIONS	Genesis 18:18	Galatians 3:8
BLESSINGS TO GENTILES	Genesis 22:18, 26:4	Galatians 3:8, 16; Hebrews 6:14
THE TRIBE OF JUDAH	Genesis 49:10	Revelation 5:5
NO BROKEN BONES	Exodus 12:46; Numbers 9:12	John 19:36
THRONE OF DAVID	2 Samuel 7:12-13, 16, 25-26; 1 Chronicles 17:11-14, 23-27; 2 Chronicles 21:7	Matthew 19:28; 21:4-5; 25:31; Mark 12:37; Luke 1:32; Acts 2:30; 13:23; Romans 1:3.
DECLARED SON OF GOD	Psalms 2:1-12	Matthew 3:17; Mark 1:11; Acts 13:33; Hebrew 1:5; 5:5; Revelation 2:26-27; 19:15-16
JESUS' RESURRECTION	Psalms 21:4	Acts 2:27; 13:30-35; 26:23
HIS HANDS/FEET PIERCED	Psalms 22:1-31	John 20:27; Luke 24:38-39
ACCUSED/FALSE WITNESSES	Psalms 35:11	Matthew 26:59-61; Mark 14:57-58
BETRAYED BY A FRIEND	Psalms 41:9	Matthew 26:14-16, 47, 50; Mark 14:17-21; Luke 22:21-23; John 13:18
HATED WITHOUT REASON	Psalms 69:4	John 15:25
HIS ASCENSION	Psalms 68:18	Ephesians 4:8
GIVEN GALL AND VINEGAR	Psalms 69:21	Matthew 27:34, 48; Mark 15:23; Luke 23:36; John 19:29.
SPEAKS IN PARABLES	Psalms 78:2	Matthew 13:34-35
PRAYS FOR HIS ENEMIES	Psalms 109:4	Luke 23:34
EXALTED BY GOD	Psalms 72:1-19	Matthew 2:2; Philippians 2:9-11
BORN OF A VIRGIN	Isaiah 7:14	Matthew 1:22-23
REJECTED BY HIS PEOPLE	Isaiah 52:13-53:12	Matthew 27:1-2, 12-14, 38-40
CRUCIFIED WITH THIEVES	Isaiah 53:12	Luke 23:32-33
A NEW COVENANT	Jeremiah 31-34	Matthew 26:27-29; Mark 14:22-24; Luke 22:15-20; 1 Corinthians 11:25; Hebrews 8:8-12; 10:15-17; 12:24; 13:20.

to do the same, will be called least in the kingdom of heaven, but whoever does them and teaches them will be called great in the kingdom of heaven. For I tell you that unless your righteousness exceeds that of the scribes and Pharisees, you will never enter the kingdom of heaven." (Matthew 5:17-20).

It is also reasonable to surmise if God intended the Christian Bible to consist of the New Testament alone, it would make no sense to arrange it to include the Old Testament. The truth is he did, and that is all the evidence we Christians need to vouch for its importance and indispensability to our understanding of God's intentions for all of us.

Journal Your Thoughts

_____

_____

_____

_____

_____

_____

_____

_____

_____

_____

_____

_____

_____

_____

_____

_____

_____

_____

_____

_____

4

GOD'S GREAT BIBLE RESETS # 1-2

"A thorough understanding of the Bible is better than a college education!" –President Theodore Roosevelt

OUR WORLD TODAY IS BEING DISRUPTED BY MASSIVE CHANGES IN THE areas of technology, economics, politics, environmental issues, and culture. All this change is affecting the way we interpret today's reality, and our view of history. These changes are so dynamic, forceful, and powerful, they are not only complicated to understand, but also difficult to keep up with due to the rapidity of changing events. It seems like no one is in control, and our world appears to be heading over a cliff. It is quite tempting to think these changes will be short lived, and we will soon be returning to normal. However, in this current environment, it appears the changes taking place will make our world far different in the future, from what it was since the end of World War II.

As I mentioned in the introduction, there are some very powerful and wealthy people who are calling for a "Great Reset" to the current world order. They want to establish a "New Covenant," made by man for the benefit of man, or at least for the benefit of a few men at the expense of the many. There are lots of conspiracy theories out there, and many should be dismissed out of hand. However, what I am talking about is real, and can be easily verified. At the forefront of this new economic system is the World Economic Forum (WEF), which meets annually to host a group of elite leaders from the world of business, media, government, and culture. The WEF is the most visible of the organizations I mentioned in the introduction.

Since the end of World War II, we have witnessed the creation of the United Nations, the World Bank, the International Monetary Fund, the World Health Organization, and the International Court of Justice at the Hague, just to mention a few, which are all designed to promote peace, unity, and stability. They have all been created to prevent a repeat performance of the 20th century, the bloodiest century on record. Previous U.S. presidents have been supportive of these organizations, especially George H.W. Bush, who was a key player in the new global world order. This trend was accelerated after the fall of the U.S.S.R. in 1991.

So, the idea of creating a new world order is nothing new, and the WEF is simply one of the current organizations promoting it at their annual meetings, typically held in Davos, Switzerland. They have been around since the 1980s, and whether we realize it or not, their members already run much of the world. They produced a video in 2016, stating the United States would no longer be the number one economy in the world by 2030. A book they wrote in 2021, during the pandemic, is called, *Covid-19: The Great Reset*, and they discuss the forecast of a post-pandemic world where countries work much closer together to solve the problems of mankind.

The members of the WEF, and members of other elite groups, are what we refer to as *transnationalists*, who do not necessarily think in terms of national loyalties. They think that nation-states, and their borders, are nothing but obstacles needing to be removed (our Mexican border is a good example). A nation-state to them, is nothing more than a convenient place for many global operations, such as Amazon, Apple et al, to serve the needs of a global community.

The forward thrust towards a fully integrated global economy is relentlessly pressing forward, with most multinational companies no longer considering themselves as large national companies. With offices all around the globe, with call centers connecting customer service people in India, for example, with people in America, Europe, and many other people groups, it seems obvious that converting to a global, digital currency would be a simple next step. Along with this new reset of global values would be the idea of creating universal values for all the world's citizens.

The WEF believes the "social contract" between the individual and the state has failed, because it has not produced equity, freedom and justice for all people. Therefore, a new social contract is necessary, but it tends to be vague on the details of what this means.

We do know there is discussion about revamping our financial system due to the deplorable debt our government owes, now pushing towards $35 trillion! We all agree this is unsustainable, but the idea of moving from a capitalistic system to a form of socialism, whereby private property rights are eroded or eliminated to give more power to a central government, is not the answer. The WEF believes the equitable distribution of wealth around the world is not fair, and should be flattened, so everyone has an equal amount. Unfortunately, there are simply too many books in print, with real history to back up the facts, demonstrating socialism and communism simply do not work. Capitalism, on the other hand, though it has many faults, has proven to be the best system of all when we consider the economic uplifting of millions of people around the world, from the miserable conditions existing in prior centuries.

Capitalism has also made a great contribution, thanks to Christian principles, to the overall freedom and enlightenment of mankind, and the United States has played a major role in implementing many of these positive forces. Unfortunately, today there is another aspect to America's declining position, which is tied to the cultural divide subverting our national will, and causing us to fight amongst ourselves. Jesus Christ himself, once said, "And if a house is divided against itself, that house will not be able to stand." (Mark 3:25). Current groups behind the idea of a great-reset appear to have a definite agenda to curb U.S. influence by lending support to China's aspirations of becoming the dominant world power. Meanwhile, the European Union is on a similar mission to shape a world that is favorable to their historic culture and vision.

The capitalistic system that has worked so well for America, and the Western countries of Europe, Australia and New Zealand, and has brought economic freedom to millions around the world, will be completely revamped by the year 2030, if the WEF crowd have their way. The result will be a greater amount of power and wealth placed in the hands of fewer people. We are already witnessing three major American companies (Vanguard, Blackrock and State Street), now controlling a very large percentage of the stock in many of the Fortune 500 companies, which no doubt provides them with huge voting rights. This allows them significant influence on decisions made by the many Boards of Directors.

As men grapple for wealth and power, they fail to realize in many ways this is all part of what the Bible foretells. Already we are seeing chips implanted in the hands of workers in Sweden, and a number of large countries are involved in the creation of digital currencies. If and when they are implemented into the mainstream of social life, they could allow governments to cutoff certain citizens from the currency system if they don't act according to government expectations. Something akin to this is already happening in China, and the last book of the Bible predicts all this. Futuristic writers such as Aldous Huxley (Brave New World), George Orwell (1984), (Animal Farm), Ray Bradbury (Fahrenheit 451), and Soylent Green (screenplay), and many others, all attest to a future managed by a few to control the many.

So, in an attempt to shed some overall perspective on our modern-day problems, I refer back to the Prophet, Jeremiah, who told us about a great reset that took place back in approximately 550 B.C. The degeneration of man had caused God to use this holy man to speak to the people on his behalf. We find God telling him, "Behold, I have put My words in your mouth. See, I have this day set you over the nations and over the kingdoms, to root out and to pull down, to destroy and to throw down, to build and to plant." (1:9-10). During that time the mighty Assyrian Empire collapsed (which had defeated the Ten Tribes of Israel, and moved them into exile), and we find the mighty empire of Egypt was relegated to a secondary power, with Judah then falling to Babylon. It was a great reset of world order, but it also served as a lens for our modern day, as we are also in the midst of social and economic upheaval, all being created by the global pandemic, and powerful people who wish to take advantage of the situation. There have been only a few times in the past when we have experienced so many transformative changes all coming together at one time. This is what is causing so much worry for vast numbers of people.

The major point being made in this chapter is the fact these elite and powerful groups, who are attempting to reset a new world order, are failing to understand the biblical world-view God has planned. While these so-called "masters of the universe" tinker around with the idea of playing God, they are blinded in not understanding God's plan has already been in place for thousands of years, and will continue to be so until the end of our world as we know it. How do we know this? The Bible tells us so.

In a later chapter we will explore what the Bible tells us about future events, so I don't want to get too far ahead of the biblical story.

All of these trends are leading to the biblical end times mentioned in the Books of Daniel, Ezekiel, Zechariah, Matthew, and others. The last book, the Revelation, talks about people having a mark placed on their hand or forehead in order to purchase survival needs. For people who do not know the Bible, they will not be aware of how the Bible's predictions for the future turn out, which can cause them great worry and angst. Christians, on the other hand, and those who do know how the story of man ends, as mentioned in the Bible, will have confidence in their future, because they know they will be living an eternal life one day, when this short life ends. This will be further developed in a later chapter.

The importance of this, and other chapters, is to mention God has reset the life of man on a number of occasions in the past through a series of Covenants, and there is another Great Covenant yet to come. Man, left to his own devices, had demonstrated during the Old Testament period, that he was not capable of living a life in accordance with God's commandments, and tended to degenerate, moving further away from God. Therefore, God has applied these resets, or covenants, to put man back on the right road toward righteousness and ultimate salvation. Just like the fairy tale, we find man acting like Humpty Dumpty, who fell off the wall, and had to be put back together again. God has had to put man back together again, repeatedly.

So, in this chapter, we will address the first two Great Resets, or Covenants, God has already created, and have already happened. In later chapters we will continue to build on more past covenants as we progress with the great plan God has for this world, and all its inhabitants. It will then be quite evident God is in charge of everything, and the Davos crowd only think they are.

The details of covenant making

The Bible tells us God has a visionary plan for all mankind, and it has been laid out in a series of special covenants, five of which have already happened in the Old Testament, and two mentioned in the New Testament, of which one has already been fulfilled, and one that will play out in the future. The Old Testament reveals important details of God's plan to produce for himself an enduring holy people. (Leviticus 20:26; 26:12; Hebrews 8:10).

There are two types of covenants in the Hebrew Bible, which include the obligatory type, and the promissory type. The obligatory type was common among the Hittite people, which dealt with the relationship between two parties of equal standing. By contrast, the promissory type dealt with the relationship between the suzerain and the vassal, with the suzerain being superior to the vassal. The suzerain and the vassal are similar to the royal grant type of legal document, which covered such items as border delineations, witnesses, blessings and curses. All these conditions were implemented with the idea of loyalty to the suzerain. This type of covenant was typical of ancient near east treaties, and we can find evidence of this in the Aba-El deed, which was put together by the son of Hammurabi, who provided us with the first code of law.

Another example of a promissory type of covenant was when Ashurbanipal, an Assyrian, gave a grant to his servant, Bulta. This type of covenant can be seen in the Abrahamic and Davidic Covenants, which were implemented between God and man. We find critical to any covenant, is the concept of a lasting commitment to a clearly defined relationship. Usually, a covenant is a long-term agreement between two or more parties formalizing a binding relationship between them. It highlights the essential obligation and commitment between each other.

Other examples of the above covenant type would be the Shoe Covenant mentioned in Ruth 4:7, and the Salt Covenant, mentioned in Leviticus 2:13, and Numbers 18:19. There is also the Blood Covenant mentioned in Genesis 15:7-18, and Matthew 26:28. You will find the Jews took their covenants very seriously, and the Jewish *brit,* with God, is codified in their Torah. The real value of these covenants is in the substance of the commitments made, for it is through God's divine obligation, that he binds himself to perform all of the promises he makes. We find in such a divine covenant, God defines the basic obligations he imposes on himself, and on the other parties to the covenant. The covenant is also a formal declaration of God's will and purpose, and by so doing, he expresses his deep love for humanity.

Let us now begin to take a closer look at the covenants God has made with mankind, which all form a revelation leading up to the end times discussed later. These covenants, or Great-Resets, all come about due to the degeneration of man's morality, and his self-destructive behavior, creating the need for a reset in order to get man back on track with God's overall plan.

The Adamic Covenant - God's Great Reset # 1

This covenant is a two-part statement of God's promise to the first man, Adam. The first part of the covenant took place during the time of man's innocence, when Adam lived in the beautiful Garden of Eden. He had been created in the image of God, and was given dominion over all the animals. He was later given a wife, Eve, and they enjoyed the gift of relationship between each other, and with God, along with the blessing of bearing children. With an ability to name all the animals, it is obvious Adam had superior intelligence and memory, and was blessed in numerous ways.

The first part of the Adamic Covenant is sometimes referred to as the Edenic Covenant, a covenant of innocence, and is found by a reading of Genesis 1:26-31 and 2:16-17. It outlines the conditions imposed on Adam while he lived in the Garden. It consisted of blessings, but also a warning to Adam. He could eat from any tree in the Garden, but not from the tree of the knowledge of good and evil. Unfortunately, Eve did not heed God's warning, and she obeyed Satan (the serpent and enemy of God), and ate from the one forbidden tree. This caused her husband to do likewise. This disobeying of God's command, resulted in both of them being banished from the Garden.

The second part of the promise (the Adamic Covenant) known as a Covenant of Grace, was not given to Adam until after he had sinned. This part details the conditions imposed on Adam while existing outside the Garden, and it includes the curse (Genesis 3:15-19).

God cursed the serpent above all livestock and the beasts of the field. God went on to say, "I will put enmity between you and the woman, and between her offspring and your offspring; he shall bruise your head, and you shall bruise his heel." This has been interpreted to mean the defeat of the serpent by a future descendant of the woman. This defeat is implied by the serpent being bruised in the head, which is more serious than the offspring of Eve being bruised in the heel. For this reason, verse 15 has been labeled as the "Protoevangelium," the very first announcement of the coming Gospel.

God went on to tell the woman, "I will surely multiply your pain in childbearing; in pain you shall bring forth children. Your desire shall be contrary to your husband, but he shall rule over you." Then God said to Adam, "Because you have listened to the voice of your wife and have eaten from the tree of which I commanded you, you shall not eat of it, cursed is the ground because of you; in pain you shall eat of it all the days of your life; thorns and thistles it shall bring forth for you; and you shall eat the plants in the field. By the sweat of your face, you shall eat bread, till you return to the ground, for out of it you were taken; for you are dust, and to dust you shall return."

Survival in this new, natural world, was going to be a struggle for Adam, Eve, and all their descendants going forward through the ages (Romans 8:22-23). Finally, death would become the fate of every living thing (Genesis 3:19). This was God's first Great Reset caused by the degeneration of the first human couple. God was providing Adam with a second chance, by providing redemption based on a covenant of grace.

The Noahic Covenant - God's Great Reset # 2

After Adam had broken the Adamic Covenant by disobeying God, we find all mankind moving further away from the gracious presence of God, and corruption and immorality increased to the point God could stand it no more. Consequently, he created a world-wide flood to destroy mankind. However, before doing so, he elected Noah to build an ark for his family, and to house numerous animals. Thankfully, for all human beings, God was demonstrating he was not content to allow the destruction of mankind to last forever, and he created another covenant to correct Adam's transgression.

God saved righteous Noah, his family and the animals, through his Covenant of Grace, to correct the transgression of Adam. The Noahic Covenant is explained in Genesis 8:20-21; 9:8-17, where God says, "I will never again curse the ground because of man, for the intention of man's heart is evil from his youth. Neither will I ever again strike down every living creature as I have done. While the earth remains, seedtime and harvest, cold and heat, summer and winter, day and night, shall not cease." God goes on to instruct Noah to go forward, be fruitful and multiply, and fill the earth. He allows him to eat meat, and provides a rainbow as a sign that he will never destroy the earth again by flooding. This covenant is saying God's pledge is to preserve the stability of nature thus creating an environment where people can flourish, and to provide an entrance for history, whereby God can bring about man's salvation (John 1:14). This pledge from God, never to destroy the earth again, is also an earthly sign that one day all creation will be renewed.

We are often tempted to think the cycle of seasons, and the setting of the sun, are all due to the orbiting of our planet, and its revolution on its axis. Although these facts have been proven by the scientific community, we must never forget it is God at work through these means, helping to keep the Noahic Covenant in force. Therefore, when we witness each sunrise, sunset, and change of season, it should be a reminder and proof that God never breaks his promise. This is God's second great reset, once again proving necessary due to the fall of mankind.

Journal Your Thoughts

_____

_____

_____

_____

_____

_____

_____

_____

_____

_____

_____

_____

_____

_____

_____

_____

_____

_____

5

GOD'S GREAT BIBLE RESETS # 3-4

"It is impossible to mentally or socially enslave a Bible-reading people. The principles of the Bible are the groundwork of human freedom!" –Horace Greeley

The Abrahamic Covenant

GOD'S THIRD GREAT RECESS CENTERS AROUND A MAN NAMED ABRAHAM, who was asked by God to journey from the pagan city of Ur, in Mesopotamia, to the Land of Canaan, where he eventually built a great legacy leading to the formation of the Jewish people. The Bible tells us the Abrahamic Covenant was given by God to Abraham and his seed, whether by natural birth or adoption, and although God makes promises, he does not make any stipulations or conditions on Abraham for the covenant's fulfillment. We first learn about Abraham and the promises he is given by God in Genesis 12:1-3. Long before the covenant is carried out, we find God's grace at work in his attempt to redeem the people he has chosen for an exclusive relationship. God promises Abraham new land, and the creation of a great nation. His name will be revered, and there will be many more blessings that will eventually be extended to all the families of the earth. This is a wonderful example of how God, and he alone, makes sure the covenant will be a success.

Later, in Genesis 15:1-6, God promises Abraham a great reward with a son of his own. Abraham wondered how he would have an heir due to his advanced age, but God tells Abraham he will have many descendants. Abraham believed God, and therefore was found righteous in God's eyes (Genesis 15:6). The promise of descendants was not fulfilled until Abraham was 100 years of age, and his wife Sarah was 90, which meant Abraham and his wife had to rely on God alone for a very long time before the promise became a reality.

In the final part of the story, we find God informing Abraham his offspring will be servants of another place, which foreshadowed the later enslavement of the Israelites in Egypt under Pharoah's control. God goes on to say they will return to the Land of Canaan after 400 years, along with great possessions. Then, they will rightfully rule over the promised land.

We must also remember the Abrahamic Covenant is part of a tradition of covenantal sacrifices dating back to the third millennium B.C. Animals are slaughtered in the covenant in Genesis 15, and are considered sacrificial offerings. It is the covenant that helps preserve the sacrificial element side-by-side with the symbolic act itself.

The three main take-aways from the Abrahamic Covenant state the Israelites will:

1. Receive the promised Land of Canaan (Genesis 12:1)

2. Receive the promise of numerous offspring (Genesis 15:4-6)

3. Receive the promise of blessing for the whole world (Genesis 12:3).

4. This covenant came about due to mankind once again degenerating into a moral abyss, causing God to select a group of people to be his special, chosen people, who could set an example for all other people groups in loving and obeying the one true, monotheistic God. The passages mentioning the chosen people, can be found in the Book of Deuteronomy 7:6, 14:2.

Previously, I introduced some of God's covenants, tracing them back to traditional ways that business was conducted in the ancient Near East. I mentioned suzerains and vassals, and the difference between Obligatory and Promissory forms of covenants. We concluded the Adamic, Noahic, and Abrahamic covenants were forms of the Promissory type of covenant. The next covenant is of a similar kind, with God acting as the suzerain.

The Sinai Covenant – God's Great Reset # 4

The Sinai Covenant is also known as the Mosaic Covenant, a biblical covenant between God and the Israelites, including their proselytes. You will find it recorded in the first five books of the Hebrew Old Testament Bible, and collectively called the Torah, or the Pentateuch. It is also called the Law of Moses, the Mosaic Law, or commandments. Many people do not realize the Old Covenant, or Mosaic Covenant, was essentially a marriage contract by which God became a husband to Israel (Jeremiah 31:32). You find in this covenant, Israel, the wife, had agreed to submit to God and obey his laws. Unfortunately, the Israelites became disobedient. Israel's adultery with foreign gods, was found to be so outrageous to God, he divorced his people, except for a few "remnants," who tried to serve him (Jeremiah 3:8; 31:32; Isaiah 50:1).

The Sinai Covenant was meant to reinforce the covenant God had given to Abraham, and it told the Israelites what they had to do in order to fulfill their side of the covenant. Once again, we find God stating he would stay with the Israelites and never abandon them, because they were his chosen people.

Upon confirmation of the Sinai Covenant, which also includes the famous Ten Commandments, (which are so important to humanity, we will address separately in later chapters), we find Moses and the Israelites put in the position of living according to certain stipulations and conditions, in order to comply with their end of the covenant. This, of course, called for a level of interpretation of the commandments. Reading further, we find Moses instructing and issuing ordinances to solve specific situations, many of which he was able to do from case law already in existence. However, the insight needed in determining their selection and application, undoubtedly came from the "Tent of Meeting." This was a simple sanctuary tent located outside the camp area, where God, or Yahweh, spoke to Moses personally. Anyone who breached the covenant had to make atonement. This required the creation of a priesthood to manage proper worship procedures and sacrificial conditions. Sinai was the place where a great deal of Hebrew culture evolved, and it was here the Twelve Tribes of Israel were identified.

A little perspective

Before we do our deep dive into the Ten Commandments, it is important to see where our society has progressed to, since many people have either abandoned, disrespected, or simply think these commandments are no longer valid. So, let's take a summary look at where we are today regarding our moral standards.

If our national cultural indicators are anything to judge by, we can certainly make the case American morality has slipped drastically over the last 50 years or so, as it has in many other places around the world. High rates of murder, rape, armed robbery, human trafficking, and huge spikes in pornography, all go against God's commandments. We are also witnessing high increases in fornication, adultery, and thievery. Sad to say, in America today, we find almost 50% of our children spend their lives in split-family situations, and one in four pregnancies end up being aborted, with more than 60 million babies having been aborted since abortion became legal in 1973. This is a form of infanticide that was practiced in the pagan times of ancient Greece and Rome. Out of wedlock births, are as high as 70% in the Black population, and we have one of the highest STD rates of all the countries in the world. The question on many people's lips, is how much longer will God allow this behavior to continue?

The word sin is mentioned more than 500 times in the Bible, so when we apply the law of proportionality, it is easy to see why God places a great deal of emphasis on this subject. Sin is a small word, but it is packed with a lot of meaning. It is simply the breaking of God's law. Sadly, the last time an American president used the word *sin* in a speech, was President Dwight Eisenhower back in the 1950s, when he quoted from Abraham Lincoln! Note that President Clinton did say, "I have sinned," during his sex scandal, but that is not what I am talking about.

Sin is pervasive in today's society, having infiltrated all corners of American life, including the media, politics, the Internet, and our educational system. There is also a growing disrespect for religion in general. As a result, we find the Pew Research Center, now stating the "nones," (people not associated with any religion, and do not attend church), now constitute 29% of American adults! That is up from 23% in 2016, and 19% in 2011. Pew goes on to say if these unaffiliated were a religion, they would be the largest religious group in the United States!

Christians today are facing a rear-guard action against atheists, agnostics, and people who just don't care about developing the spiritual part of their human nature. Even our highest court, SCOTUS, ordered a small town in Indiana to remove the Ten Commandment monument from the front of city hall. The people and the courts are losing the message that God gave us these laws for a reason. He knew we could never achieve our true-life potential, unless we live our lives according to his commandments.

Can man live without absolutes? We only have to look back to the 19th and 20th centuries to realize millions of people listened to Karl Marx, who insisted man is not controlled by the absolutes of God, but rather by economic factors. Remember also, Friedrich Nietzsche, the admired German philosopher, who famously stated "God is dead," also said the only thing controlling man is the quest for power. I also bring to your attention, Sigmund Freud, who stated man is controlled by his sexual desires, and not by the law of God. And let us not forget Charles Darwin, who vowed the only consequential law that mattered was the survival of the fittest!

Let us now take a brief look at the legacy these men handed down to us during the last 200 years.

To start, the communist empire built on the teachings of Karl Marx is now in shambles. Nietzsche? Well, he spent the last ten-years of his life in an insane asylum. Notwithstanding this fact, we later find Adolph Hitler being a huge fan of Nietzsche, and tried to implement some of his superman programs in Germany. As for Sigmund Freud, he is no longer revered in psychology circles, and is now considered somewhat anachronistic. And Darwin? His idea that human life began in some primeval cesspool billions of years ago, without any assistance from God, and then somehow evolved into who we are today, has been debunked on so many levels, since scientific methods have become far more sophisticated. The truth is, God's law is not relative. His law, unlike man's, is absolute, immovable, and does not change.

To wrap up the Mosaic Law, before we later discuss the Ten Commandments, it should be noted God gave Moses three types of laws worth mentioning:

Civil Laws:

At that time in history, Israel was a theocracy, which states God was the king, judge and leader of his people. This means there was no legislature or parliament in Israel in order to pass new laws, or to amend existing ones. God was the chief legislator, and you will find when reading God's civil laws, they always mention a punishment if they are broken. It could be a fine, a beating, or even execution. Further, ignorance was not accepted as an excuse, and punishment was swift. Interestingly, under Mosaic Law, there were 16 crimes that could cause the death penalty to be enacted. During the time of the Anglo-Saxons, there were only four. However, in the early 1800s in England, there were more than 200 death penalty crimes! The pendulum on capital crimes has swung drastically over the centuries, to the point it is rarely used in modern societies, with the exception of a few countries.

There were no prisons in ancient Israel. Instead, they had cities of refuge to prevent vigilantism. Babylonians had prisons, as did the Assyrians, Greeks and Romans, but not ancient Israel. So, what happened to the civil laws of Israel? Well, when the Romans destroyed Jerusalem in 70 A.D., the civil laws were also abolished.

Ceremonial Laws:

The second type of law is found in the Pentateuch (the first five books in the Old Testament). These ceremonial laws pertain to sin offerings, trespass offerings, along with all the other sacrificial offerings of the Jewish religious system. We later find all these sacrifices simply act as a foreshadowing of Jesus Christ, the coming Messiah. By faith in the atoning future death of the Messiah, which was set forth in the sacrificial offering of bulls and goats, Jews were able to have their sins covered temporarily.

Though the sins could not be forgiven, the payment allowed an extension for a period of time. However, when Christ gave his life as a ransom for many (Matthew 20:28), the sacrificial system was abolished, because it was no longer necessary. Why? Because Jesus Christ paid the price for our sins, once and for all (Hebrews 10:11-14). In other words, when Christ died and rose again, the requirements of the ceremonial laws were canceled. We are saved and forgiven, through the purified blood of the Lord Jesus Christ.

Moral Laws:

Thirdly, there were moral laws, as detailed in the Ten Commandments. These laws define God's moral character, which never changes. For instance, would it be foolish for us to think when God gave us the Ten Commandments some 3400 years ago, it was wrong to steal then, but okay today, because he has changed his mind? Does it make sense to say God thought adultery was sinful back then, but it is OK in these modern times? Many people appear to think that way today, as if God has softened his position on those and other commandments. No, he has not! The good Scriptures tell us God is fair, applies consistent justice and application of the law, and his law is to be respected by everyone throughout history, and into the future. We find both the Old Testament and the New Testament provide us with numerous examples of the importance of obeying God's law. In a later chapter, we will discuss St. Paul, who gives us his summation of the Christian Gospel, and ends by saying, "Do we then make void the law through faith? Certainly not! On the contrary, we establish the law." (Romans 3:31). Hebrew Scripture promises us the commandments of God, his law, would one day be written on the hearts of all humans, and Christians have already discovered this promise to be true.

The Ten Commandments, as part of the Sinai Covenant, will be explored in more detail in the next chapter, once again serving as another Great Reset, established by God to steer his people toward the right path in life, in order to win God's favor. The chapters following, are designed to open people's eyes and minds to these great commandments, which are just as relevant today as when first given to us. Unfortunately, they have been somehow thrown onto the "scrap heap" of history as no longer having the same meaning, or importance to our lives. Many people fail to realize that these commandments have, over these many centuries, represented the "glue" holding our moral standards together, and have allowed man to gain such tremendous progress as a result.

Journal Your Thoughts

_____

_____

_____

_____

_____

_____

_____

_____

_____

_____

_____

_____

_____

_____

_____

_____

_____

_____

_____

_____

_____

_____

_____

6

OVERVIEW AND PURPOSE OF THE TEN COMMANDMENTS

"The Ten Commandments have lost their validity. Conscience is a Jewish invention. It is a blemish like circumcision!" –Adolf Hitler

WHEN WE READ THE BIBLE, WE ARE INTRODUCED TO EXODUS 20:3, which contains perhaps one of the greatest sections of religious literature the world has ever known – the Ten Commandments of God, which he gave to the Israelite leader, Moses, for the benefit of his people, and for all future mankind. It is also known as the *Decalogue,* Ten Words, or *deka,* which is Greek for the word, "ten," and *logos* meaning "word."

God gave these words to the Israelites during their journey from Egypt, where they temporarily stayed at Mount Sinai. As we meditate, we find these commandments unveil to us the very heart of the human soul, and its rebellion against God's law. History has proven people want to do it their way, and do not like anyone telling them what they can and cannot do, including what God says. Here are God's Ten Commandments, which convey God's laws.

The Ten Commandments:

1. You shall have no other gods before me

2. You shall not make for yourself a carved image, or any likeness of anything that is in heaven above, or that is in the earth beneath, or that is under the water of the earth. You shall not bow down to them or serve them, for I the Lord your God am a jealous God, visiting the iniquity of the fathers on the children to the third and fourth generation of those who hate me, but showing steadfast love to thousands of those who love me and keep my commandments

3. You shall not take the name of the Lord your God in vain, for the Lord will not hold him guiltless who takes his name in vain

4. Remember the Sabbath day, to keep it holy. Six days you shall labor, and do all your work, but the seventh day is a Sabbath to the Lord your God. On it you shall not do any work, you, or your son, or your daughter, your male servant, or your female servant, or your livestock, or the sojourner who is within your gates. For in six days the Lord made the heaven and the earth, the sea, and all that is within them, and rested on the seventh day. Therefore, the Lord blessed the Sabbath day and made it holy

5. Honor your father and your mother, that your days may be long in the land that the Lord your God has given you

6. You shall not murder

7. You shall not commit adultery

8. You shall not steal

9. You shall not bear false witness against your neighbor

10. You shall not covet your neighbor's house; you shall not covet your neighbor's wife, or his male servant, or his female

servant, or his ox, or his donkey, or anything that is your neighbor's.

Modern reality check:

I will now share with you two stories that provide a type of litmus test regarding the attitudes of many people, toward the Ten Commandments, in our modern-day culture. The first took place a few years ago, when a number of students were asked by their teacher to arrange the Ten Commandments, by prioritizing them in order of importance. In other words, they were expected to rate the most important commandment first, down to the least important. After some deliberation, the students decided, *thou shalt not murder,* was the most important of the commandments, which was followed by *thou shalt not steal.* The next one, they figured, was, *thou shalt not bear false witness,* (lying), and so they went down the list, prioritizing the rest as they went. When they got to the end, they could not decide which of two commandments should be last. After further considerable discussion, it was found half the class stated, *thou shalt not commit adultery,* and the other half stated, *thou shalt have no other gods before me.* When the vote was finally decided, this last commandment was chosen to be the very last! In other words, the very first and most important commandment set down by God in Exodus 20:1, more than 3,000 years ago, turned out to be the least of the commandments in the eyes of these young students! They had completely turned God's law upside down![1] Who was it who said in the end times, right will be wrong, white will be black, up will be down, and truth will be replaced with constant lying?

---

1   Source: Anonymous to protect the teacher

The second story involves a CNN website article entitled: "Behold, Atheists' New Ten Commandments." Airbnb (the property leasing company), the sponsor, offered a $10,000.00 reward to anyone who would like to be the modern version of Moses. Contestants simply had to present their version of the ten, "non-commandments." In reviewing almost 3,000 responses, they selected a panel of judges to preside over the winning version, which is mentioned as follows:

1. Be open-minded and be willing to alter your beliefs with new evidence

2. Strive to understand what is most likely to be true, not to believe what you wish to be true

3. The scientific method is the most reliable way of understanding the natural world

4. Every person has a right to control their own body

5. God is not necessary in order to be a good person or to live a full and meaningful life

6. Be mindful of the consequences of all your actions and recognize that you must take responsibility for them

7. Treat others as you would want them to treat you, and can reasonably expect them to want to be treated. Think about their perspective

8. We have the responsibility to consider others, including future generations

9. There is no one right way to live

10. Leave the world a better place than you found it.[2]

---

2   CNN – Behold Atheists' New Ten Commandments 12.20.2014.

The purpose of sharing these stories is to point out where our moral code has devolved to in such a short period of time in man's history. In the first story, the students demonstrated complete ignorance of the original intent of the biblical Ten Commandments. In the CNN story, there is no doubt the adults involved were educated people, according to our modern-day definition. However, they had developed their own thinking based on an individual sense of what is right and wrong, irrespective of what God thinks.

There is a little hypocrisy to their answers, when you dig a little deeper. First, they say you don't need God in your life in order to be a good person, or to know the proper way to live (#5). This appears to be contradicted by their seventh commandment, (#7), which appears to represent the Golden Rule, which was given to us by Jesus Christ himself in Matthew 7:12. They mention the scientific method (#3), without mentioning the fact it was invented by a Christian, back in the 16th century. Francis Bacon invented the inductive reasoning method, which later became known as the scientific method. This method later helped Christian leaders to know God better. They also mention their #10 commandment, stating we must leave the world a better place than we found it, which causes us to compare it with their #9 non-commandment, which says there is no right way to live. We know this was a publicity stunt, but it does provide us an additional lens into seeing how far we have strayed from God's original intentions in today's society.

In all fairness to Americans, though, a survey conducted by Pew Research asked citizens living in some European countries, how important religion was to them. The answers below are based on each country's citizen's responses as a percentage of the population:

Portugal	37%
Italy	27%

Ireland	24%
Germany	21%
Spain	21%
United Kingdom	19%
Netherlands	18%
Norway	17%
Finland	13%
France	12%
Sweden	10%[3]

The United States, incidentally, still has more than 50% of the population who claim religion is very important to their lives, but the numbers are admittedly going down.

Clearly, if moving further away from God's word is helpful to our social system, and apparently many believe so, then our world should be a much better place to live in than it is, right? Obviously, that is not the situation today, and therefore a good case can be made that getting back to the basic fundamental laws God laid down for us a long time ago, is a much better option for us as we advance forward.

Are There Good Reasons for Studying the Ten Commandments?

There was a time when the answer to this question was not necessary, because it was self-evident to a large majority of the population. Today, however, we find in many Christian churches, there appears to be a reluctance to discuss the Commandments, or even the subject of sin for that matter. Therefore, taking a trip down memory lane can provide us with a reminder of manyforgotten principles, and the great importance of inculcating God's

---

3   Pew Research 12.5.2018 – How do European Countries differ in Religious Commitment?

commandments into our everyday life. So, here are a number of reasons for reiterating God's commandments:

COMMON IGNORANCE: Our public schools do not teach the Ten Commandments anymore, and children are not being taught them in the home. People have a fleeting understanding of the commandments, but most cannot recite most of them. Many people cannot recite even five of the ten, according to Barna & Associates. Here are a few troubling examples:

1. 82% of Americans think, "God helps those who help themselves," is a Bible verse.

2. A majority think the Bible teaches the most important purpose of life is taking care of one's family.

3. 12% of adults think Joan of Arc was married to Noah.

4. Some 50% of students thought Sodom and Gomorrah were husband and wife.

5. A considerable number of respondents thought that Billy Graham preached the Sermon on the Mount.[4]

We don't expect secularized Americans to be fully knowledgeable about the Bible, because America's civic dialogue has been stripped of all biblical references and content. Our citizens are now living in Scripture-free public space, as evident in many media outlets. Therefore, ignorance of the Bible's content should be assumed in a post-Christian America.

Unfortunately, an even larger concern is the growing ignorance of Scripture among Christians. Irrespective of what survey you choose, you will find Christians in general know less and less about the Bible, and it shows in the way they act in society, as

---

4   Barna.com – archives.

they are gradually conforming to the demands of our secular culture. This dilution of the Christian faith is affecting us at all levels of society.

Forgetting our historical heritage

Throughout church history, we find the Ten Commandments have always been emphasized. This has been particularly true with regards to children, and new members of the faith. For hundreds of years, the church has prioritized the importance of Christian education through the Ten Commandments, and in the New Testament era with the Apostles' Creed, the Council of Nicaea, the Council of Ephesus, the Council of Chalcedon, and the Athanasian Creed, to name a few. The Ten Commandments, along with the creeds, and the Lord's Prayer, were recited orally to provide a practical guide on how to live, and they are still emphasized in the Lutheran Larger Catechism, and the Shorter Westminster Catechism.

New Testament validation

The Ten Commandments are emphasized in the New Testament by Jesus himself. In Matthew 19:16-22, we find a rich man asking Jesus: "Teacher, what good deed must I do to have eternal life?" "Why do you ask me what is good? There is only one who is good. If you would enter life, keep the commandments." He then said to Jesus, "Which ones?" And Jesus went on to list the Second Table of the Law (The first three of the commandments represent the First Table, and the remaining seven detail the Second Table). Jesus said, "Do not murder, do not commit adultery, do not steal, do not bear false witness, honor your father and mother, and, you shall love your neighbor as yourself."

Interestingly, Jesus never mentioned the tenth commandment to the rich man, which is, do not covet. Perhaps Jesus knew that this was the one commandment that would be difficult for the rich man to honor due to his great wealth, and his reluctance to share it.

The Jews turned the ten commandments into 613, but they can all be summarized in the Ten Commandments, which in turn can be summarized by just two commandments mentioned in Matthew 22:36-40, where Jesus says, "Love the Lord your God with all your heart, soul, and mind, and love your neighbor as yourself." By living up to these two commandments we have lived up to them all. Later, Paul reiterated the same message when he said, "You shall love your neighbor as yourself." (Romans 13:8-9). Later, as we examine the New Covenant of Jesus Christ, you will find that Jesus, in transforming the Ten Commandments, never intended to abolish them. (Matthew 5:17).

A lot of good comes from obeying the commandments

The commandments are intrinsically good, and there is no question our social condition would be much improved if everyone understood and obeyed them. As mentioned earlier, we know from history that man continuously rebels against obeying rules and laws. However, here is an interesting thought. Try to imagine for a moment what life would be like if the Ten Commandments of God had never been given to Moses at Mount Sinai. Most people would agree that crime statistics would be much higher. Rape burglary, armed robbery, kidnapping, murder, with locks and chains on everything, would be the order of the day. Our two-million plus prison inmate population would be a much higher number, and every conceivable law you can think of would be broken. We would no doubt return to the pagan world of the past, when life was brutal, and very short. So, keeping the Law of God is a very good thing if it allows us peace of mind, security, and an inner-feeling that we are in lock-step with God's instructions for our lives.

I have just mentioned several reasons for studying the Ten Commandments. Studying them is very important for the reasons given, but obeying them is even more important. With this thought in mind, let us now look at several reasons why obeying the commandments can bring more love, joy, peace, patience, kindness, goodness, and faithfulness into our lives:

Obeying the Ten Commandments is fulfilling

Surveys tell us many people today feel they cannot live up to the Ten Commandments as an attainable goal, although they wish they could. The fact is a number of these commandments can be obeyed by ordinary people, at least in the outward letter of the law. This is true, even if they have not received the gift of the Holy Spirit. It is possible for instance, not to worship idols, not to take the Lord's name in vain, and to rest on the Sabbath, and keep it holy. It is also possible for people to respect and honor parents, not to commit murder, adultery, or commit thievery. Right from the very beginning we find God expecting much more from his creation of human beings, because he is interested in what comes out of their heart, which is judged by their actions. However, when we receive the Holy Spirit into our heart, which will be reviewed later when we discuss the New Covenant of Jesus Christ, we become more fortified to obey the commandments. We must first, however, seek repentance for our transgressions.

Reasons for obeying the Ten Commandments:

Other than in the Book of Daniel 5:5, where God wrote the famous handwriting on the wall, we find God, just like Jesus Christ, never put any of his words in writing, with the exception of his Ten Commandments, and his divine words through his chosen people. Therefore, the law provides us with a unique peek into God's heart and character. It is important for us to think about this before we say his commandments have no meaning in today's society. The commandments not only show us what God wants, but they also indicate to us what God is like. These commandments tell us a great deal about God's honor and majesty. By framing the conversation this way, it becomes obvious we cannot disrespect God's law without also disrespecting God himself!

The dictionary tells us freedom is having an exemption or liberation from the control of some other person or arbitrary power. It stands for independence, and being able to act without restraint. On the other hand, the biblical definition of freedom is not doing everything you want. We find many people think the Ten Commandments are too restrictive on their freedom, in that it prevents them from doing whatever they want. They feel the commandments inhibit their ability to reach their true potential, and fulfill their dreams. A reading of the Bible, however, tells us it is God's intention to give us life and to have it abundantly. (John 10:10). The Bible also tells us, "We will know the truth and the truth shall set us free." (John 8:32). Jesus tells us, "Come to me, all who labor and are heavy laden, and I will give you rest. Take my yoke upon you, and learn from me, for I am gentle and lowly in heart, and you will find rest for your souls." (Matthew 11:28). We are also told God's commandments are not burdensome. (1 John 5:3).

For people who think trying to live according to the ten commandments is tough, they should take a closer look at the number of laws we already have on the books of the United States. American laws run into the hundreds of thousands, with federal laws dealing with firearms alone, exceeding 300,000! Living by man's laws can be tricky, with the ever-present possibility of being sued under civil law, to say nothing of exposure to potential criminal offenses due to circumstances.

So, when we compare God's law with man's law, it becomes easier to see God is not trying to bog us down with a lot of regulations and red-tape. Think instead, of God's commandments as traffic laws, designed to keep us from having an accident. It is more positive to think this way, rather than assuming that by obeying God's law, it is somehow a type of jail sentence restricting our freedom.

In John 14:15, we find Jesus simply saying, "If you love me, you will keep my commandments." For all Jesus has done for us in providing us with redemption for our sins, through his shed blood at Calvary, it is the very least we should be doing!

7

God's Great Bible Reset #5

"God operates the world by covenants. These covenants have specific jurisdictions and responsibilities, not just infringed upon by another covenant." –Pastor Tony Evans

The Davidic Covenant:

OD'S FIFTH GREAT BIBLE RESET CENTERS AROUND WHAT IS KNOWN AS the Davidic Covenant, which was given by God through King David, to establish a clear linkage between the previous other four Great Resets, or covenants, in the Old Testament, and the New Covenant of Jesus Christ in the New Testament. This covenant serves as a prelude and preparation for the later coming of Jesus Christ. It establishes a clear bloodline easily traceable from Christ to David, and back to Abraham, the founder of the Jewish faith.

King David lived a very colorful life, which resulted in much success, as well as tragedy. He was born in Bethlehem about 907 B.C., during the time of the great prophets, and during the same time the Israelites were given their first human king, a man named Saul. Prior to that, the Israelites were a theocracy, but yearned for a monarchy, which God finally granted to them by charging Samuel, a prophet, to appoint Saul to be king. Meanwhile, David, grew up tending the sheep of his father, Jesse.

Parenthetically, Jesus the Messiah, would later be born through the bloodline of this great King David. Listen to what the Gospel of Luke says: "And the angel said to her, 'Do not be afraid, Mary, for you have found favor with God. And behold, you will conceive in your womb and bear a son, and you shall call his name Jesus. He will be great and will be called the Son of the Most High. And the Lord God will give to him the throne of his father David, and he will reign over the House of Jacob forever, and of his kingdom there will be no end.'" (Luke 1:30-33).

King Saul later fell from grace in the eyes of God, and thus began a spiritual search to replace him, which resulted in David becoming king after King Saul died fighting the Philistines. King David married many times, but only eight are mentioned in the Bible: Michal, Ahinoam, Abigail, Maacah, Haggith, Avital, Eglah, and Bathsheba. Unfortunately, David's adulterous affair with Bathsheba, and David's involvement in the death of her husband, caused great pain, and he was full of remorse. They had a child together, but he died, and later they had another child named, Solomon, who would later replace David as king.

David was a warrior, a man of war, and he caused much loss of blood during his kingship. For this reason, God would not allow David to build the Temple (1 Chronicles 22:6-9). Instead, God told David he would build a house (dynasty), that would last forever. God also advised David that his son, Solomon, would be the one to build the Temple.

Jewish custom tells us David died at age 70. Before his death he wanted to know when he would die, but God would not tell him. God simply told David he would die on Shabbat (the Sabbath). It is said David made it his duty to study the Torah every Shabbat, in order to prevent Satan from taking his soul. We are further told the Angel of Death distracted David from his Shabbat learning by shaking the trees in his garden. This caused David to climb the stairs to see what was happening. Just then, one of the steps broke under his feet, and he died from the fall.

We find God always provides us with progressive revelation, as he unfolds his plan for mankind a little at a time. It appears everything God does, it builds on itself, as he unveils how he intends to cause what he promised. Looking at the previous covenants, we can easily see how they build on each other – The Adamic, Noahic, Abrahamic, and Mosaic, because they are designed to create milestones of redemption in order for mankind to atone for sin. The covenants were initially given to the Israelites, who later became known as Jews, and God's chosen people. The idea of a new kingdom and a redeemer, had been percolating through the Bible all the way back to the first book, Genesis. However, with David, it became more precise as you will soon see.

After God had established the Ten Commandments, it became necessary to pave a clear way for the Messiah to come to earth, which was on the lips of the Israelites for a very long time. This dream became clearer with the birth and reign of King David in Judea.

God created the Davidic Covenant with King David, almost 1000 years before Jesus Christ would be born, which was a grant type of covenant, similar to the Abrahamic Covenant. It was an unconditional covenant. It was different from the Mosaic Covenant, that was more similar to a Suzerain – Vassal type, with clear conditions attached to it. We consider the Davidic Covenant as unconditional, because God did not place any restrictions in order to fulfill it. The promise contained in the covenant rests solely on the faithfulness of God, and was not conditional upon anything David or Israel had to do in order to maintain it.

God's promise to David, through the prophet, Nathan, tells us how God promised David and Israel, that the Messiah (Jesus

Christ), would descend from the bloodline of David, and the Tribe of Judah. God promised a kingdom that would last forever. The Davidic Covenant itself comes in two-parts. The first part represents promises that will come true during the lifetime of David.

The second part contains other promises that came after David's death. In the Book of 2 Samuel 7:11-13, it says, "The Lord declares to you that the Lord himself will establish a house for you ("house" meaning "dynasty."). When your days are over and you rest with your fathers, I will raise up your offspring to succeed you, who will come from your own body, and I will establish his kingdom. He is the one who will build a house for my name." The promise continues, "I will establish the throne of his kingdom forever." It also goes on to say, "Your house and your kingdom will endure forever before me; your throne will be established forever." See also 2 Chronicles 6:16.

Davidic Covenant terms:

The Davidic Covenant contains four declarations God made with his people:

1. **Establishing a place for Israel:** In Genesis 17:8, God says, "And I will give to you (Abraham), and to your offspring after you, the land of your sojourns, all the land of Canaan, for an everlasting possession, and I will be their God." Later, we find God telling Abraham's son, Isaac, in Genesis 26:3, "Sojourn in this land, and I will be with you and bless you, for to you and your offspring I will give all these lands, and I will establish the oath that I swore to Abraham your father. I will multiply your offspring as the stars of heaven and will give to your offspring all these lands. And in your offspring, all the nations of the earth shall be blessed, because Abraham obeyed my voice and kept my charge, my commandments, my statutes, and my laws."

Finally, the Bible tells us Isaac's later son, Jacob, is told by God in a dream, "I am the Lord, the God of Abraham your father and the God of Isaac. The land upon which you lie I will give to you and to your offspring. Your offspring shall be like the dust of the earth, and you shall spread abroad to the west and to the east, and to the north and to the south, and in you and your offspring shall all the families of the earth be blessed. Behold, I am with you and will keep you wherever you go and will bring you back to this land. For I will not leave you until I have done what I have promised you." (Genesis 28:13-15).

2. A Royal bloodline: In Luke 1:31-33 we find an angel saying to Mary, "And behold, you will conceive in your womb and bear a son, and you will call his name Jesus. He will be great and will be called the Most High. And the Lord God will give to him the throne of his father David, and he will reign over the House of Jacob forever, and of his kingdom there will be no end." Also, in Isaiah 9:6-7 it says, "For unto us a child is born, to us a son is given; and the government shall be upon his shoulder, and his name shall be called, *Wonderful Counselor Mighty God, Everlasting Father, Prince of Peace.* Of the increase of his government and of peace there will be no end, and he will reign on the throne of David and over his kingdom, to establish it and to uphold it with justice and righteousness from that time forth and forevermore. The zeal of the Lord of hosts will do this." It is interesting that when we trace the bloodline leading to Jesus, we find it includes men, women, adulterers, prostitutes, heroes, villains, and Gentiles. Jesus became the Savior of them all!

3. A sustainable kingdom: Further evidence of the restored seed of David ruling over the Jewish kingdom and the world, is amplified when we see what happened to the great powers of the Babylonians, Medo-Persians, Greeks, and Romans, who were all later destroyed. In the Book of Daniel 2:44-45, we find the prophet,

Daniel, explaining the king's dream as follows, "And in the days of those kings, the God of heaven will set up a kingdom that shall never be destroyed, nor shall the kingdom be left to another people. It shall break in pieces all these kingdoms and bring them to an end, and it shall stand forever, just as you saw that a stone cut from a mountain by no human hand, and that it broke in pieces the iron, the bronze, the clay, the silver and the gold. A great God had made known to the king what shall be after this. The dream is certain, and its interpretation sure." With these great powers all later coming to an end, we can readily see why Christ's realm is David's kingdom forever.

A throne and dynasty that will last forever

As previously mentioned, when the twelve tribes split into ten tribes forming the State of Israel, and the tribes of Judah and Benjamin formed Judah, with their principal capital in Jerusalem, we find only the kings of Judah retained the Davidic kingship. God was faithfully fulfilling his promise to preserve David's bloodline by seeing to it each Davidic king became a rightful heir to the Davidic throne. Each succeeding king then had the right to rule based on the bloodline of David.

Now this is where it gets interesting. Just before the Babylonians captured Judea, God had become outraged with the Davidic Judean King Jeconiah (who was also known as Coniah), and so God instructed the prophet, Jeremiah as follows: "As I live, declares the Lord, though Coniah the son of Jehoiakim, King of Judah, were the signet ring of my right hand, yet I would tear you off and give you into the hand of those who seek your life, into the hand of those whom you are afraid, even into the hands of Nebuchadnezzar, king of Babylon, and into the hands of the Chaldeans (modern day Iraq). I will hurl you and the mother who bore you into another country, where you were not born, and there you shall die. But for the land for which they long to return, there they shall not return." (Jeremiah 22:24-27). Then, in verse 30, God says this: Write this man down as childless, a man who shall not succeed in his days, for none of his offspring shall succeed in sitting on the throne of David and ruling again in Judah!"

It appears from the above declaration by God, that all descendants of Solomon's bloodline were basically cursed by God, and would never fulfill the Davidic king line of succession. However, we know that Jesus will later receive the Davidic Covenant, giving him the legal title to rule forever. The question then becomes, how can this be? Upon further study, we find Jesus, in his humanity, actually descended from David's other son, Nathan, through Jesus' mother, Mary, rather than through the Solomon bloodline. In the Book of Luke, chapter 3:23-38, we find a complete genealogy of Jesus Christ, tracing his human lineage back to Nathan, the son of David, and then all the way back to Adam, the first man.

It should also be noted that Jesus also obtained the legal right to rule from his step-father, Joseph, who was a direct heir to Solomon. Check the bloodline in Matthew 1:1-16, for further clarification. The bottom line is, that although the bloodline of the Davidic King Jeconiah (Coniah), was cut-off by God, we find, thanks to the work of Luke, that Jesus did in actual fact descend from the Davidic bloodline, through Nathan, the brother of Solomon (Nathan was the son of David and Bathsheba). Furthermore, Jesus' bloodline can also be traced legally from his step-father, Joseph, back to Solomon. Here again we give thanks to Matthew. The evidence is in, and it is solid that Jesus did descend through the bloodline of King David, just like the Bible says. This story serves as a classic example of how the Bible can be misinterpreted when passages are taken out of context. There is a valuable lesson to be learned here as we pursue our Bible study.

In summary, the Davidic Covenant is unalterable. There is nothing that can change God's plan for mankind. God's promise made to David is unconditional, and unbreakable. A reading of Psalm 89 attests to the permanency of the covenant. It is rather long, but the key verses three and four say this: "You have said, 'I have made a covenant with my chosen one; I have sworn to David my servant: I will establish your offspring forever, and build your throne for all generations.'"

8

THE OLD TESTAMENT IN LESS THAN 30-MINUTES

"It is impossible to rightly govern the world without God and the Bible!" –President George Washington

BEFORE PROVIDING YOU WITH A PANORAMIC OVERVIEW OF THE OLD Testament, it is important to first mention there is a difference between the Hebrew or Jewish Old Testament, and the Christian Old Testament version, but only in book order, rather than in substance. So, allow me to provide more detail in order to eliminate any confusion when comparing one against the other.

First, the Jews consider the Old Testament their complete Bible, and therefore they don't consider it "old" for that reason. Also, the Jewish Bible has 24 books, which are arranged in a different order than the Christian Old Testament books, which contain 39. However, the 24 books and 39 books are the same, only categorized differently, which I will explain in a moment.

The Hebrew Bible is divided into three sections:

Section One is The Torah, or Pentateuch, which represents the

Law, and is referenced by the first five books: Genesis, Exodus, Leviticus, Numbers, and Deuteronomy.

Section Two is called Nevi'im, or the Prophets, and consists of the following books: Joshua, Judges, Samuel, Kings (all known as the Former Prophets), and Isaiah, Jeremiah, Ezekiel, and the Twelve Minor Prophets, all in one book, (referred to as the Latter Prophets). This gives us a total of eight books.

Section Three represents the Ketuvim (Writings), which includes: Psalms, Proverbs, Job, Song of Solomon, Ruth, Lamentations, Ecclesiastes, Esther, Daniel, Ezra-Nehemiah, and Chronicles, for a total of eleven books. The total of these three sections represents 24 books.

Using the English Standard Version (ESV) bible as an example, the Old Testament for Christians is categorized into four sections:

Torah or Pentateuch Books: Genesis, Exodus, Leviticus, Numbers and Deuteronomy. (Five Books).

Historical Books: Joshua, Judges, Ruth, 1 & 2 Samuel, 1 & 2 Kings, 1 & 2 Chronicles, Ezra, Nehemiah, and Esther. (Twelve books).

Poetic and Wisdom Books: Job, Psalms, Proverbs, Ecclesiastes, and Song of Songs. (Five books).

Prophetic Books: Isaiah, Jeremiah, Lamentations, Ezekiel, Daniel, Hosea, Joel, Amos, Obadiah, Jonah, Micah, Nahum, Habakkuk, Zephaniah, Haggai, Zechariah, and Malachi. (Seventeen books). The total of these four sections represents 39 books.

The Jewish 24 books are expanded to 39 books by taking Samuel, Kings, and Chronicles and changing them into six books (1 & 2 Samuel, 1 & 2 Kings, and 1 & 2 Chronicles). Then the Twelve Minor Prophets (one book), are turned into twelve separate books.

Ezra-Nehemiah is also split into two separate books, which gives us a total of 39.

The Torah:

In opening the first book, Genesis, we find chapters 1–11 represent dates before recorded history. They tell us stories providing us with not only history, but more importantly they teach us something about ourselves. They unmask the human condition. We become acutely aware of our lifelong struggle with sin, and our attempts to avoid and resist temptation. We are also exposed to our struggle with pride, and our propensity for violence. In these chapters we are also introduced to God's first two Great Resets, or Covenants, both the Adamic and Noahic Covenants.

From chapter 12 through the rest of the book, it contains the story of the Israelites, and how they were appointed as God's special, chosen people (God's third Great Reset, the Abrahamic Covenant discusses this). God called the Israelites to become his people, and entered into a covenant with them. The storyline goes on to tell us how these people often failed, and were unable to fulfill the covenants, due to their sins and disobedience to God. This led to their captivity and slavery in Egypt.

We discussed earlier how God gave the Israelites a narrow piece of land between the Saudi Arabian Desert to the east, and the Mediterranean Ocean to the west, which is referred to as the Promised Land. The land was very valuable because it controlled commercial trade between Asia and Egypt, and the rest of Africa. Consequently, there would always be a strong military power wanting to control it, thus placing the Israelites in the crosshairs of these invading forces.

In the Book of Exodus, we are told how God rescued the Israelites from 400 years of slavery in Egypt, by appointing the man, Moses, to deliver them to the Promised land – (modern day Israel,

PLO, Gaza Strip, Lebanon, and Jordan). God enters into his fourth Great Reset by creating a Covenant with Moses and the Israelites. It is called the Sinai Covenant, or Mosaic Covenant. In it are the famous Ten Commandments, and the rest of the law needed in order to create their new society, or kingdom, which was to be a theocracy, with God as their king. These laws included criminal, ceremonial and civil laws. The Israelites were then expected to become a light for all other people groups by serving as an example of the correct way to manage their lives according to the principles of God. It was Joshua, after Moses died, who was given the responsibility to conquer the Promised Land, and defeat the Canaanites.

So far, we have now covered the first five books, Genesis, Exodus, Leviticus, Numbers and Deuteronomy, known as the Torah, and part of the Book of Joshua.

Judges and kings:

Once the Israelites settled in the land they began to regress spiritually. Their morals became more lax, and they practiced worshiping idols, similar to other people groups around them. God is pushed further into the background as they concentrate on gaining wealth and enjoying pleasure. This caused God to withdraw his grace, and the people suffer until redemption takes place once again. This trend continues to repeat itself for many years.

The Book of Judges describes a transitional time in Jewish history in which Israel was made up of a loose federation of city-states. It started after the death of Joshua, about 1405 B.C., through to the anointing of Israel's first king, Saul, in about 1050 B.C. During this 350-year period, there were thirteen judges, both men and women. They were not judges in the Western sense, but rather leaders who were empowered by the Holy Spirit to help deliver Israel from her enemies, while at the same time exercising priestly duties, like Samuel, or providing military leadership, like Samson. Also, a great woman, Deborah, demonstrated a talent for administrative skills. The book provides many folk stories that are compelling to read, especially in the way they describe these leaders' heroism in battles with the Canaanites, Midianites, Ammonites, or Philistines, all during a time when there was no king in Israel.

Eventually, the people cried out for a king to lead them, and God allowed Saul to become their king. Saul, however, later falls from grace due to his disobedience to God, and David becomes the new king. God enters into a fifth Great Reset by creating the Davidic Covenant with David, (see previous chapter), which established a clear bloodline leading from Abraham to David, all the way through to the birth of Jesus, almost 1000 years after David dies.

After King David's death, his son, Solomon becomes king, and God allows him to build the temple. Solomon becomes the wisest man in the world, but later, due to marrying some 700 foreign wives, cohabitating with 300 concubines, while worshiping their gods, he became corrupted, and lost favor with God. Upon his death, his son, Rehoboam, became king. It did not take long before many of the tribal leaders complained to Rehoboam about unfair taxation and unbalanced distribution of favors benefiting Judea more than the northern tribes. Rehoboam, however, listened to poor advice from his priests, and resisted their demands for a more just system. Consequently, ten of the tribes broke away under a new king, Jeroboam, and created their own new State of Israel. King Rehoboam retained the House of Judah, the Benjamite tribe, and control of the holy city in Jerusalem, along with the Holy Temple.

God was very angry with the ten northern tribes due to their idolatry and immorality, and as the facts disclose, they were taken over by the Assyrians in 722 B.C., who then exiled and scattered them to many parts of Mesopotamia and Persia. Judah also practiced idol worship, and lost favor with God. This resulted in the Babylonians, some 130 years later, after having already defeated the Assyrians, to defeat Judea also. This happened over a period of years from about 605 B.C. to about 586 B.C. as previously mentioned. It was during this time the Babylonians destroyed Jerusalem and the Holy Temple. Many Jews were exiled to Babylon, where many remained for the next seventy plus years.

We have now summarized the books of Joshua, Judges, Ruth, 1 & 2 Samuel, 1 & 2 Kings, and 1 & 2 Chronicles.

After some 70 years in Babylonian captivity, we find once again God rescuing his people from their bondage. He enables the Jews to return to their homeland, and begin construction on the Second Temple. This was due to the approval of King Cyrus and the Persians, who had already defeated the Babylonians, and taken over the Holy Land area. This phase of Jewish history covers the books of Ezra, Nehemiah, and in some ways touches on the Book of Esther, which highlights the antipathy other people groups had towards the Jews.

The above three books complete the Christians' group of historical books, and from the first book, Genesis, through Esther, we have summarized Israel's history from the beginning of the world through to the return from Babylonian captivity, in more or less chronological order. The time period, excluding all that happened in Genesis 1 – 11, covers the year 2000 B.C. all the way through to about 450 B.C. During that time, we find the Jews involved in covenant making and covenant breaking, as God gave them, time and time again, the opportunity to redeem themselves. We can readily see Jewish history covers almost half of the Jewish Bible.

Next comes the poetic and wisdom books, which starts with the Book of Job, followed by Psalms, Proverbs, Ecclesiastes, and the Song of Solomon (aka: Song of Songs). The words in these books are more like poetry than prose, although Hebrew doesn't necessarily rhyme as much as it tends to repeat. Jewish poetry begins with a statement, and then the next line ends up repeating the first statement using different words, or it states just the opposite. In either case, the whole idea is to reinforce or emphasize the message to ensure effectiveness.

These five poetic and wisdom books are located in the center of the Jewish Bible. This may have been planned in that these books help to capture the heart and soul of the Jewish people, including both agony and ecstasy, joy and anguish. They appear to indicate all their suffering came from their unfaithfulness to God. The Book of Job, however, serves to counteract the other four books because Job was a very righteous man, yet he suffered terribly. This story clearly demonstrates suffering is not always a result of sin.

After Job, we come to the Psalms, commonly referred to by the Jews as their hymn and prayer book. There are 150 psalms that have been authored during the complete history of the Jews, whether during the good times or the bad. They include many joyful songs of praise, a number of laments, and the Jewish cries to God for his support in times of need.

Proverbs comes next, and they comprise short, concise sayings, providing us with knowledge we can use throughout our lives. Such short sayings are to be found throughout the Near East, and Egyptian wisdom contains a number of sayings that appear to parallel Jewish sayings. King Solomon is said to have spoken some 3000 proverbs and created 1005 songs. but we have only 31 proverbs in the Old Testament book. Proverbs states its overall theme at the book's beginning, where it says its goal is to describe and instill "wisdom" in God's people, a wisdom that is founded in the "fear of the Lord," as it works out covenant life in practical details of everyday circumstances and relationships. Proverb 6:16 serves as a good example:

> "There are six things the Lord hates, seven that
> are an abomination to him: haughty eyes, a lying
> tongue, and hands that shed innocent blood, a heart
> that devises wicked plans, feet that make haste to
> run to evil, a false witness who breathes out lies,
> and one who sows discord among brothers."

The fourth of the wisdom books is the Book of Ecclesiastes, which is the story of a wealthy man nearing the end of his life, who has come to realize the foolishness of all he has worked for, and gained throughout his existence. It stresses there is a time and a season for everything; a time for every matter under the sun. The theme of the book, however, is the necessity of fearing God in a fallen, and confusing world. It can be interpreted in many different ways, and runs the gamut of optimism to pessimism about life in general. Similar to the rest of the wisdom books, Ecclesiastes is mainly concerned with passing wisdom and knowledge along to the people of God, while at the same time teaching them to fear the Lord.

Finally, the fifth wisdom book is called the Song of Solomon, or the Song of Songs, which contains beautiful, sensuous poetry expressing romantic love between a young man (a shepherd), and a young woman in ancient Israel. This book was generally understood by the early Jews as a type of allegory of God's faithful love for Israel. However, down through the centuries, Christians have interpreted it as Jesus Christ's love for the Christian church, or love for the soul. A key theme to the book is God's covenant, which requires sexual purity, within the confines of a marriage relationship. God's honor is therefore upheld when God's people demonstrate with their lives, that their obedience in obeying God brings them joy and peace.

Song of Solomon completes the historical, or poetic and wisdom books of the Old Testament, which causes us to now turn to the prophets.

First, you will find the prophets' section are divided into two groups, the Major and Minor prophets. They are separated by the length of the books, not necessarily by order of importance. Within each group, you will find the books are roughly grouped chronologically, but not exactly. You will find the earliest prophets in both categories lived between the 8th and 5th centuries B.C., about a 400-year period. They began just before the Northern Kingdom (Israel), fell to the Assyrians. It was a time when Israel had turned from God and adopted other gods and worship practices of their Canaanite neighbors. At the same time, Judah was also being influenced by Assyrian gods, and the Mosaic Law was being forgotten. Each time the people forgot their covenant with God, the prophets were there to remind them, to reason with them, and to cry out to them about the coming disaster that would come, if they did not change their immoral and idolatrous ways.

The Latter Prophets, consisting of longer books, are referred to as the Major Prophets. They are Isaiah, Jeremiah, (who also wrote Lamentations), Ezekiel, and Daniel. The remaining twelve are referred to as the Minor Prophets, mainly due to the brevity of their books. They include: Hosea, Joel, Amos, Obadiah, Jonah, Micah, Nahum, Habakkuk, Zephaniah, Haggai, Zechariah, and Malachi.

The prophets came from varying walks of life. Isaiah, for instance, is remembered as coming from an upper-class family in Jerusalem, whereas Amos was a "herdsman" from a small Judean village. Each of these men were called to carry out God's message to the people. Their writings would often start with, "Thus says the Lord," which was a calling few would ever want to wish on themselves, due to the fact they were given the responsibility of exposing unpopular truths to the people. They also had to speak to powerful rulers about their lack of faith, and the likely results, if they did not change their ways. We are told no one wanted to listen, and these prophets were thrown out of courts and worship places, were vilified, and in some cases killed. Needless to say, the prophets were relentless, and continued to offer the people hope provided they amended their ways. They were truly the heart, and spiritual conscience, of the nation.

In summary, the Old Testament is the story of the people of Israel, and their faith relationship with God. It is also a story of their God, and what his will and purpose was for his people. The Old Testament does not read like it was ordained by God as much as it reads like a variety of writings, including law, short stories, court histories, poetry, along with the many prophetic warnings and predictions. As we read the story of the Israelites, we find our own story, and as they share their stories, their experiences, and reflections about their God, we also find God speaking to us as well.

JOURNAL YOUR THOUGHTS

THE NEW CHRISTIAN TESTAMENT

9

THE NEMESIS OF GOD AND MAN

"Like a good chess player, Satan is always trying to maneuver you into a position where you can save your castle only by losing your bishop." –C.S. Lewis

BEFORE DELVING INTO THE NEW COVENANT OF JESUS CHRIST, IN CHAPTER eleven, it is important to provide some background to help us better understand the motivation that caused the New Covenant, and all the previous covenants, to be enacted by God in the first place.

Living in an advanced nation like America, it is easy to be lulled into believing life on earth has never been better, when compared to the violence, disease, and famines of the past. We have gotten used to having plenty of food in our refrigerators, convenient in-door heating and air-conditioning, independent transportation, and easy access to higher education. Add to the list our health industry, with state-of-the-art equipment to fix almost every health malady known to man, along with the other great strides achieved in technological advancements, such as smart TVs, Internet, and smartphones, capable of researching anything, and it becomes easy to see why many of us have been lulled into thinking that way.

Meanwhile, if we take a 30,000-foot view of the larger picture of our globe, we witness another story entirely. Every night some 800 million people go to bed hungry, wondering if they will have anything to eat tomorrow. Each and every day about 40,000 children around the world die of starvation, or disorders attributed to chronic malnutrition. Americans represent about five-percent of the world's population, yet we consume about 20% of the world's resources. The distribution of wealth is clearly not equitable around the world, and Americans may one day lose the advantages they presently enjoy.

With about 200 countries in the world, we find at least 14 of them have nuclear warheads. Here is a quick summary: Russia (4350), France (300), China (280), United Kingdom (215), Pakistan (145), India (145), Israel (80), N. Korea (150), Italy (80), Turkey (70), Germany (20), Belgium (15), Netherlands (15), and the United States (3830). According to *Earth's Future,* a scientific journal, it would take just 100 nuclear detonations to create a worldwide climate catastrophe causing massive famine and death. Add to this list chemical and biological weaponry, and there is enough to kill every man, woman and child on earth many times over! Only the Holy Spirit of God prevents it.

We also experience diseases taking the lives of tens of thousands of people every day. Cholera, malaria, tuberculosis, and typhoid, which have been almost eliminated in developed countries, but remain deadly throughout much of the rest of the world.

In the 20th century, the bloodiest century on record to date, up to some 200 million men, women and children died, due to catastrophic warfare and oppression, according to a consensus of Atrocitologists. Even now, as we are well into the 21st century, there are more than 30 armed conflicts going on at any one time around the world. Why so much hatred and violence? Where can we find the answers to explain it?

Perhaps religion is the answer. Unfortunately, reality tells us otherwise. Many of the armed conflicts going on today are centered around religious differences. There is clearly much confusion in the more than 40,000-religious faiths around the world. Even the big five major religions cannot get along. Consider just for a moment, the conflicts between Muslims, Jews, Hindus, Buddhists, and Christians.

Ralph Waldo Emerson once said, "The law of cause and effect is the 'law of laws.'" Every cause has an effect and every effect becomes the cause of something else. In other words, we "reap what we sow!" (See also Galatians 6:7). Keeping this point in mind, we can find a cause for every evil: crime, war, religion, famine, confusion, disease, and early death, all exist for a reason. There are always reasons behind broken marriages, broken families, and broken relationships in general. The totality of this list all add up to a broken society, and a broken world. These things don't just happen by themselves, they are caused by something.

There is one, major primary cause behind all the maladies mankind faces, and until we are willing to address the subject we will remain in ignorance. The Bible, however, provides us with the answer, because it reveals a very powerful, intelligent being, who is actively involved in creating all the sin and wickedness that takes place on earth. The Bible calls him Satan, the devil, or the dragon, which are the most common terms, and often used interchangeably.

Christology vs. Demonology

Before discussing Satan, or the devil, it is important to know we cannot truly understand Christian theology without an understanding of demonology, and in doing so we must remember to always bring God into the conversation when demonology is discussed. You will soon see why as we explore this chapter further. Meanwhile, it is worthwhile for us to take a quick trip through history during the last millennia to see how Satan has been perceived by man down through the centuries. In this way, we will be better equipped in understanding the tricks Satan continues to use even in this modern era.

Going back to the Middle Ages, the devil was seen as a long-tailed, cloven-hoofed jester, with two horns and a red suit. He was exposed as a clown and cartoons depicted him that way. The people, however, did not for one moment think he was not an evil spirit, with powerful abilities to do much harm to mankind. Though they feared him, they nonetheless made jokes about his caricature, mainly to strike him where he was most sensitive, his pride. The people, many who were illiterate, were consequently influenced by very talented writers and producers of plays. Here are three examples:

In 1320, Dante Alighieri wrote, *Inferno,* as the first part of an epic poem, *A Divine Comedy.* Dante took his audience on a journey through Hell with the great Roman poet, Virgil. He discusses nine concentric circles, citing human sins such as lust, greed, wrath, gluttony, heresy, thievery, treachery, and so on. His readers see demons tormenting the pitiful sinners. Retribution is doled out according to a person's sins, with hypocrites located at the lowest circle. There are two problems with this masterpiece. First, the devil is seen as a tormentor in Hell, but Dante misinterprets the devil's role in the world of the living. Also, Dante neglected the teachings of the New Testament doctrine of salvation, and substituted salvation based on works instead of faith.

Later, during the years 1667 and 1674, John Milton, though totally blind, wrote a 12-book collection called, *Paradise Lost.* It depicts the fall of man from the Garden of Eden, which causes Milton to attempt to make sense of this fallen world. Interestingly, we find Milton being somewhat sympathetic towards Satan, causing other writers, such as William Blake, to think Satan becomes the real hero of the story.

Then, in 1829, Johann Wolfgang Goethe wrote, *Faust*, the story of a successful, well-educated man, who is dissatisfied with his life. He wants to commit suicide, but instead decides to sell his soul to the devil to gain unlimited knowledge and worldly pleasure. In part two of the poem, we find Faust actually does go to Heaven, because he lost only half of the wager.

We moderns gain great insight through these three masterpieces, in determining how the devil has been viewed by the general public over the last thousand years. Although these great epic poems and tragic plays provided great entertainment, they were unrealistic according to the Bible. Later, however, during the Age of Enlightenment (primarily the 18th century), we find our history going through a change of thinking supported by reason and evidence of the senses. The old order was critically scrutinized, and ideals of liberty, tolerance, progress, constitutional governments, and separation of church and state, were all forced to change. Royal monarchies, and the churches, were also undermined, as Satan was pushed more into the background. Rationalism became the focus, and fewer historians discussed the subject of evil and the devil.

Instead of identifying the devil, great writers like Samuel Richardson, Daniel Defoe, Jane Austin, et al, began placing more emphasis on satanic persuasion, explaining a process of people becoming corrupted by evil and sinful ideas. Although the devil does not appear alive himself, he remains "alive" in scenes of satanic persuasion.

This background of how the devil was perceived in the past, has caused millions of people today to laugh at the idea of an evil force responsible for all the suffering mankind experiences. For instance, we find the famous socialist, Robert Wuthnow, once stating our belief in the devil today often depends on our social class. He said, "Look at the parking lot outside any church, if you see Lexuses and Cadillacs, you won't hear Satan preached inside. If you see a lot of pickup trucks, you will."

Given what we know, is it possible to arrive at the truth of who this devil really is? Does Satan, or the devil, actually exist or not? The answer to these questions is critical in helping us understand the current state of humanity. To date, history has educated us to understand Satan's two most effective strategies: 1) getting the people to underestimate him, or 2) getting people to overestimate him. Either way, Satan is happy when we ignore him, or when we elevate him to a higher level of power than he actually has.

Writers have written millions of words attempting to explain Satan and the spirit world, but you will find only one credible source to get to the truth. Look no further than the Bible, for when we open its pages, we find God, the Creator of all things, speaking to us. The Bible is the only source we have where God communicates directly to us. Any other information outside the Bible, is found in mythology, and man's futile explanation and speculation. When we study the Bible, we find it contains enough internal evidence to convince us it truly is the Word of God. Our spiritual knowledge of a reality beyond our five senses, can only be found in the Bible, and nowhere else. **And it tells us in no uncertain terms, Satan does exist, and the spirit world is just as real as our own world is.**

Satan is mentioned many times in the Bible, where he is presented as a formidable spirit, allowed to exercise great influence over mankind. He leads an army of demons, or evil spirits, all designed to obey him. The Bible describes Satan's origin, later changing from a beautiful angel of light, into the enemy of God, and later against mankind. The Bible tells us Satan's goals, and the strategy he uses to win. The Bible also provides insights into Satan's character, nature, and the plans he has set for himself.

We also read about his great influence on each individual, as well as humanity in general. Finally, the Bible explains Satan's future and how it all ends (see chapter eighteen). This truthful knowledge, provided to us only by God in the Bible, is supplied from a source that cannot be equaled in any other way.

New Testament evidence supporting the reality of Satan

Name	Meaning	Bible Quotation
SATAN	Adversary	Matthew 4:10
DEVIL	Slanderer	Matthew 4:1
EVIL ONE	Intrinsically Evil	John 17:15
GREAT RED DRAGON	Destructive Creature	Revelation 12:3; 7, 9
ANCIENT SERPENT	Deceiver in Eden	Revelation 12:9
ABADDON	Destruction	Revelation 9:11
ROARING LION	Opponent	1 Peter 5:8
BEELZEBUB	Lord of the Flies	Matthew 12:24
BELIAL	Worthless	2 Corinthians 6:15
GOD OF THIS AGE	Controls the World	2 Corinthians 4:4
PRINCE OF THIS WORLD	Rules World System	John 12:31
RULER OF THE KINGDOM OF THE AIR	Control of Unbelievers	Ephesians 2:2
TEMPTER	Entices people to sin	Matthew 4:3
MURDERER	Solicits people to eternal death	John 8:44
LIAR	Perverts the truth	John 8:44
ACCUSER	Accuses believers before God	Revelation 12:10
PRINCE OF DEMONS	Controls demonic forces	Matthew 12:24

If you are still having trouble wrapping your mind around Satan being directly responsible for all the evil in our world, The Bible identifies him in a number of other ways, which demonstrates quite clearly Satan really is who the Bible says he is. On the previous page is a short list.

Jesus verifies Satan as our enemy

Jesus Christ himself states Satan is our true enemy. For the sake of brevity, here are a few examples of some of Jesus' quotes using some paraphrasing:

"And the enemy who sowed them is the devil." (Matthew 13:39)

"Now will the ruler of this world (Satan) be cast out." (John 12:31; 14:30)

"He (the Devil) was a murderer from the beginning." (John 8:44)

"For he (the Devil) is a liar and the father of lies." (John 8:44)

"I saw Satan fall like lightning from heaven." (Luke 10:18)

"How then will (Satan's) kingdom stand?" (He has a kingdom). (Matthew 12:26)

"The weeds are the sons of the evil one." (Evil men are his sons). (Matthew 13:38)

"The evil one (Satan) snatches away the word sown in man's heart." (Matthew 13:19)

"Satan bound a woman of Abraham for 18 years." (Luke 13:16)

"Simon, behold, Satan demanded to have you, and sift you like wheat." (Luke 22:31)

"Into the eternal fire for the devil and his angels." (Devil has angels). (Matthew 25:41)

You will have no other gods before me!

The very first of the Ten Commandments makes it very clear God is a jealous God who will accept no rivals. The word "god," using a lower-case "g," refers to anything or anyone, who worships something or someone other than Almighty God Himself. The word "God" with a capital "G," refers to our Creator, and the only one deserving to be called God. Only God, and his only begotten Son, Jesus Christ, are uncreated and have existed forever. God is omniscient, meaning he is all knowing, with infinite knowledge. He is omnipresent, meaning he is in all places at the same time. God is also omnipotent in that he has unlimited power and authority. We can now see more clearly why only God could have created us, provided for our needs, healed us when we needed it, while at the same time offering us a free gift of salvation for an eternal life. This gift is available to all those who accept and obey him as the most powerful, positive force in their lives.

Unfortunately, there are millions of people alive today, who have been affected by the dark side, and who believe in alternative ways to practice their faith. Here are just a few:

Pantheism – It is one of the oldest religious theories believing all *(pan)* is God *(theos)*. In other words, Pantheists believe the whole universe, and everything in it, is God! One believer in this religious practice was once asked, "Do you believe Satan is God?" His response was, "of course!" On the other hand, we find in Exodus 3:14, God saying, "I AM." This statement reveals God is a person by saying, "I think, I feel, and I act." God is not, as Pantheists would have us believe, an impersonal force. The case is made that Pantheism is the worst type of religion in that if all is God, there can be no distinction between good and evil.

Polytheism – Believers in Polytheism worship many gods, and the country of India is the center point for the religion of Hinduism, where some 850 million people worship some 330 million gods or types of deity, according to some Hindu scholars. God Almighty, however, never said, "We are the Lords your gods." God said, "I am the Lord your God." He is one and only, and there are no other gods. The apostle, Paul, says in 1 Corinthians 10:20, those who worship the so-called gods of the pagan world are bowing before demons in disguise.

Deism – It is known as the religion of the clockmaker, mainly because they believe God created the world, wound it up like a clock, and then took off and forgot about us. They believe God has no interest in this world, and therefore there is no point in praying to him, because he is just not listening. In other words, his phone is off the hook! We know through a large amount of empirical evidence God is very much involved in worldly affairs.

Communism – Karl Marx is the founder of this movement, which is a form of religion. Communists believe in the idea of creating a society controlled by the few, for the benefit of the many. They wish to distribute wealth according to need, as depicted in Marx's magnum opus, *The Communist Manifesto.* In his writings, Marx believed man should be in charge of his own destiny, and God was not needed. We can translate this to mean Marx was in favor of a godless, atheistic society for all men. In hindsight, the results of Communism have been horrific.

In the 20th century, we only have to look at the communistic record of Josef Stalin in Russia, Mao Zedong in China, Pol Pot in Cambodia, Fidel Castro in Cuba, and Kim Jong Un in North Korea, to witness the catastrophe brought upon its people, and by default many other people groups around the world. This is what happens when men forget God and try to replace him with a man. Think also, for instance, of Adolf Hitler, and Mussolini in World War II.

At this point in our discussion, we will now look at the dark side of the spirit world, while also remembering to keep a sharp eye on our Savior, Jesus Christ. In this way, we can learn about dark forces, while also remembering who we serve, the Lord Jesus Christ. Knowing our enemy should strengthen our faith, not weaken it.

The Spirit world's dark side

Theologians often tell us we know little about the spiritual world, because our five senses limit our ability to know anything beyond our current, mortal existence. Yet we are aware spirit beings do exist even though we cannot see them. God, Jesus, the Holy Spirit, Satan, angels, and demons, all play a role in the spirit world, and as a result they have a direct influence over our lives and our world.

As traditional Christianity is losing its popularity with many people, they try to fill the void in their lives in other ways. Some turn to drugs, others to sex or alcohol, or some other form of deviant behavior as they experiment in order to find meaning for their lives. Others seek alternative religious sources such as Eastern religions like Hindu, Zen Buddhism, or even Animism. Some people join cults, while others engage in occultist practices such as witchcraft, and even Satan worship. True, some people are just bored or curious, but whether they know it or not, they are flirting with dangers that are well beyond their capability to understand. That's what occultism is, something secretive, mysterious or concealed.

Young people especially, are being attracted more and more towards Wicca, Santeria, voodoo, seances, palm reading, channeling, tarot cards, Ouija boards, consultations with mediums, and many other occultist practices, that are growing in popularity. Satan is the originator of them all, including many other manifestations that include adding a suffix to regular words.

Isms

An ism is a simple suffix in the English language, but it has nefarious implications when it is added to the end of a word, because it then becomes a distinctive doctrine, cause, or theory, that is usually oppressive and discriminatory regarding attitudes or beliefs. Many of the isms have been developed since about 1700 and have done much to undermine Christian principles, thus diluting the Word of God, and pushing mankind further from his presence. You can be sure Satan is behind anything that takes away our love for God. Here are a few examples: relativism, humanism, evolutionism, materialism, atheism, agnosticism, communism, fascism, Nazism, secularism, progressivism, multiculturalism, hedonism, Marxism, cronyism, feminism, satanism, cultism, barbarism, narcissism, sexism, pessimism, totalitarianism, masochism, sadism, socialism, new ageism, anti-Catholicism, anti-intellectualism, and the list goes on.

The ism disease has crept into our Western culture causing much confusion, especially when they create alternatives taking away our straight road to God as laid down in the Bible.

Some people may say that capitalism is an "ism," which it is. There is no doubt capitalism, in its purest form, is a force of nature that can be used for wealth gain, without too much regard for the negative consequences that it might create in the process. However, the history of capitalism has created far more-good for societies around the world, than any harm it has caused, thanks to the restrictions imposed on it by Christian principles. The reason for this, is the fact capitalism comes from the principles of the Christian faith. Not to get too much off this chapter's subject, I refer you to my previous book, *Your Last Chance to get it Right!* where you will find how the Christian faith formed and shaped capitalism for social good, which led to stronger rights from women, children, and more dignity for the support of the elderly.

Christianity has many other firsts, including the elimination of cannibalism, slavery, equal rights for women; protection of children and the elderly. It has elevated and democratized education for all. Overall, Christianity led to the formation of democratic forms of government, and greater compassion for the common man. Yes, capitalism is an ism, but I believe it should not be part of the above-mentioned block of isms that create evil, and dilute the Word of God, putting further distance in our relationship to him.

What the Bible says

God warns us to have nothing to do with the occult, because he knows exactly how Satan operates. God tells us to "give the devil no opportunity." (Ephesians 4:27). There are certain passageways to our minds that should be reserved for our own thoughts and entrance of the Holy Spirit, and nothing else. By allowing evil spirits into our minds, we lose a certain amount of control over our own senses, which can lead to dangerous living. The apostle Paul advises us to be aware of such practices, "lest Satan should take advantage of us, for we are not ignorant of his devices." (2 Corinthians 2:11). In Deuteronomy 18:10-12, we find God saying:

> "There shall not be found among you anyone who burns his son or his daughter as an offering, anyone who practices divination or tells fortunes or interprets omens, or a sorcerer or a charmer or a medium or a necromancer or one who inquires of the dead, for whoever does these things is an abomination to the Lord."

Also, in Leviticus 19:31 it says,

> "Do not turn to mediums or necromancers; do not seek them out, and so make yourself unclean: I am the Lord your God."

If someone does get involved with evil spirits, they must be removed by genuine ministers of God through exorcism. This subject, however, is nothing to fool around with. Acts 19:14-16, tells us of seven sons of a Jewish high priest who were attempting to remove an evil spirit from a man, but the evil spirit answered, "Jesus I know, and Paul I recognize, but who are you?" Then the evil spirit jumped out of the man and beat the seven brothers, causing them to flee naked.

Protection from the Devil

So, how do people protect themselves from the devil? God provides specific guidance on combating the devil and his manipulations. In James 4:7, it says, "Resist the devil and he will flee from you." This is a promise made only to those who are willing to submit to God, because the passage goes on to say, "Draw near to God and he will draw near to you." How do we do that? The passage continues, "Cleanse your hands you sinners, and purify your hearts, you double-minded." Some effort is required by us in making sure we actively seek to eradicate the devil's way of thinking and acting from our lives. The problem we all face, is the fact the devil is so clever and resourceful, none of us can successfully resist his influence, without the help of God.

Here are some other Bible sources you can look up to help protect you from the evil of the Devil: 1 John 4:4, Philippians 4:8, James 4:7-8, Matthew 4:3-10, 1 Peter 5:8-9, Jude 9, Psalms 23; 27; 34; 37; and 91. This list, and many other Bible verses, show us how we can be protected from the devil when we have accepted Jesus Christ as our Lord and Savior. Unfortunately, all those who do not believe in Jesus as their Lord and Savior, are totally unprotected, and subject to the manipulation of Satan, which leads to a bad end.

In summary it is important to point out Satan was technically defeated the moment he sinned. This is because Satan is one of God's creatures, and therefore is dependent upon God for his continued existence. Satan is like a mangy dog on a very long lease, being controlled by his master. (See Job, chapter one as an example). The only power he possesses is always subject to God's will. So, the only trouble Satan can cause is to the benefit of the saints (people who are saved and fully protected by the shed blood of Christ). These saints cannot be harmed by Satan, but non-believers, however, are under no such protection, and are fully exposed to the manipulations of Satan. This should give pause to anyone who has not accepted the free gift to accept Jesus as Lord and Savior, if they have not already done so.

In future chapters we will develop further ways to ensure we walk with God, and enjoy the assuredness of knowing we will live in eternity with him when this brief life ends.

Journal Your Thoughts

10

THE PAGAN WORLD AT THE
TIME OF CHRIST

"Women are somewhere between a free man and a slave." –Aristotle

*"If a man is a coward in this life, he would come
back as a woman in the next."* –Plato

THE BOOK OF MALACHI REPRESENTS THE LAST BOOK IN THE OLD
Testament, and it was written in the mid-5th century B.C.
The Bible mentions nothing about what happens during the next
400 years, as mentioned earlier. The Prophets are silent and so
is God. Historians are therefore forced to seek out non-biblical
sources to determine what happened during that time period,
which is referred to as the Intertestamental or Second Temple period. We do know, however, as mentioned in Chapter Two, that a
great deal of history took place during this time period.

The Persians were the great world empire at the time Malachi was written, but later they would be overthrown by Alexander the Great, creating the Hellenization of the known world.
After Alexander's death, his four generals divided the Greek
empire, which later resulted in two generals jockeying for ul-

timate world power. One of the generals, Ptolemy, controlled Egypt and North Africa, and the other, Epiphanes, controlled Syria. Both of these generals were vying for possession of the land between their empires, which was the Palestine of the Jews. After much back-and-forth fighting, the Syrians took control, but their oppressive actions led to a Jewish revolt under the Maccabees. The Jews eventually won their freedom, which lasted for about 100 years before being taken over by the Romans in 63 B.C. This was the state of affairs leading up to the birth of Jesus, around 4 B.C.

The Romans were polytheists, who worshiped many gods, and they even worshiped the emperor himself. Rome's conquered provinces felt their national gods had betrayed them, because they had not helped to defend them against the might of Rome. Consequently, atheism began to spread everywhere, and they no longer believed in their own gods, although they practiced a form of diluted religion to protect their cultural bonds. As they looked further for meaning, they courted mystery religions, where they thought they could gain salvation.

The central point for Judaism, of course, was Jerusalem and the Temple. It was actually called Judea at that time, and it only became Palestine, or the land of the Philistines, after the Jews last revolt against Rome in 135 A.D. This was Rome's punishment for all the trouble the Jews had caused them.

At this time in history, it was reckoned there were approximately 500,000 Jews living in the area of Judea, and many more who had moved to other Roman provinces. Many had stayed in Babylon after the exile, and about one-third of the population of Alexandria in Egypt, were Jews.

This made proselytism a promising proposition for Jewish conversion, as the Jews held a favored status in the empire. They were able to send taxes to their Temple, be exempt from military service, and honor the Sabbath. In reality, the Jews were controlled by two separate jurisdictions: the Roman emperor, and the Sanhedrin, the Jewish leaders in Jerusalem.

Overall, it was a very unrestful time for the Jews, and although they were allowed to practice their own religion, they were subject to heavy taxation. The majority of Jews were poor, and illiterate. In such an environment, superstition and mystery cults abounded. The small minority, however, lived very sumptuous lives. They included the sovereign, King Herod, and his court, priestly aristocracy, the successful merchants, tax collectors, and the great landowners, mostly from Galilee. There was also a middle class made up of craftsmen, and country priests. The small farmers were often in heavy debt, and were part of the peasant class.

At the heart of the economy was the great Jewish Temple, where the priests and Levites practiced their business activities. Craftsmen and stonecutters were always working there, and it was the place where thousands of sheep, goats and bulls were sacrificed every year. Skins were tanned and treated, and then exported for profit. You would also find precious woods and perfumes being used and sold. Thousands of pilgrims visited the Temple each year, providing even more opportunities to sell food, trinkets and other souvenirs. Pilgrims were also expected to spend a portion of their annual income at the Temple, as well as paying their usual tithes. The Second Temple, now some 500 years old, was clearly being used for commercial and financial gain, and not for its original purpose. This was not pleasing to God.

The poorest of the poor were the day laborers, and the unemployed, who often had to turn to begging in order to survive. The slaves were better off because they were provided with food and shelter from their masters. Those who were sick, such as the lepers, which appears to have been quite common, lived off the alms of the people, as did anyone unable to take care of themselves.

There was no government or church safety net, no welfare or un-employment checks, and no hospitals or medical centers to treat people with serious health issues. Under such circumstances, life was harsh and cruel for many.

The Social Scene

Jewish society at this time was divided into a number of social groups, which we need to identify in further developing our understanding as to why Jewish leaders sought to ultimately have Christ, one of their very own, sacrificed and killed.

Clergy: The priestly aristocracy resided at the top of the hierarchy, as they were quite distinct and separate from the rest of the clergy. The high priest was the chief authority regarding the law and the Temple. He was also the president of the Sanhedrin. The high priest position changed each year, but during his time as high priest, he was the only one who could enter the Holy of Holies. Clearly, he was the undisputed leader of the Jewish people. There was a time when the high priest was nominated for life, but then the kings, and later the Romans, changed high priests to meet their own needs. In other words, the position became very politicized. As a result, the high priests always tried to please the governing powers, which happened to be the Romans at this time. The high priest's position was also extremely lucrative. He was given a share of the offerings, and part of the profit on the sale of animals. It should also be noted the high priest post was drawn from only four powerful families. This allowed them to enjoy both political and economic power. These types of benefits were hard to give up, and they therefore would do whatever it cost to maintain the status quo, by promoting social calm, and thus pleasing their overlords, the Romans. This fact became very evident later when Jesus is put on trial.

There were about seven thousand country priests, who remained close to the people, sharing in their lives, their work, and their poverty. These country priests were divided into 24 sections functioning in the Temple in a round robin fashion for one week per year. They were deeply involved in the three major annual festivals. At this time, the Levites, who numbered about 10,000, had become more of an inferior clergy, losing most of their former power. They were also divided into 24 sections, with a once-a-year function in the Temple. Their duties generally included collecting tithes, preparing sacrifices, and providing music. Some acted as Temple police.

The Elders: In some ways the elders were a type of lay aristocracy, but the lines are somewhat blurred when compared to some other groups such as the village chiefs and the rich merchants, who had a seat in the Sanhedrin. Most elders held on to their power by courting both the Romans and the high priest. The majority appeared to be Sadducees.

Doctors of the Law: These people were given official recognition due to being specialists in the law. They went through a long course of study, until about the age of 40. Some were priests, while many were Pharisees and lay people. They were advocates for the people, and often shared in their poverty. As interpreters of the Scriptures, they enjoyed great influence in presiding not only on rules for everyday life, but also recommending legal judgments in court. Perhaps the most famous were men like Hillel, Shammai, along with Gamaliel, who was Paul's teacher (more about him later). The elders protected the law by creating a number of prescriptions, which appeared to be a form of bondage. In actual fact, they served the purpose of providing a form of liberation by extending the rule of purity to all the people, instead of just the priests. By doing so, it allowed the people to get closer to God in their everyday life.

The Publicans: By collecting taxes from the people on behalf of the Romans, publicans were hated by the people, and were considered public sinners. They were known to increase taxes in order to gain more profit for themselves. A rich man by the name of Matthew, who wrote the Gospel of Matthew, was a tax collector, who later gave his wealth away to follow Jesus.

The Religious Scene

During the period of the Maccabees, three main religious sects were formed, which were all in existence at the coming of Jesus.

The Sadducees: As high-ranking aristocratic priests, the Sadducees were supporters of the Hasmoneans. They were bent on protecting their own power and prerogatives at all costs, making them pliable when working with the Romans. The Pentateuch appears to be the only law they accepted, and they did not recognize the prophets. They also did not believe in an afterlife, angels, or the resurrection. They took the position there is no resurrection of the dead, or any type of life after this one ends. Their position was to reject any type of belief in angels or demons. In fact, the whole idea of a spiritual world was anathema to them. They did accept oral law as authoritative, and appeared to place everything based on free will.

They did, however, interpret the Mosaic law in a more literal way than the Pharisees did. They were very stringent in Levitical purity, for instance, and only the books of Moses, as I mentioned, were considered canonical scripture. You will find they were later very cruel to Jesus, and the fledgling Christian faith. After the Romans crushed Jerusalem and tore down the Temple in 70 A.D., the Sadducees were greatly weakened and were no longer a viable force.

The Pharisees: Known as the "separated ones," the Pharisees were part of the Hasidim, a strict orthodox Jewish faith prevalent in the 3rd and 2nd centuries B.C., who had resisted the influence of Hellenism. They were big supporters of the Maccabees. The Pharisees were holy men who had separated from the Hasmoneans, whom they thought had broken from faith. They were very concerned in preserving the holiness of God and obeying his law. Pharisees accepted the Torah along with equally inspired and authoritative material within the oral tradition. Regarding the subject of free will, they held to a mediating view, making it impossible for either free will, or the sovereignty of God to cancel out the other. Unlike the Sadducees, they believed in life after death, and they accepted the reality of both angels and demons in the forms of hierarchy. They were also champions of human rights, and therefore placed great emphasis on ethical teachings rather than theological.

The Bible tells us the main fault of the Pharisees was in thinking their holiness, and their lineage from Abraham, would guarantee them a place in heaven. This is the one thing Jesus was so firmly opposed to. He thought they were relying on their genetic heritage and religious piety, and had subverted their holiness. This was affecting the people who held them in high esteem. There were only about 6,000 Pharisees, but they were able to preserve Judaism after the fall of Jerusalem in 70 A.D, whereas the Sadducees sank from view.

The Essenes: The Essenes originated during the Hasmonean period about the same time as the Pharisees, but they later separated. The source for these facts comes from the non-canonical book of 1 Maccabees 2:42; 7:13. They were strict Jews who took part with the Maccabees during their rebellion against the Syrians around 165 – 155 B.C. They lived close to the Dead Sea in a type of communist society by sharing in communal property. They followed strict observance of the purity laws in the Torah, and placed great importance on the daily study of sacred scripture, along with taking sacred oaths of piety and obedience. They offered sacrifices on holy days, and although marriage in principle was avoided, they did not prevent it.

With the discovery of the Dead Sea Scrolls in 1946/47, modern scholars gained great access to how the Essenes lived. They were a type of monastic order, who were led by a priest, whom they referred to as The Teacher of Righteousness. They had formerly parted from other Jews, and preferred to live alone. They lived a life of prayer and meditation, preparing for the coming of God's Kingdom. Meanwhile, they lived their lives by focusing all that had happened to them on fate. Their monastery was also destroyed by the Romans in 70 A.D.

Baptist Movements: There were many Baptist movements at this period in history, which began about 150 B.C. and lasted to about 300 A.D. Their main emphasis was on baptism as a formal rite to forgiveness. They looked at the Temple rituals with contempt, and were against sacrifices. John the Baptist, who baptized Christ, was part of this movement. Their policy was open to all, and they did not reject any elements of traditional faith.

The Samaritans: After the defeat by the Assyrians in 721 B.C, many of the Jews were deported, but some remained in Samaria. Meanwhile, the Assyrians brought other people groups to Samaria, who came with their own idols and gods. Later, these various people groups became mixed blood, and were looked down upon by the Jews in Judea. Although these people were separate from official Judaism, they nonetheless held on to the Pentateuch in common with the Jews. They worshiped in their own temple located at Mount Gerizim. The New Testament later testifies that the relationship between these Samaritans and the Jews in Judea was hostile, but they shared the same common destiny. It was not until Jesus later spoke to a Samaritan woman, that things began to change. In fact, after the death of Jesus, we find his 12 apostles directing their energies towards conversion of the Samaritans.

Jewish converts: As far as Judaism is concerned, there were two groups of people in the world: the Jews, who were circumcised, and the people of other nations, Gentiles, who were not. The Gentiles who converted, were expected to be circumcised, and as a consequence were expected to accept the whole of the Jewish law.

The Institutions: The Second Temple, which at one time housed the ark of the covenant, was renovated by King Herod to much of the glory of the first temple. It had been built in the eastern part of Jerusalem, and stood in the center of a courtyard measuring some 984 feet by 1640 feet. This was the holy place of God where he would make himself present, provided proper protocol was followed. Only the high priest could enter the Holy of Holies, which took place once a year, on the Day of Atonement, commonly referred to today as Yom Kippur. This holy place was an empty room, and sealed off by the curtain of the Temple. There was also an altar surrounded by the first courtyard for the priests. Outside of there, was the courtyard of Israel, for males, and a courtyard for women, which was separated from the courtyard of the Gentiles by a balustrade. Any Gentile found crossing the balustrade was subject to death.

Temple sacrifices were offered on the great altar, which was about 82 feet long, and 24 feet in height. Day and night, there was a continuing sacrifice of a lamb, along with many other private sacrifices. The sacrifices increased dramatically during festival times. The paschal lamb had to be sacrificed there before being eaten at any family meal. This practice was discontinued, however, after the Temple was destroyed, and Passover henceforth was celebrated without a lamb. The Temple, when you think about it objectively, served as the center of the Jewish faith, its political center, due to the Sanhedrin meeting there, and the economic center, since all the activity taking place there resulted in much profit.

The Synagogue: For Jews who lived some distance from the Temple, the synagogue was the place where they could practice their faith and religious practices. Services generally took place three times each day. The synagogue provided teaching, and a reading of the law, which often included a reading of a prophetic passage, followed by a sermon. Although anyone was allowed to preach, generally it was restricted to Pharisees and scribes, who structured the message according to their doctrine. The people recited psalms, and their prayers centered around the three great benedictions. These in turn provided for the recitation of the Shema, which was a summary of the faith of Israel. The meeting would end with the eighteen benedictions, and the wonders of God toward his people.

The Political Scene

The Jewish Monarchy: After the Romans had taken control of the Holy Land in 63 B.C., they later installed Herod to be King of the Jews. Herod tried hard to appease the Romans, and imposed heavy taxes on the Jews, along with harsh and brutal treatment of his subjects.

Herod's father was an Edomite Arab, and his mother was a princess of Nabatean origin, thus making Herod an Arab on both sides of his bloodline. Nonetheless, he was raised a Jew, but because of his decadent lifestyle, he was hated by the average Jew under his control. He banished his wife, Doris, and their child, in order to marry another woman, and had three of his sons killed. Emperor Augustus is known to have said, "It is better to be

Herod's pig than his son." This was a reference to the fact Herod would not kill pigs. Herod the Great is perhaps the only figure in ancient Jewish history who has been hated by both Jew and Christian alike. In Matthew 2:16, for instance, he ordered every child in Bethlehem and its vicinity, under two-years of age, to be killed in order to insure the death of the coming Messiah. Both the Pharisees and the Sadducees opposed him because of his brutality, and he ended up dying a very painful death soon after Jesus was born.

The Roman Empire: Superimposed over all the known world was the Roman Empire, which demanded absolute fealty from all the kingdoms and people under its control. The Romans managed a pagan government, and worshiped many gods. As I have already mentioned, many of the people groups who were subjugated under the yoke of the Romans, abandoned their own religion, thinking their gods had betrayed them by allowing the Romans to overpower them. As a result, atheism began to spread. The Romans, however, allowed the Jews certain privileges, because they knew they took their Jewish faith seriously, and were willing to die in order to defend it. Provided they obeyed Roman laws, and paid their taxes, the Jews were given a semi-form of self-rule. The Sanhedrin and other power brokers were only too happy to accommodate the Roman officials in order to maintain their own privileged positions.

The Zealots: As a result of Jewish oppression, a number of Jews, known as the Zealots, began to form during the reign of King Herod the Great, around 6 B.C. Zealots opposed paying taxes to a pagan emperor, claiming their only allegiance was to God alone. They fiercely defended Jewish traditions, and resented Hellenism, particularly the Greek language being used in Palestine. They also prophesied a future salvation.

Unlike the Pharisees, who began a protest movement of non-violence, the Zealots wished to provoke the Romans through violence. Some of the Zealots were called *Sicarii*, based on a name for a short sword that could easily be hidden under their garment. They became particularly forceful about 66 A.D., and were mainly responsible for the revolt resulting in the destruction of Jerusalem in 70 A.D., that killed between 600,000 and 1,000,000 Jews. The rest of the Jews were scattered throughout the empire.

A gruesome reminder of Masada

Three years later, the Romans were able to capture Masada, a mountain fortress close to the Dead Sea, once the summer palace of Herod the Great. Having visited the place myself, I can easily imagine how the 960 zealots who had control of it, thought it to be impregnable. However, they finally came to realize the Romans were now using Jewish labor to build a rampart up the side of the mountain. Not wishing to kill their own countrymen by throwing down rocks, they decided, on the day before the Romans were to overpower them, to kill themselves, rather than surrender to the cruelty of the Romans.

As the story goes, each man was responsible for killing his own wife and children. Then each man was assigned to kill another man, until there was only one left. He then had the responsibility to ensure that everyone was dead before committing suicide. When the Romans took the fort, they found, according to the historian, Josephus, a woman and two small children, who provided an eye-witness account of what happened. To this day, each young man and woman, when entering the Israeli military, must recite the slogan, "Masada shall not fall again."

This chapter, I believe, has provided considerable insight into the social and political makeup of Jewish society in Palestine under Roman occupation, and the world in which our Lord Jesus Christ entered as a baby being born in Bethlehem, about six-miles south of Jerusalem. This chapter, along with the previous chapter, where we discussed the role of Satan, has now fortified us to be fully prepared for our understanding of the purpose for God's next Great Reset.

JOURNAL YOUR THOUGHTS

11

GOD'S GREAT BIBLE RESET #6

"A man who was completely innocent, offered himself as a sacrifice
for the good of others, including his enemies, and became the
ransom of the world. It was a perfect act!" –Mahatma Gandhi

The New Covenant Of Jesus Christ

IN UNDERSTANDING THE BIBLE, WE HAVE DISCOVERED HOW THE JEWS HAVE played an extremely important role in giving us our Christian faith. We have also come to realize the "spine" that holds the Bible together, both the Old and the New Testaments, are the Major Covenants, or Great Resets, which God has instituted from time to time throughout man's history. You might refer to them as contracts or agreements to help us understand the relationship God would like to have with each living person. They reveal God's promises, and help us understand the conditions each of us is expected to meet, in order to enjoy the blessings of those promises.

The trouble with man's heart

These covenants represent God's divine plan, and are created by him for our benefit. They are the foundation upon which God's plan for our future is based. God has a specific goal in mind, which is to create a divine family of sons and daughters striving to reach the same righteous character displayed by Jesus Christ. This type of character can be developed only through a process taking place between God and each individual. In other words, it is a personal process. The reason for this, is the fact man's heart is corrupt, and he needs God's intervention to stay on the right track towards righteousness and holiness. Here are two quick references regarding man's heart. The first is found in Genesis 8:21, where God says, "I will never again curse the ground because of man, for the intention of man's heart is evil from his youth." Secondly, in Jeremiah 17:9, it says, "The heart is deceitful above all things, and desperately sick; who can understand it? I the Lord search the heart and test the mind, to give every man according to his ways, according to the fruit of his deeds."

This is the reason explaining the need for God to create the necessary Great Resets or covenants. They are still needed to keep us all on track towards an eternal life with him, when this one ends. We just can't trust ourselves, or our fellow man, to do it for us. We all need God to create a rebirth in our hearts and minds, directing us towards righteousness. It is our only hope.

Our world is a testing ground

In order to develop our spiritual character, and to ensure we are all maturing in our spiritual growth, God tests us, as he has done more than 200 times in the Bible. One such test is when God provided us with the gift of personal choice, which means each person has to decide between two extremely important options. A person can metaphorically decide to "drive their own car" through life so to speak, by experimenting with their own future, which often leads to endless mistakes. Or, they can put their total trust in God by allowing him to "drive the car" for them. God knows where the road leads and ends, but do we?

I mentioned earlier about a horizontal line leading to eternity, and the dot and bubble that represents each of our lives. And it is through our education and experiences that cause us to seek enlightenment. The hope, of course, is that we will eventually find God, who gives us all an opportunity to either drive "our own car" through life, or allow God to take over as the driver.

The more we learn about God's ways, through study of the Bible, the more we come to realize that God is a much better driver than we are, because he will always get us safely to our destination. When we drive, do we have the same confidence?

As you study the Bible, you will learn more about God's spiritual gifts made available to those who love and accept him, but they are denied to those who do not. Those people who do not understand the Bible, and do not have a relationship with God, are at a severe disadvantage in not knowing the many benefits that can be made available to them. More on this later.

The need for revelatory covenants

Besides the corrupt nature of man's heart, coupled to the lack of Bible knowledge, we find Satan taking full advantage of this situation, which allows him to cause much trouble and chaos all around the world. So, time and again, God has stepped in primarily to save man from himself.

Before we discuss the details of the New Covenant, it is important to reinforce and summarize the previous covenants, to make plain the necessity of Jesus Christ providing us all with the gift of the New Covenant, which also provides solid answers to man's dilemma, and a way forward towards an eternal life with Christ when we leave this earth.

As mentioned earlier, it started with the first man, Adam, who was induced by Satan to disobey God, and was consequently exiled from the Garden of Eden, thus causing the first Great Reset or Covenant to take place, called the Adamic Covenant, in which Adam was given a second chance to redeem himself and all mankind.

Later, man degenerated again to a state where he became an abomination to God, which caused God to flood the world and destroy everyone in it, except Noah and his immediate family. God then entered into a second Great Reset, which we call the Noahic Covenant, whereby God promised never again to use a flood to destroy the world. The rainbow is a sign of this pledge. God created a new covenant with all humanity, and it marks a new beginning for the world after the flood. God pledged that he would preserve the stability of nature, which allows his people to grow in numbers, and provide an opportunity for salvation.

Later in history, man again fell into moral decay, and this time God selected one man, Abraham, to become the founder of a chosen people of God, ultimately the Jews, who would set the standard for righteous living, and become an example for all other people groups. Unfortunately, the Jews, along with the rest of mankind, again slid into degeneracy, requiring another lifeline from God to prevent them from drowning in their accumulated sin. That is when God provided Moses with the fourth Great Reset, which is known as the Sinai Covenant. In it, God provided the Ten Commandments in writing, that we still live by today, but under a newer and better covenant explained later in this chapter.

The fifth Great Reset came about when David was anointed King, which established a clear bloodline between David, tracing back to Abraham, who had been called by God to be the founder of Judaism, thus creating God's chosen people. The identity of this bloodline is very important because from David we can further trace the bloodline down through the centuries for another 900 years, directly to the Messiah, Jesus Christ. During that time, multiple generations in David's bloodline came and went, including thieves, adulterers and prostitutes, before it finally culminated with the birth of Jesus.

Bridging the Testaments

The "bridge" between the Old Testament and the New Testament, demonstrates Jesus fulfilled the hopes and promise of the Old Testament through his messianic genealogy, fulfillment of the Old Testament prophecies, and the complete fulfillment of the Old Testament law. The Christophanies, with various shadows, and types of messianic images portrayed in the Old Testament, became a reality in the New Testament with the birth of Jesus.

As previously mentioned in chapter three, upwards of 25% of the Bible contains prophecy, many of which have already been fulfilled. According to John F. Walvoord, former chancellor of Dallas Theological Seminary, he stated there are 52 prophecies fulfilled in Christ's birth, life and death, which are stated in 81 passages of the Old Testament, and fulfilled in the New Testament. Here are a few to whet your appetitive for further exploration:

He would be a descendant of King David (Isaiah 11:1-5; Matthew 1:1, 6)

He would be born in Bethlehem (Micah 5:2; Matthew 2:1)

Someone would announce his coming (Isaiah 40:3, 5; Malachi 3:1; Matthew 3:1-3)

He would be rejected by his own people (Isaiah 53:3; John 1:11)

He would be betrayed by a friend (Psalm 41:9; John 13:18-30)

Reward for betrayal would be 30 pieces of silver (Zechariah 11:12; Matthew 26:15)

They would pierce his hands and feet (Psalm 22:16; Luke 24:38-40)

He would be crucified without breaking any bones (Psalm 34:20; John 19:33-36)

They would cast lots for his clothes (Psalm 22:18; John 19:23-24)

He would be buried in a rich man's tomb (Isaiah 53:9; Matthew 27:57-60)

He would be resurrected from the grave (Psalm 16:10; Acts 2:30-32).

These prophecies create a "bridge" between the two testaments not only confirming the authenticity of these events, but also validating the bloodline from Abraham and King David, down to Jesus. This proves beyond a doubt, Jesus Christ truly is the Messiah.

With the birth of Jesus Christ, who was God in the form of man, everything about us humans changed. The impact of Jesus' ministry was so powerful, the Julian calendar was eventually replaced with time stopping at Jesus' birth. Remember, there is no zero year between B.C. (Before Christ), or BCE (Before the Common Era), and A.D. (Anno Domini) meaning, the Year of Our Lord. B.C. numbers run backwards, and A.D. numbers run forward from Christ's birth. For instance, 1B.C.; 2 B.C., 3 B.C., and 1 A.D., 2 A.D., 3 A.D. etc.

The Old Jewish law and the Old Testament came to an end, and the New Covenant of Jesus Christ was made available to everyone in the New Christian Testament once Christ began his ministry.

So why a New Covenant?

The short answer is we are all created incomplete, because there is a missing dimension in our thinking that needs to be added so we can properly control our thoughts, and the actions they produce. God is willing to provide us the knowledge and power we need to manage our thinking, how we feel, how we behave, subject to us giving God our sincere obedience to his law. History provides much evidence to confirm man cannot make right choices without God's divine help. All of history proves this unalterable fact. So, whether our life is temporary, or eternal in heaven, it all depends on whether we allow God to actively change our hearts and minds, or not.

You see, the Mosaic Covenant supplied the Israelites with a complete package of laws, and the first five books: Genesis, Exodus, Leviticus Numbers, and Deuteronomy, covered all aspects of national life in ancient Israel. It offered solid solutions on how to judge criminal acts, protect the people against poverty, and the proper way to conduct the priesthood. The law also covered the management of the tabernacle, proper ceremonial cleanliness, tithing, animal control, moral issues, sanitation and health issues, as well as agricultural methods, and the conduct of sacred festivals. In other words, it devised a complete system of government, **but it was without God's Holy Spirit, with perhaps the exception of a few, such as some priests, prophets, and a few others.** The system took into consideration the fact God knew people's hearts were spiritually hardened, and whose minds were not able to understand the spiritual intent of God's teachings. (Matthew 13:15; Acts 28:27, and Isaiah 6:9-10, all confirm this fact).

A primary distinction between the Old and New Covenants resides in where God's law is written, as mentioned in Jeremiah 31:31-34, and Ezekiel 36:26-28. Under the New Covenant the spiritual intent of the law is to be inscribed on the **hearts** of the people who are converted by receiving the Holy Spirit. This, of course, requires a change in the law, as to who holds the office of high priest. It has to be someone who can execute the role, and can assist us in obeying God from the heart (Hebrews 7:12). So, the new focus is on heartfelt repentance leading to forgiveness of sin through faith in the sacrificial blood of the Lord Jesus Christ. Later, Paul tells us we are told "not to conform to this world, but be transformed by the renewing of your mind." (Romans 12:2). This happens with the assistance of the Holy Spirit.

The Bible tells us the New Covenant had to be offered first to the Israelites, who were the very same people who received the Old Covenant at Mt. Sinai, and who were also the physical descendants of Abraham. Later, you will find all of Jesus' apostles, including Paul, honoring this requirement by communicating the message of the New Covenant, first to the Jews, and later to the Gentiles. In fact, Paul (the great apostle to the Gentiles (non-Jews), demonstrated that whenever he visited a new city, he first preached in the synagogues, and then to the Gentiles.

The Apostle, Peter, also explained why the Jews had to be given the first opportunity to accept Jesus Christ as their Savior, when he said, "And all the prophets who have spoken, from Samuel and those who came after him, also proclaimed these days. You are the sons of the prophets and of the covenant God made with your fathers, saying to Abraham, 'And in your offspring shall all the families of the earth be blessed.' God, having raised up his servant, sent him to you first, to bless you by turning every one of you from your wickedness." (Acts 3:24-26).

Another very important point separating the two laws is found when we read Deuteronomy 28, and Leviticus 26. In these Bible passages we find God providing many blessings for obedience, and punishment for disobedience, if his commands were disobeyed. What is missing in both chapters, and in the Old Law, is there is no promise of an eternal life. However, the New Covenant of Jesus Christ, does provide us with eternal life for our obeyance and fidelity to God's law.

Looking back, we can clearly see without the gift of the Holy Spirit, the people of Israel, just like anyone today, would not be capable of obeying a promise to God. Some Israelites did obey what they were taught, and this is evidenced when, in some time periods, they were observant of God's instructions. This can be seen in a reading of Joshua 24:31, and 2 Chronicles 32:26. For the most part, however, they disobeyed God, and went their own way. It appears the Israelites were provided with every natural advantage to obey God, but they simply lacked the supernatural help of God's Holy Spirit, which would have put them on the right track to developing a righteous heart. We have much to learn from the experience of ancient Jews.

Does the New Covenant abolish the Old Testament Commandments?

There are many people who believe the New Covenant does away with the Old Covenant, which is a misunderstanding of both covenants. There was a weakness in the Old Covenant, but it was not in the covenant itself, but rather in the people who could not live up to its terms. In the Old Covenant, God had written the law on tablets of stone. It was external to the people, and although it became a part of their literature, it was not in their hearts because they did not at that time have the Holy Spirit to guide them.

Another problem is our own weak human nature is manipulated by Satan, and he uses our fleshly desires to serve his own ends, which is to destroy what God has created. Paul the Apostle, tells us in Galatians 5:19-21, "Now the works of the flesh are evident: sexual immorality, impurity, sensuality, idolatry, sorcery, enmity, strife, jealousy, fits of anger, rivalries, dissensions, divisions, envy, drunkenness, orgies, and things like these. I warn you, as I warned you before, that those who do such things will not inherit the kingdom of God."

Paul goes on to summarize as follows: "But their minds were hardened. For to this day, when they read the Old Covenant, that same veil remains un-lifted, because only through Christ is it taken away. Yes, to this day whenever Moses is read, a veil lies over their hearts. But when one turns to the Lord, the veil is removed." (2 Corinthians 3:14-16).

At every turn, Satan takes advantage of our weak and greedy nature by influencing us to rely ever more on our own emotions, our own needs and wants. Without the positive influence of God's Spirit, we are simply not prepared to live according to his instructions.

The idea of a New Covenant was discussed deep in the Old Testament when we find God saying, "The time is coming, declares the Lord, when I will make a new covenant with the house of Israel and with the house of Judah. It will not be like the covenant I made with their forefathers when I took them by the hand to lead them out of Egypt, because they broke my covenant, though I was a husband to them," declares the Lord. "This is the covenant I will make with the house of Israel after that time," declares the Lord, "I will put my law in their minds and write it on their hearts. I will be their God and they will be my people. No longer will a man teach his neighbor, or a man his brother, saying, 'Know the Lord,' because they will all know me, from the least of them to the greatest," declares the Lord. "For I will forgive their wickedness and will remember their sins no more." (Jeremiah 31:31-34; Hebrews 8:10).

As mentioned earlier, some people mistake the above Bible passage to mean the Old Covenant is done away with once the New Covenant is enacted. The new thing promised in verse 33, however, is neither a new law nor freedom from law. It is, rather, a sincere inward desire, with self-determination on behalf of God's people to obey the law that has already been given to them. **In other words, it is now an internal motivation, rather than an outside effort.**

The New Testament confirmation of the Old Law

I mentioned earlier the Old Testament is the New Testament concealed, and the New Testament is the Old Testament revealed. So, here is a list of examples that confirm how both Jesus and his apostles viewed the Ten Commandments as being a necessary part of Christian living:

Old Testament	New Testament
COMMANDMENT NUMBER ONE	Matthew 4:10; 22:37-38
COMMANDMENT NUMBER TWO	1 Corinthians 6:9; 10:7, 14; Ephesians 5:5
COMMANDMENT NUMBER THREE	Matthew 5:33-34; 7:21-23; 1 Timothy 6:1
COMMANDMENT NUMBER FOUR	Luke 4:16; Acts 13:14; Hebrews 4:4; 9
COMMANDMENT NUMBER FIVE	Matthew 15:3-6; 19:17-19; Ephesians 6:2-3
COMMANDMENT NUMBER SIX	Matthew 5:21-22; 19:17-18; Romans 13:9; Galatians 5:19-21
COMMANDMENT NUMBER SEVEN	Matthew 5:27-28; 19:17-18; Romans 13:9; 1 Corinthians 6:9
COMMANDMENT NUMBER EIGHT	Matthew 19:17-18; Romans 13:9; Ephesians 4:28
COMMANDMENT NUMBER NINE	Matthew 19:17-18; Colossians 3:9; Ephesians 4:25
COMMANDMENT NUMBER TEN	Luke 12:15; Romans 7:7; Ephesians 5:3, 5.

A marriage between God and his people

You perhaps noticed in the Jeremiah 31:32 quote mentioned earlier, the Lord is like a "husband" to his people. I mention this to point out the Old Covenant was like a marriage contract, where God acted as the "husband," and his people were his "wife." In the covenant we find Israel agreeing to submit to God and obey his laws. Unfortunately, Israel did not, and her "adultery" with foreign gods was so terrible, God "divorced" his people with the exception of a remnant who continued to obey him. (Jeremiah 3:8, 14; Isaiah 50:1). This happened because the people never had the right heart or mind for the "marriage." (Deuteronomy 5:29; Romans 8:7). Hebrews 8:7 tells us if there had been nothing wrong with the Old Covenant, there would have been no need for a new one. God had found fault with the people, however, and decided to make a new one in the future, which came later with the birth of Jesus Christ. More on this subject later.

A one-time miracle

The greatest miracle ever witnessed by mankind took place some 2,000 years ago, and it is just as vivid in our minds today as when it actually happened, due to the tradition of us celebrating the occasion every Christmas season. At the time of the miracle, the invisible God, the Creator of all things, came to earth in the form of a baby human being who would evolve into the only sinless, and perfect man. His name was Jesus, who was God's only begotten Son. His purpose in doing so, was to bring new hope to man by offering a better way to live, in fact the best and most righteous way to live, even to the present day and beyond.

Now hold on for a moment, you say. How can God be the Father and the Son at the same time? This is where the Holy Trinity needs to be explained before we go any further.

The Holy Trinity of God

God, in his infinite wisdom, decided ages ago to communicate with mankind in three different ways. He has spoken to man as the Father, as his only begotten Son, Jesus Christ, who is also God, and he also speaks to us through the Holy Spirit, who is also God. This does not mean there are three Gods, because God is a mono-theistic God – there is only one God! We must realize that no one metaphor can capture or explain everything God is trying to con-vey to us. Someone once said that if God were small enough for our minds to comprehend, he would not be big enough to solve our problems! However, that being said, let's think of the Trin-ity as an egg, which has three parts: the shell, the white, and the yoke. It is one product with three parts. Or, an apple consisting of skin, seed and flesh. Water is another example, where depending on temperature, it can be liquid, gas or a solid. In each case they are all one product made up of three different parts.

The early church fathers had difficulty defining the Trinity of God, but through divine revelation, it was "hammered" out through a number of church councils and creeds, such as the Apostles Creed (140 A.D.), The Council of Nicaea (325 A.D.), along with the Council of Ephesus (431, 449, 475 A.D.), and the Council of Chalcedon (451 A.D.). These events, along with the Athanasian Creed, established in the 400s, allowed the concept of the Trinity to be finally worked out to the satisfaction of Christian leader-ship. The Athanasian Creed did not add any new interpretation of the Trinity, but rather represented a summation of previous councils. However, it takes the Trinity of God seriously, and pres-ents a very straightforward, refreshing approach in its 42 arti-cles. It partially says: "For there is one Person of the Father, an-other of the Son, and another of the Holy Ghost. But the Godhead of the Father, of the Son, and of the Holy Ghost, is all one; the Glory equal, the Majesty coeternal. Such as the Father is, such is the Son; and such is the Holy Ghost. The Father uncreated, the Son uncreated, and the Holy Ghost uncreated. The Father unlimited, the Son unlimited, and the Holy Ghost unlimited. The Father eternal, the Son eternal, and the Holy Ghost eternal. And yet they are not three eternals, but one eternal." Note that the terms, *Holy Ghost* and *Holy Spirit,* are interchangeable terms.

The Bible tells us God can express himself as the Father when we read Ephesians 4:6, and 1 John 3:1. God is expressed as the Son when we read John 1:1, 14; 1 John 5:20, and John 3:16. Also, God is expressed as the Holy Spirit when we read 1 Corinthians 2:10, and Ephesians 4:30. With this concept explained, we can now continue forward with the reasoning behind the New Covenant of Jesus Christ.

So, why did God come to Earth as a man?

This intriguing question needs to be addressed in order to appreciate the magnitude of what happened when our Savior came to earth, and what has happened to date and in the future. With this thought in mind, let us delve into the history of man's past relationship with God in order to appreciate what God did, and continues to do for all those who believe in his Son, Jesus Christ.

By the beginning of the 1st century A.D., the mighty Roman Empire ruled most of the known world with brutal force. All countries with access to the Mediterranean Sea were all part of a huge Roman lake. All subjugated people accepted Roman pagan gods as part of the price they paid for a semblance of peace and semi-autonomy in self-rule, provided they paid proper taxes to Rome, and complied with Roman law and regulations. The Jews were perhaps the main exception to this state of affairs in that they refused to worship Roman gods, or their emperor, and subsequently were a constant problem for their Roman overseers.

At this point in history, it had become obvious to all that human nature made it impossible for man to manage his life in a righteous way that was pleasing to God, and our human nature has not changed to this day. You see, the original sin of the very first man, Adam, has tracked down through the bloodline of subsequent generations, and the historical record of man's inhumanity to man is plain for all to see. Clearly, God was set to implement a sixth Great Reset, or covenant, which we know as the New Covenant of Jesus Christ. This would be the one and only time God would take the form of a man, in order to demonstrate the proper way for man to live out his short life here on earth before entering an eternal life after this mortal existence ends.

Jesus, in fact, was to become our new High Priest, setting the gold standard of what we should all be striving for. However, Jesus was doing far more than just setting an example of how we should live our lives, as is clearly demonstrated by other world religious leaders. Jesus was doing far more than just setting an example. He sacrificed his own life, and allowed his shed blood to cleanse his believers from all their sins, past, present and future. But it doesn't stop there. Jesus actually lives in all believers. **He is living in and through us!** (Galatians 2:20). Without this "born again" experience, we would all be truly lost and damned.

Jesus' example provides us with a pathway to an eternal life, but with a condition attached. A person must accept, and have faith in Jesus Christ as their Redeemer and Savior. Compliance with this condition is what will save the soul of man for eternity. However, it is man's choice to accept or reject the offer. Some people think this offer is so simplistic, it can't be that easy. There has to be something else involved. Actually, there isn't. So, I ask such people to simply open their minds and hearts, clear out their preconceived thoughts and ideas, and just allow God to speak, instead of always letting their own thoughts guide them, thus creating "roadblocks," which need to be cleared in order to make progress in their spiritual journey. If they don't, then Hell, which is mentioned numerous times in the Bible, will become their new home when this life ends. (More on the subject of Hell later).

The High Priest under the Old Law

The concept of a priesthood did not begin with the nation of Israel, but rather during the patriarchal period. At that time the head of each household performed the role of a priest for his family members, by offering sacrifices to God on behalf of his family (Genesis 12:7-8; 13:18; 22:9-12; Job 1:5). God had informed the nation of Israel that if they obeyed him, it would become a "kingdom of priests and a holy nation." (Exodus 19:6). This theocracy gave Israelites direct access to God, which came with a responsibility to spread God's holiness to the world.

Unfortunately, the Israelites sinned against God and broke the covenant he had made with them at Mt. Sinai. This caused them to forfeit their privilege of becoming a kingdom of priests. As a result, it became necessary for God to choose certain priests from among the people, who would then represent the nation of Israel before him. Moses was told by God to select his brother, Aaron, to minister to God as a priest. This resulted in the tribe of Levi functioning as priests, and Aaron's sons would later take on the same role of high priest. The term, *priest*, (Hebrew, *kohaya*), means "one who officiates." So, the Aaronic priesthood began. The high priest was not meant to be an angel with supernatural qualities. He was simply a man with the same nature and passions as any other man.

Under the Mosaic Covenant, Israelites were not able to go directly to God's throne for communication. They obtained access to God through the high priest who was only allowed into God's presence once a year, on the Day of Atonement (Yom Kippur). When the priest entered the tabernacle, he did so with fear and trembling. Under the New Covenant, believers are continually asked to come to God's presence with boldness, confidence, with free and open speech. They are asked to open up their hearts at the throne of grace, rather than a throne of judgment as with the Mosaic Covenant.

So, the tribes of Israel fully respected the Aaronic high priest, and perhaps with Moses as the exception, the high priest enjoyed access and fellowship with God more than any other Israelite. Although God provided the high priest with many privileges, God knew the high priest was imperfect like all men, and subject to death like any other men. However, the New Covenant of Jesus Christ was superior in that Jesus serves as our High Priest forever.

To qualify for the Aaronic high priest position in ancient Israel, a man had to be mortal, and come from the seed of Abraham, and from the tribe of Levi. He was neither self-appointed, nor elected, but rather divinely elected. "No man takes this honor for himself, but he who is called by God, just as Aaron was." (Hebrews 5:4). The high priest was expected to sympathize with men so that he could "have compassion on those who are ignorant and going astray, since he himself is subject to weakness." (5:2). High priests, just like other Israelites, were subject to temptation and sin, and would one day die and give account to God for their actions.

The high priest's duties included offering sacrifices for his sins and those of the people. At that time, there were five sacrificial offerings of five animals, along with incense, that the priest was to offer daily and on various feast days, in accordance with their tradition, according to the Jewish calendar. For instance, on the Day of Atonement, the high priest alone was allowed to offer incense and blood sacrifices in the Holy of Holies for the sins of Israel. (Leviticus 16).

Jesus as our new High Priest

Now that we have an understanding of how the high priesthood operated under the Mosaic Covenant, we will now look at the qualifications of Jesus Christ as the new High Priest. He needed to be human, divinely appointed, compassionate, and be able to offer himself as a sacrifice for sin. Jesus Christ met all these qualifications, with the difference that, unlike Aaron, Jesus would be an eternal priest. The author of the Book of Hebrews cites two Messianic psalms, Psalm 2 and 110, and as we look at Psalm 2:7-8, for instance, he shows that as the eternal Son of God, Jesus Christ was appointed High Priest by God the Father.

Hebrews 5:5 says: So also, Christ did not exalt himself to be made a high priest, but was appointed by him who said to him, "You are my Son, today I have begotten you"; as he says also in another place, "You are a high priest forever, after the order of Melchizedek."

When we look at the phrase, *I have begotten you,* it does not refer to the Son's origin, his eternal generation, or incarnation, simply because there never was a time when Jesus never existed. Instead, the Book of Hebrews verified that at Christ's resurrection, he was uniquely appointed as High Priest, and declared to be so by God, the Father. God never said this about Aaron, or the other Old Testament high priests. Jesus took on flesh (Phil 2:7, 8), which limited his use of the divine attributes, but Jesus is and always will be the Son of God.

Christ's priesthood is from a different realm than was Aaron's. In quoting from Psalm 110:4, he called Christ "a priest forever according to the order of Melchizedek." We find that Melchizedek was a king-priest, but Aaron was only a priest. Also, no Israelite king ever dared to enter the Temple to function as a high priest without suffering God's punishment. (2 Chronicles 26:16-21). However, Christ, just like Melchizedek, was both a King and a Priest. The Aaronic priesthood was handed down to many sons over the centuries, but Melchizedek stood alone, and just like Jesus, he neither inherited his kingly priesthood, nor transferred it to successors. Just like Christ, Melchizedek had no recorded beginning or ending, even though Aaron had to be replaced upon his own death. It should also be noted that the Aaronic priesthood came to an end with the destruction of the Temple by the Romans in 70 A.D.

In order to be a high priest, Jesus had to become human, and so he became a man of flesh and blood. In Hebrews 5:7, where it says, "in the days of his flesh," refers to Christ's entire earthly pilgrimage as a mortal until he was later resurrected and glorified. (See 2:14, 17 also). Christ knew he had to become a sin offering for us, and so through his death he satisfied the righteous demands of a holy God, making it all possible for him to provide salvation and forgiveness to everyone who believes in Jesus Christ. Although Jesus suffered spiritual separation from the Father during his death on the cross, he was later eternally united at the right side of God the Father after his resurrection.

Summing up the New Covenant

After carefully reading this chapter, I believe it should leave no doubt in one's mind that the New Covenant of Jesus Christ, is a much better covenant, offering superior promises, with the opportunity of enjoying the gift of an eternal life when this one ends. This gift was not offered in the Sinai Covenant, as God chose not to make those promises to the Israelites, especially the forgiveness of sin, through the sacrificial blood of his only begotten Son, Jesus. In the New Covenant, God provides all believers with another wonderful gift, that of the Holy Spirit, which only became available after Jesus had been crucified. The whole concept of the New Covenant is to set in motion a process of transforming the hearts and minds of those who respond to God's call, which is to repent and accept Jesus as their personal redeemer. (Hebrews 9:15).

The heart of the New Covenant

In the book of Matthew, chapter five, we are told of five great discourses, one of which is known as the Sermon on the Mount, which gets to the very heart of what the New Covenant is all about.

It includes eight Beatitudes, which are divine blessings for those who obey God, and we will discuss them further in the next chapter.

> In the Sermon on the Mount, Jesus explains his view very early on when he states that he did not come to abolish the Old Covenant, but rather to fulfill it. (See Matthew 5:17-18).

This tells us that Jesus, when mentioning the Law, was referring to the first five books of Moses, the written Law at that time. Also, when Jesus was referring to the "Prophets," he not only meant the biblical prophets, but also the historical books of the Old Testament. By fulfilling the Law, Jesus fulfilled what was lacking in the old Law.

12

JESUS AND THE JEWS

After 2,000 years there is still no official Jewish view of Jesus!

WHY IS IT, TO THIS VERY DAY, THAT JEWS DO NOT ACCEPT JESUS Christ as their true Messiah, with the exception of some Messianic Jews? The answer lies in the Jewish expectation of what the Messiah would do when he finally appeared. The Jews were indeed looking forward to the Kingdom of God, but they were expecting a political kingdom, which was much different than what the Old Testament prophets had described. This perception eventually led the Jewish leaders to reject Jesus, leading to much tension between the two.

At this particular time in history, the Jewish people had been under the oppression of the Roman Empire since 63 B.C., and they were very restless for change and freedom. Remember, the Jews had been subjugated under the Assyrians, Babylonians, Persians, and Greeks, and they were weary of paying high taxes, and operating under the rules and regulations of foreign officials. Although they had a brief period of about 100 years of independence under the Hasmoneans, thanks to the revolt by the Maccabees, they were once again under the control of a foreign power.

Throughout all this time, however, the Jews never gave up hope of a coming Messiah. So, where did this hope spring from?

Jewish hope came from a literal reading of the Old Testament. At face value, they would often read about an earthly kingdom created by God through the Messiah, the unquestioned King of Israel. The Book of Job 19:25, sets the tone: "I know that my Redeemer lives, and he shall stand at last on the earth." They also believed that the Kingdom teaching of the Old Testament was found in the biblical covenants: Abrahamic (Genesis 12; 15; 17), Davidic (2 Samuel 7; Psalm 89), and the New Covenant (Jeremiah 31). In the Abrahamic Covenant, God deeded the land of Israel to Abraham and his descendants forever, and the promise continued with the Davidic Covenant, which promised the throne of the Kingdom of Israel to the descendants of David in perpetuity. And then, a final son of David, who the Bible says is Jesus Christ, would then rule and reign forever.

In the New Covenant, God promised a spiritual restoration of Israel in the end-times. This included, and is sometimes forgotten, that this spiritual restoration involves Israel being a nation forever. (Jeremiah 31:31-37). As you delve into the Bible, you find numerous examples of specific predictions and promises in the Old Testament related to the end-times Kingdom of Israel. In Amos 9:15, for instance, God said of his people: "I will plant them on their land, and they shall never again be uprooted out of the land that I have given them," says the Lord your God. This is a prophecy rendered in the 8th century B.C., when the kingdom was divided, and it promised a later unification of the nation.

We also find in the same century, the prophet Isaiah giving frequent prophecies about the coming Kingdom for Israel, although he is better known for predicting the Messiah's death, which was fulfilled in the First Coming of Jesus Christ, as an atonement for sin. This is what Isaiah said in chapter 9:6-7:

"For unto us a child is born, unto us a Son is given; and the government will be upon his shoulder. And his name will be called Wonderful, Counselor, Mighty-God, Everlasting Father, Prince of Peace. Of the increase of his government and peace, there will be no end, on the throne of David and over his kingdom, to establish it and uphold it with justice and righteousness from this time forth and forever more."

This passage is both spiritual and political, as it discusses the birth of Jesus, as well as a divine Messiah who will control his rule, as he sits on the throne of King David forever.

There are many other Old Testament passages that mention a future Messiah, and I will briefly mention another one. The prophet Ezekiel spoke of a future Kingdom for the restoring of the Jewish nation:

"I will take the people of Israel from the nations among which they have gone, and will gather them from all around, and bring them to their own land. And I will make them one nation in the land, on the mountains of Israel. And one king shall be a king over them all, and they shall be no longer two nations, and no longer divided into two kingdoms." (Ezekiel 37:21-22, 25).

It is interesting to note that when we review the Old Testament prophecies, only a couple of which I have mentioned from many, you find the children of Israel yearned for a coming Messiah. This is very similar to Christians who yearn and look forward to the Second Coming of Christ. This Jewish sentiment was clearly on the minds of many Jews when the events that led to the New Testament began to take place.

The fulfillment of Old Testament prophecies was now being realized, as Jesus had come to earth to preach the gospel message. Jesus was communicating an offer of the kingdom, as long as the Jews repented and accepted Jesus as their Messianic King. Unfortunately, only a few Jews accepted Jesus as Messiah, which caused the Apostle, John, to comment many years later: "He came to his own, and his own did not receive him." (John 1:11). Jewish rejection of Christ is what led to a delaying of the installation of the kingdom.

For Israel, their rejection of the Messiah had devastating effects. It was not because the kingdom was being redefined, it simply meant that the kingdom was no longer available at that time, and was being postponed. Instead, there would be an interregnum, (Latin for "between reigns."). In other words, there would be an interval, or pause of some time without a ruler, until some future date when the King and the Kingdom would reappear. We humans have all been living in that state of interregnum up to the present time. In Romans 11:25, Paul says, "Lest you be wise in your own sight, I do not want you to be unaware of this mystery, brothers, a partial hardening has come upon Israel, until the fullness of the Gentiles has come in. And in this way all Israel will be saved . . ." In John 12:40, it goes on to say, "He has blinded their eyes, and hardened their heart, lest they see with their eyes, and understand with their heart, and turn, and I would heal them." So, the Jews must wait until a future time when God brings Israel into a state of true repentance.

A similarity can be drawn between this story, and the story of Joshua sending twelve spies into the Promised Land (Numbers 13). When the spies came back, we find ten of the twelve showed fears of taking the land. This caused the people to reject the plan, which also meant they were rejecting God's plan for their future. Consequently, God subjected the people to wandering in the desert for 40 years until all of the people over the age of twenty had died off. The only exceptions to entering the Promised Land were Joshua and Caleb, the two spies who wanted to conquer the land and honor the Lord's plan.

The life of Jesus

The story of Jesus began in a small town in the Near East, about six-miles south of Jerusalem. The name of this small town was, and still is, called Bethlehem. It was there that God chose to have his only begotten Son be born a man. In Hebrew, we find the name, Bethlehem, is actually two-names. The first part, Beth, means "house," and the second part, "lehem," means 'bread." In other words, Bethlehem is the House of Bread, which is quite symbolic for Christians in that they participate in regular communion by eating bread and drinking the fruit of the vine as a symbolic, spiritual gesture of their commitment and connection to Jesus.

What is quite amazing about the birth of Jesus, is the fact that two ancient prophets both predicted his birth some 700 years before he was born! In Isaiah 7:14, we find the following words, "Therefore, the Lord himself will give you a sign. Behold, the virgin will conceive and bear a son, and they shall call his name, Immanuel." In Hebrew, the name Immanuel means, "God is with us!" Isaiah's words are also confirmed in the New Testament book of Matthew 1:23, which was written in the early 70s A.D. It says, "Behold, the virgin shall conceive and bear a son, and they shall call his name, Immanuel." Also, the prophet, Micah, who was active between 742 and 687 B.C., also predicted the coming of the Messiah. Micah also stated that the birth would take place in Bethlehem Ephrathah (Micah 5:2). The word, Ephrathah, means "fruit," as in, for instance, "By their fruit you shall know them," a phrase uttered by Jesus.

The bloodline of Jesus can easily be traced back to Abraham, the founder of the Jewish faith, as mentioned earlier. Also, there is no need to repeat the generations leading up to Christ as they too have already been detailed. However, it is perhaps important to point out it was when traveling to Bethlehem, where Rachel, wife of Jacob (the third of the Jewish patriarchs), died giving birth to Benjamin. Later, in the book of Ruth, who was a Moabite from east of the Jordan River, we find she later marries a Jew, Boaz, who becomes her kinsman redeemer. Later, Ruth is grafted into the Jewish bloodline. They have a son, Obed, who later has a son named Jesse, who had many sons. His youngest son was named David, who was also born in Bethlehem. Later, David is anointed king by the prophet, Samuel, which also took place in, you guessed it - Bethlehem!

Obviously, Bethlehem is a very special place in Bible history, and it becomes clearer as we trace the bloodline of Jesus, and why, of all places, he would be born in Bethlehem out of all the many possibilities available. Bethlehem is known as the City of David, and if you visit the town today, you will still find the Church of the Holy Nativity, which claims to be the place where Jesus was born. It is one of the oldest existing Christian churches in the world!

We know very little about Jesus' upbringing, other than his parents were from a small town in the Lower Galilee area, called Nazareth, which at that time had a population of about 150 people. It is located about 90 miles north of Bethlehem, about a six day walk. It is located close to Megiddo, which the Bible claims to be the last great battle of mankind before the end comes, as mentioned in the last book of the Bible, the Revelation. It is in Nazareth, where Jesus grew into an adult, doing carpentry work. Imagine for a moment, Jesus' upbringing was in the very vicinity where millions of people would be killed at the last great battle on earth, before Jesus would later descend from heaven to bring it all to an end. (Discussed later).

Jesus began his three-year ministry at about the age of 30, having been born about 4 B.C. Before starting his ministry, however, he had to fulfill two critical objectives. First, he had to be tested for 40 days in the wilderness, where God's nemesis, Satan, tried to tempt Jesus in a number of ways, without success. Secondly, Jesus had to build up a group of dedicated followers to help him accomplish his mission of bringing hope to the world.

From his many disciples, he chose 12 apostles, who were then expected to leave their families, their jobs, their businesses, and their homes to follow Jesus. They had to be willing to travel from town to town, frequently in hostile and dangerous territory. According to the Gospel of Mark, the apostles had very little resources – just a staff, a pair of sandals, a single tunic, and no bread, no bag, and no money. They traveled strictly on faith. All 12 answered Jesus without hesitation, which gives us insight into the greatness of who Jesus was, and his influence on all who came across his path.

During his three-year ministry, and in the name of brevity, I will briefly summarize some of his great accomplishments:

1. He performed some 38 miracles that we are aware of, but he also performed many others that were not detailed according to the book of John.

2. Included among his miracles were a number of "nature" miracles such as:

    a. Raising a dead man back to life

    b. Calming a great storm on the Sea of Galilee

    c. Feeding 5000 people with only five loaves of bread, and two fish

    d. Feeding 4000 people with only seven loaves and a few fish

    e. Creating a miracle catch of fish after his apostles had failed

    f. Cleansing ten lepers

    g. Casting out demons.

3. Jesus often spoke directly, but sometimes in aphorisms of short, clever phrases that simply expressed an important concept. He also spoke at least 50 parables, in which he would tell vivid stories to convey his teachings. Many scholars believe Jesus spoke in parables to invite discussion, encouraging interpretation, and to ask everyone to find some meaning in them. Consequently, his parables have been discussed in many different ways over the centuries.

4. Jesus was often found to be antithetical, meaning he would take the exact opposite view or position in traditional ways of thinking, especially with the Jewish leaders, the Pharisees and the Sadducees. Jesus told us to love our enemies, and if someone strikes you on the cheek, then offer the other one. He also told us to do good to those who hate us. He told us the stories of the Good Samaritan, and a Samaritan leper who was the only one out of ten lepers that thanked Jesus for healing him. These stories were undoubtedly told so that the Jews would learn to love the Samaritans, whom they hated.

5. It seems whereas the Old Testament tended to take people in the opposite direction of their natural inclinations regarding physical issues, the New Testament Covenant takes us in the opposite direction of our natural inclinations regarding spiritual issues. The teachings of Jesus appear to tell us that if we want to keep our lives, we must lose them. In order to be strong, we must be gentle, and if we want to receive, we must give and help others. In order to be first, we must put ourselves last, and in order to be great in the eyes of Jesus, we need to become servants to help others.

We find during Jesus' brief life, he led a rather austere, and humble existence. He lived a simple life, and treated everyone with respect, irrespective of their station in life. He worked among thieves, prostitutes, tax collectors, and the poorest of the poor, and by doing so expressed his love for all mankind. As God, Jesus could have easily lived like the kings, public officials, or so-called Godly men of the Sanhedrin of his day, but that was not his purpose for coming.

In the first four books of the New Testament, known as the gospels, written by Matthew, Mark, Luke and John, we learn more details of his life, such as where he was born, his teachings, his ministry, and his disciples. We also learn about his travels, prayer habits, and many of the great words he spoke in his lengthy speeches. We find out about the objections he experienced from the Jewish leaders and educated men, which prompted Jesus to reply in a way that provided us with even keener insight into his thinking. This was a great blessing to all of us as we mine into his treasure trove of wisdom, which guides us to this day.

The details I provided earlier in this chapter, have provided the background to help explain why the Jews did not accept Jesus as their Messiah, and the terrible price they paid for this non-acceptance. We can now move forward with the story of Jesus that eventually led to his crucifixion and death on the cross.

Through the Gospels, and other Old Testament prophets, we also learn about Jesus' betrayal, his unjust arrest, his corrupt trial, his shameful death on the cross, and the miracle of his recovery at the Resurrection. In Isaiah 52–53, we are provided with a description of how much Jesus suffered during the crucifixion. In several passages, we find Isaiah telling us Jesus' appearance was so disfigured beyond that of any man, and his form marred beyond human likeness. Isaiah further describes Jesus as someone who had no beauty or majesty to attract us to him, and he was despised and rejected by men. He was a man of sorrows and familiar with suffering, like one from whom men hid their faces. He was despised, and we esteemed him not. Isaiah goes on to say that Jesus took up our infirmities and carried our sorrows, yet we considered him stricken by God, smitten by him, and afflicted. He was pierced for our transgressions, he was crushed, for our iniquities, and the punishment that brought us peace was upon him, and by his wounds we are healed.

Theologians all over the world have written 1,000s of pages on the life of Jesus, but in the almost 90 chapters contained in the Gospels, there is a special passage providing us great insight into the heart of Jesus. It is found in Matthew 11:28-30, where Jesus says: "Come to me, all who labor and are heavy laden, and I will give you rest. Take my yoke upon you, and learn from me, for I am gentle and lowly in heart, and you shall find rest for your souls. For my yoke is easy, and my burden is light."

Focus for a moment on the two words, "gentle" and "lowly." These words still confuse Jews to this day, because Jesus was the antithesis of the military leader, they were expecting to overthrow the mighty Romans. Yet Jesus tells us he is gentle, and he is lowly. This insight indicates no matter how sinful a person's life has been to date, he or she can still seek repentance through Jesus, who will welcome them into his world, and forgive all their sins. No contract has to be signed, no cash down payment is required. Jesus simply says, "I will give you rest." This is a pure gift of grace just for the asking.

13

JESUS AND HIS TEACHINGS – PART ONE

"The Word of God I think of as a straight edge, which shows us our own crookedness. We cannot really tell how crooked our thinking is until we line it up with the straight edge of Scripture!" –Elisabeth Elliot

THE BOOKS OF THE NEW TESTAMENT, AND ESPECIALLY THE FOUR GOSPELS, provide us with an understanding of the mind of God, as Jesus provides us with a treasure trove of wisdom sayings we need to apply in our everyday lives, in order to enter the Kingdom of God. Of the many sermons Jesus gave us during his brief ministry, perhaps the greatest of them all is known as the Sermon on the Mount. This sermon was given on a mountain, known as the Mount of Beatitudes, where to this day you will find the Church of the Beatitudes, built by the Roman Catholic Church. With Jesus delivering the sermon on a mountain, it appears to be no coincidence, in that Moses delivered the Ten Commandments on Mount Sinai (Exodus 20:1). Now, Jesus was delivering a New Covenant on a mountain, which provides another similarity between Jesus and Moses. The sermon took place on the north shore of the Sea of Galilee, in what is today known as the State of Israel.

It could be said this sermon was Jesus' inaugural address, which masterfully explains the countercultural values of God's Kingdom, and what Jesus expects of those who follow him. Although Jesus sets very high moral and ethical standards for his followers, we must realize we Christians cannot meet its demands in our own power. It is only through Jesus' power we can attain a Spirit-filled life, through a yearning to know him better. This means we must show a willingness to live our lives in the best possible way, with the assistance of the Holy Spirit, as we navigate this life in preparation for the next, eternal life.

In the Sermon on the Mount, Jesus provides us with eight Beatitudes, which come from the Latin word, *beatidudinem*, meaning state of blessedness. In Matthew there are eight, but in Luke there are four, with four woes. The Beatitudes are relatively easy to remember, but more difficult to implement in our lives without the help of God.

Some theologians state the Beatitudes shine a light on our sins by holding them up to a mirror, which is true. By doing so, we realize we need God's grace to enter the Kingdom of God, while at the same time it shows us the blessedness of life in God's Kingdom. By setting a moral standard, which we should strive to achieve, it provides the type of values the Holy Spirit gives us, while indicating the moral character we should all be striving for. The Kingdom of God, and the term, The Kingdom of Heaven, are mentioned some 55 times in Matthew.

In John 18:36, Jesus tells us about the kingdom, when speaking to Pontius Pilate, the Roman governor. Jesus said, "My kingdom is not of this world. If my kingdom were of this world, my servants would have been fighting, so I might not be delivered over to the Jews. But my kingdom is not from the world."

Jesus is stating his kingdom is not a political one, but rather a spiritual one. We also find in Luke 17:20b-21, Jesus saying, "The kingdom of God does not come with your careful observation, nor will people say, 'Here it is,' or 'there it is,' because the kingdom of God is within you!"

Below, and also in the next chapter, you will find an insightful overview of the eight Beatitudes, which Christ challenges us all to strive for, as we go about strengthening our commitment to him. We all realize, of course, these eight goals are difficult to achieve without the help of Jesus rendering to us through the Holy Spirit:

> **Blessed are the poor in spirit for theirs is the Kingdom of Heaven – Matthew 5:3**

One of our biggest temptations is trying to fit in and being like everyone else. In this way, we avoid criticism and friction. Jesus, however, expects us to change our value system, and endorse the idea that aptitude plus attitude equals altitude! In The Sermon on the Mount, Jesus demonstrates we are expected to be different and separate from other people. These differences are laid out in the Beatitudes. Blessed are the poor in spirit means total dependance on God versus independence from God. Our world says it does not need anyone, including God, but believers say they cannot move forward with their lives without God guiding them.

Millions of people today are seduced by living a comfortable lifestyle, believing they have everything they need. So, why worry about attending regular church services for spiritual development, especially when they can watch the electronic church on TV in their pajamas, or use some excuse for not attending. Christians need the support of other Christians as they travel through a world becoming more hostile towards Christians.

Whether we realize it or not, we need to recognize our own spiritual poverty in order to begin to grow spiritually. The beginning of repentance is the recognition of one's spiritual bankruptcy, and our inability to become righteous on our own. We note a few words from Charles Spurgeon, the great 19th century English pastor, who once said: "A ladder, if it is to be of any use, must have the first step on the ground. This gospel blessing (being poor in spirit), reaches down to the very spot where the law leaves us." This should make us all glad the first beatitude is to be poor in spirit.

So, in essence, what Jesus is essentially saying, is when we finally accept our own spiritual bankruptcy, and then accept the redemptive blood of Christ in our lives, it is only then we can begin the sanctification process leading to ultimate salvation, and eternal life with our Lord and Savior, Jesus.

> **Blessed are those who mourn for they will be comforted – Matthew 5:4**

We are told there are three types of mourning: natural, sinful, and spiritual. Natural mourning is grieving for someone you have lost, which is a normal response. Secondly, there is sinful mourning, where people are pining for something God has not given them. There is no sin in natural mourning, but there are other types of sin that can lead to death. Thirdly, there is spiritual mourning. This is sorrow over our sins against God, and therefore is a Godly sorrow, which Paul also spoke about in 2 Corinthians 7:10. It is blessed because it produces a repentance leading to life.

Yes, we all know about natural mourning, and sinful mourning, but what does the church today know about spiritual mourning? Many Christians today find themselves surrounded by a form of faith that has been so emaciated, diluted, it is sometimes unrecognizable to what Jesus was talking about. What Jesus is stating, is spiritual mourning follows naturally from becoming poor in spirit. When we finally realize we do not have what it takes to enter the Kingdom of God, we mourn over our sins, and the righteousness we do not have.

> **Blessed are the meek for they shall inherit the Earth – Matthew 5:5**

In modern life, when we think of the word "meek," it conjures up submissiveness, being impressionable, or easily led. An English literal meaning is "gentle," but the Greek version has a deeper meaning. The Greeks saw the word as a picture of great power to do harm, but instead choosing to suffer insult upon themselves, rather than using the power to cause injury. Meekness means "God-tamed." It is like a wild horse that is of no use to us, until it has been tamed. In the Christian life, God breaks us in order to make us like his Son Jesus.

A portrait of the meek signifies four main characteristics:

1.   They trust God, and by doing so, they believe he will work for them and vindicate them when others oppose them. Meekness in the Bible sense, simply provides confidence God is for you, and not working against you.

2.   They totally rely on God. They do this by turning over all their problems, their business, financial, health, emotional challenges, and their fears to God for remedy. By doing this, they are openly admitting they lack the understanding to deal with the complexities of life, and totally trust in God for sustenance and protection.

3.   They are quiet in waiting for the Lord, with patience and endurance. They have discovered God can be trusted by committing their ways to him, while waiting for God to work in their lives. Does this mean they are shiftless? No! They are simply not worrying about the twists and turns of life, and are calm under pressure knowing God has their situation under control.

4.   Their steady, confident approach to life's problems, means they do not become bitter, or angry, or frustrated, when challenges arrive. Refraining from anger, they believe all their family, their possessions, and future, are all in God's hands.

Here are two examples of Bible figures who demonstrated meekness. In reading Numbers 12:1-4, 10, we find Aaron and Miriam arguing with Moses because he had married a Cushite woman. In defending himself, Moses does not say a word, but instead he waits patiently for assistance from the Lord. Meanwhile, he does not show anger or fret over the harsh words directed at him. Later, we find God turning Miriam into a leper for seven days. This story tells us meekness has the power to absorb criticism, without responding. This is a challenge for most of us. Then, in James 1:19-20, he says: "My dear brothers, take note of this: everyone should be quick to listen, slow to speak, and slow to become angry, for man's anger does not bring about the righteous life God desires."

Meekness is a teachable virtue, because those who are quick to listen and slow to speak, generally do not have a hostile spirit when they are taught. This does not mean they are naïve or over trusting, and it does not mean they never get angry, because James says we should be slow to anger, rather than never experience it. We find Jesus in Matthew 11:29, saying: "For I am gentle and lowly in heart," yet in Matthew 3:7, Jesus became angry and grieved at the hardheartedness of the Pharisees. We are also aware of the story in Matthew 21:12-13, where Jesus drove the merchants out of the temple, and turned over the tables. This would be an example of righteous anger, which can be justified. (See below).

It should also be pointed out truly wise people are also truly meek people. Let's go back to James 3:13, 17, where he says: "Who is wise and understanding among you? By his good conduct let him show his works in the meekness of wisdom."

In summarizing the characteristic of meekness, we find it begins when we put our trust in God. Then, because we trust him, we totally depend on him by transferring to him all our plans, worries, fears, frustrations, and all of our health, emotional, and financial concerns. We then patiently wait on the Lord, trusting totally in his power and grace to work matters out for his glory and ultimately our benefit.

> **Blessed are those who hunger and thirst for righteousness, for they will be filled. – Matthew 5:6**

Christians typically enjoy contented hearts, but this cannot be said for the majority of people who live restless lives. They appear to be just one step away from the ideal job; a step away from a dream home or car, and perhaps just one-step away from their ideal partner. They appear to be always yearning, but never satisfied. The Book of James identifies this well, when it says, "They quarrel and fight; they want something but they don't get it; they kill and covet because they do not ask God, and when they do ask, they don't receive, because of their wrong motives." (James 4:1-3). St. Augustine, a great 4th century Christian leader, once said, "Thou madest us for Thyself, and our heart is restless, until it rests in Thee." So, what exactly is righteousness?

Webster's New World Dictionary quotes righteousness as, "Acting in a just, upright manner, doing what is right, virtuous, and morally justifiable." You will find it as a concept in both Abrahamic and Indian religions. From a biblical point of view, righteousness is the chief property of God. This concept can be found in Leviticus 19:36-37, Psalm 1:6, and Proverbs 8:20, as ethical conduct. Righteousness is the hallmark of the Messiah's reign, and it is the main attribute of the citizens of God's Kingdom.

Isaiah's theme of righteousness is found in chapter 11:5, which says, "Righteousness shall be the belt of his loins, and faithfulness the belt of his waist." This passage lies at the heart of the Sermon on the Mount, as a belt acts as a main functional addition to a man's attire, in holding up his clothes. We also find in Ephesians 6:14, where it says, "Stand firm then with the belt of truth buckled around your waist."

When we think of righteousness in the Bible, we find it often refers to an ethical or moral standard, representing the virtuous and honorable way to conduct our lives. Unlike God's law, we find man's law directed towards corruption, leading to abuse of the common man. Jesus' rule, however, will raise us up to the standard of God's Law, which protects everyone with divine justice. (See Psalm 72:1-2). The Jewish religious leaders at the time of Jesus, believed Jesus was teaching a righteousness that went against the Law of what God demanded. (See Matthew 12:1-8; 15:1-20).

Today, we have the advantage of history, and we know for certain Jesus did not come to change God's Law, or overturn the Old Testament Covenant for that matter. Rather, Jesus came to fulfill it in the proper way. (Matthew 12:1-8; 15:1-20).

It appears Jesus was sending a message to his disciples by stating God's righteous standard found in the Old Testament will not change, and God's character will continue to prevail. The Law will continue to be the foundation of God's Kingdom here on earth. We also notice Jesus appeared to place less emphasis on judging Israel's enemies, and more focus on judging Israel's spiritual leadership, because it was Jewish leadership who abused their power in the way they ruled the people's spiritual life.

So, Jesus first addressed the spiritual well-being of his people, rather than take action against Israel's enemies who were exploiting them. First, Jesus is seen condemning the Pharisees (Matthew 6:2; 6:5), by setting a standard for entering the Kingdom of Heaven, when he said,

"For I tell you, unless your righteousness exceeds that of the scribes and Pharisees, you will never enter the Kingdom of Heaven." (Matthew 5:20). This type of righteousness was from the heart, and obedience to God comes from the inside out.

In order to emphasize true righteousness, Jesus pointed to those laws engraved on stones, would find a truer, more fulfilling meaning, when they are written on a person's heart. (2 Corinthians 3:2).

Righteousness, Jesus pointed out, was gained by the Law, and further righteousness is imputed to those who demonstrate faith in the lawgiver. A good example of this can be found in Genesis 15:6, where, "Abram believed in the Lord, and he accounted it to him as righteousness." Totally trusting in God is what made Abram righteous in God's mind. The same thing can be said about the disciples when they placed their faith in Jesus Christ alone. Thankfully, all followers of Jesus Christ have the Holy Spirit inside them, thus fulfilling another promise of the New Covenant. (Ezekiel 36:26-27).

What we have learned so far about us human beings, is that we tend to exaggerate our own virtues, while minimizing or ignoring our own faults. We are also quick to judge others, even between Christians and fellow Christians! These, and other flaws, are endemic in human nature, and explain why it is so important to understand what the term righteousness means from God's point of view. This helps us all get closer to the Kingdom. C.S. Lewis, the famous British theologian, once said, "If I find myself a desire which no experience in this world can satisfy, the most probable explanation is that I was made for another world."

So, the entrance to the Kingdom of Heaven is held up by the two pillars of Faith and Righteousness, in accepting Jesus as our Lord and Savior. Another Bible passage worth quoting comes from Matthew 7:12, where it says, "So whatever you wish others would do to you, do also to them, for this is the Law and the Prophets." Most people know this phrase as the Golden Rule, which, in one way or another, ties into many other religions around the world.

We have just covered four of the great Beatitudes of Jesus, and like rungs on a ladder, we will keep climbing by reviewing the remaining four in the next chapter.

JOURNAL YOUR THOUGHTS

_____

_____

_____

_____

_____

_____

_____

_____

_____

_____

_____

_____

_____

_____

_____

_____

_____

14

JESUS AND HIS TEACHINGS – PART TWO

"Forgiveness is at the very heart of Christianity. When Peter asked Jesus how many times should he forgive his brother, as much as seven times? Jesus replies, "Not seven times, but seventy-seven times." –Matthew 18:21-2

PUSHING ONWARDS, WE WILL NOW LOOK DEEPER INTO THE REMAINING four Beatitudes given by Jesus during his famous Sermon on the Mount. All eight Beatitudes are vital for us to understand in our attempt to measure up to the standard Jesus has established for us. But remember, however, these Beatitudes are hard to live up to without the power of the Holy Spirit, which is given to every believer.

> **Blessed are the merciful, for they shall be shown mercy – Matthew 5:7**

At this point we have detailed four Beatitudes, representing blessings Jesus gave us in order to teach us the proper way to manage our lives, and to do it in a way that is pleasing to our heavenly Father. We have learned the benefits of being blessed in being poor in spirit, as one of the keys to entrance into the Kingdom of Heaven. We also learned there are three types of mourning, but spiritual mourning, caused by our sinful nature, is very pleasing to

God. We also now know the meek shall inherit the earth one day, and we should all be hungering and thirsting for righteousness in order to be filled with the Grace of God. When we analyze these four Beatitudes, we find they are just the opposite to the statement in Proverbs 6:16-19, where it describes seven things God hates: "Haughty eyes, a lying tongue, hands that shed innocent blood, a heart that devises wicked schemes; feet that are quick to rush into evil, a false witness who pours out lies, and a man that stirs up dissension among his brothers." Haughty eyes, for instance, are just the opposite of being poor in spirit. Also, a man who stirs up dissension among his brothers, is just the opposite of a peacemaker, which is Beatitude number seven. All the others in between, such as lying, killing, scheming wicked schemes, rushing to evil, and bearing false witness, all differ considerably from the virtues God loves.

As we compare the above first three Beatitudes, which describe the emptiness the blessed person feels in developing a poverty-stricken spirit, coupled to grieving over sin, and then accepting the hardships of the meek, it is easy to find these conditions of emptiness are logically followed by Beatitude number four, a hunger and thirst for righteousness. We find later how these first three Beatitudes describe how righteousness overflows in the hearts of the hungry, in mercy (verse seven), in purity (verse eight), and peacemaking (verse nine). With these thoughts in mind, we will now look closer at the blessing of being merciful.

Mercy (Beatitude number five), we find, comes from a heart that has experienced spiritual bankruptcy, a heart that has experienced grieving, and a heart that has learned to wait patiently and meekly for the Lord. It then cries out for hunger for God's mercy to satisfy us with the righteousness we need. You will find mercy is a true blessing from God, as it grows like fruit in a broken heart. A meek spirit is a soul that hungers and thirsts for God to show his mercy.

The mercy we show to each other comes from God's mercy to us, and we find the way of becoming a merciful person is to become a broken person. When this happens, it provides us with the power to show mercy from our heart, which allows us to truly acknowledge we owe everything to God's divine mercy. So, if we want to become a truly merciful person, we need to strengthen our view of God, which helps us to say with all our heart, that every joy we experience, every virtue we cultivate, and every distress in our lives, are due to the undeserved gift of mercy from God.

In order to further understand the defining of a merciful person, it sometimes helps when we look at the opposite. For instance, when we look at Matthew 9:10-13, and Mark 2:17, we find Jesus stating he wants mercy and not sacrifice. This refers to God not wanting burnt offerings, but rather the true love of the people. We find a quote in Hosea 6:4-6, where God accuses the people, saying, "your love is like a morning cloud, like the dew that goes early away . . . For I desire steadfast love and not sacrifice, the knowledge of God rather than burnt offerings." God is stating he wants his people to be alive in their hearts, to have feelings of affection towards him, and to demonstrate mercy to each other.

Jesus views sinners and sick people, including rich people and tax collectors, as people in need of a physician. They were sick, but Jesus had the medicine. Unfortunately, all the pious Pharisees could see was a ceremonial problem contaminating them by eating with sinners. Their lives were a mechanical ritual and implementation of rules. They appeared blinded to the fact something much bigger was at stake, but they could not see it because they were "majoring in minors" on trivial issues of ceremonial cleanliness, rather than thinking about eternal sickness, which was about to be healed.

Therefore, the opposite to mercy was bondage to religious triviality. When we look at Matthew 23:23-24, we find Jesus advising the Jewish leaders they resembled blind guides who were trying to strain out a gnat, but swallow a camel. It is the opposite of mercy, for instance, when our religious impulses are drained, after we have decided whether we should tithe our gross income or our net income, or whether we should tithe from other sources of income such as gifts, job bonuses, or inheritance income. Jesus is indicating a valuable lesson when he said, "I desire mercy and not sacrifice," in which he is implying we put a great obstacle in front of our giving, and approach to mercy, when we become too preoccupied with the minutiae of life. In other words, let's stop sweating the small stuff. Instead, try to listen to, and be guided by, our hearts. Jesus is basically saying the bondage of triviality is the curse of the unmerciful.

While not being grounded in trivialities, we should also be careful not to neglect the weightier matters of the law, according to Jesus. He wants us to be aware of not going through the day focused on trivialities, doing trivial things, driven by trivial thoughts and feelings. Rather, Jesus makes the case we should pinch ourselves often in order not to fall into this mental trap. Stay away from mindless TV, and spend more mental effort on the major importance of engaging in mercy.

Just the opposite to mercy can be read in Jesus' parable of the Good Samaritan, found in Luke 10:25. In this story a man asked Jesus how a person should act who is expecting to find mercy on Judgement Day, and then enter eternal life. Jesus answered by saying, "The people who will receive the mercy of eternal life are those who have loved God with all their hearts, and loved their neighbor as they loved themselves. In other words, show mercy to your neighbor. This parable demonstrates both mercy and its exact opposite.

The Good Samaritan parable is segmented into four parts:

1. The Samaritan saw a man in serious trouble.

2. He reacted with compassion.

3. He made a heartfelt and concerted effort to help relieve the man's problem.

4. All the while he was helping, he knew the man was his enemy.

This parable ties into the point Jesus is making in Matthew 9:13, when he said, "I desire mercy not sacrifice, for I have not come to call the righteous, but sinners." Jesus was telling us to show mercy just like the Samaritan, and not like the priest or Levite.

How do we know when to apply mercy, and when to show justice? **The answer lies in getting as close to Jesus as we can.** There is no biblical rule book telling us how to manage and solve every situation we face in dispensing justice and mercy. This may be an accident by design, if we come to the realization Scripture is attempting to produce a certain type of merciful person, rather than a detailed "Yes and No" list, for all the problems we can experience throughout our lifetime.

Here is an example: A teenage boy robs three stores in the same evening and is then caught. Later, at trial, the judge asks for the recommendations of each of the store owners. The first owner says he should go to jail. This might be justice, but is it showing mercy? The second owner says he should be released and go free. This may show mercy, but is it justice? Then the third owner is asked her opinion, and she says: "Judge, give the young man to me, and I will teach him the right way to live." Now this is an example of both mercy and justice! The point is, we should all try to be merciful even when acting within the confines of dispensing justice. We need to still demonstrate being poor in spirit, being sorrowful of our own sins, while applying meekness as we hunger and thirst for righteousness. This helps us to render mercy when appropriate, based on our best judgment of the situation.

In the end, however, there are certain acts against individuals and society at large, needing to be addressed, and the appropriate punishment applied. I would hope, however, a form of grace would be adopted in order to obtain a certain balance between the severity of the crime and the punishment rendered. So, by getting closer to Jesus, and his biblical principles, mercy can be achieved.

The subject of mercy often brings up several questions. Are merciful people, for instance, the only ones who obtain mercy on Judgment Day? If this is so, how does it reconcile with salvation by grace through faith? The answer, it appears, is found in Matthew 5:7, where Jesus says, "Blessed are the merciful for they will obtain mercy." This clearly demonstrates those people who have shown mercy, will surely obtain mercy from our Lord. The answer to this question is sometimes followed up by asking if this is a form of salvation by works, which it isn't, because if mercy is earned, it would not be mercy, but would be more like earned wages. When Judgment Day comes, we will be receiving pure mercy based on our faith in Jesus Christ, because he is the key to God's Kingdom. Therefore, Christians should always do their very best to demonstrate mercy to their fellow man. An old Christian adage sums this subject up very well by saying mercy is not getting what we do deserve, which is punishment, but rather we are given God's grace, which is something we don't deserve!

> **Blessed are the pure in heart, for they shall see God – Matthew 5:8**

In discussing the last five Beatitudes, you will notice while each of the Beatitudes stands on its own, each is progressively linked to the one following it. Like the rungs of a ladder, each step elevates us higher than the previous one.

We now arrive at the sixth Beatitude – Blessed are the Pure in Heart, for they shall see God. This is a challenging Beatitude for all of us, as the next step on the ladder (as mentioned by Pastor Charles Spurgeon in the last chapter), is even higher for us to climb up. There is comfort in knowing, however, that Jesus commented with man it is not possible to obtain, but with God all things are possible. Therefore, the closer to God we get, the closer we get to reaching this ideal. You see, Jesus is very concerned about the state of our hearts. Jesus told the Sadducees they were blind (spiritually speaking), in the sense they cleansed the cup on the outside, while drinking the poison on the inside, which was damaging their souls. He recommended they first cleanse the inside of the cup, so the outside can also be clean (metaphorically speaking). Jesus was less concerned about reforming society than he was about cleansing the hearts of sinners. For example, Jesus was less focused on a society that did not commit adultery, and more concerned about our heart's approach to the subject. We find Jesus saying if a man looks at a woman with lust in his heart, he has already committed adultery.

Jesus teaches us our heart is who we are in the secrecy of our thoughts, our feelings, and what we do when no one is looking. Sometimes we forget God knows everything! Nothing is hidden from his sight.

So, our Lord is saying, what comes out of our mouth proceeds from the heart. Out of our heart comes murder, rape, adultery, fornication, theft, lying, and slander. All these things defile a man. In the Book of James, it says: "If we put bits into the mouths of horses so they obey us, we guide their whole bodies as well. Look at the ships also: though they are so large and are driven by strong winds, they are guided by a very small rudder wherever the will of the pilot directs. So also, the tongue is a small member, yet it boasts of great things. How great a forest is set ablaze by such a small fire! And the tongue is a fire, a world of unrighteousness. The tongue is set among our members, staining the whole body, setting on fire the entire course of life, and set on fire by hell. For every type of beast and bird, of reptile and sea creature, can be tamed and has been tamed by mankind, but no human being can tame the tongue. It is a restless evil, full of deadly poison." (James 3:3-8).

It is important to take a closer look at sin, because it is preventing us from developing a pure heart as we strive forward in our spiritual walk. By properly identifying the enemy, we get closer to reaching our goal with God. Notice for instance, such sins as adultery, fornication, abortion, and lying, are not punishable with prison time, but they are clearly wrong in the mind of God, even though they are acceptable in the laws of man. Identifying sin more clearly, then, is a good first step towards developing a pure heart.

A reality check on our current societal condition, tells us our government is incapable of fixing the ever-worsening moral condition of our people. In one survey, some 50% of all black babies have no father in the home, and only one-percent are given up for adoption. So, what can the government do? Lessening the economic burden appears to be the only thing they can do. All babies born without a father come through fornication, and this statistic is true irrespective of skin color. All man's problems are heart issues, and if we all strive towards developing a pure heart, then our government's inability to fix our problems would no longer be relevant.

It is of great interest to ask ourselves what does it mean to be pure in heart? What is it like to see God? How are these two questions bonded together? What should we be looking for in a pure heart? Here are some pointers to help us get closer to understanding this Beatitude:

First, a pure heart is one clean from the guilt of sin. We are already aware no one can obtain a pure heart unless by the saving grace of Jesus Christ. We can try on our own until the cows come home, but our thoughts will always remain impure until soaked in the sacrificial blood of our Lord, Jesus Christ.

Our heart is at the core of our spiritual problems, but we are also aware it is our mind that directs the heart. So, if we think impure thoughts, we know our heart will act in a similar manner.

Those people who yearn for a pure heart try to keep themselves transparent to God auditing their heart, and are therefore always willing to be tried and tested. "Search me, O God, and know my heart; try me and know my thoughts! And see if there be any grievous way in me, and lead me in the way everlasting." (Psalm 139:23). This is the tried-and-true method of helping eradicate any impurities. I know it's very hard for any of us to imagine what it is like to experience a pure heart, containing no sin, no dark motives, no negative thoughts etc. But as we get closer to God, we gain more understanding. "Through your precepts I get understanding; I hate every false way." (Psalm 119:104).

We are also aware it is possible not to sin for the wrong reasons, which people do all the time. They may not act on their sin of immorality, getting drunk, or doing illegal drugs, for fear of being exposed to public criticism. A person motivated towards gaining a pure heart, however, is motivated by not wanting to commit sin, and therefore is more concerned with what an act of sin can do to their relationship with God.

In summary, I think it fair to say we all yearn to be pure. We also understand it is a high goal for any of us to aspire to, without the help of Jesus Christ working on our hearts and minds. The apostle, Paul, was right on the mark when writing to the Romans, when he said:

> "For we know that the law is spiritual, but I am of
> the flesh, sold under sin. For I do not understand
> my own actions. For I do not do what I want, but I
> do the very thing I hate. Now if I do what I do not
> want, I agree with the law, that it is good. So, it is
> no longer I who do it, but sin that dwells within
> me. For I know that nothing good dwells in me,

that is, in my flesh. For I have the desire to do what is right, but not the ability to carry it out. For I do not do the good I want, but the evil I do not want is what I keep on doing. Now if I do what I do not want, it is no longer I who do it, but sin that dwells within me. So, I find it to be a law that when I want to do right, evil lies close at hand. For I delight in the law of God, in my inner being, but I see in my members another law waging war against the law of my mind and making me captive to the law of sin that dwells in my members. Wretched man that I am! Who will deliver me from this body of death? Thanks be to God through Jesus Christ our Lord! So then, I myself serve the law of God with my mind, but with my flesh I serve the law of sin." (Romans 7:14-25).

It is now clear, irrespective of our very best efforts to achieve a pure heart, with many people having strived hard to do so over the centuries, where we find it impossible to achieve our goal without the strength of Jesus Christ working in us to make it all a reality. There is no other way out of our situation, without having faith in Jesus Christ.

> Blessed are the peacemakers, for they shall be called the children of God – Matthew: 5:9

As we now enter into a discussion of the seventh Beatitude, we have learned Jesus has taught us a number of important life lessons we need to focus and build on in order to enter the Kingdom of God. The previous six Beatitudes all represent spiritual virtues we need to incorporate into our lives while we remain here on earth. Without a good understanding of this seventh Beatitude, however, we will not be in a position to help solve problems between people, or even trouble between nations for that matter. This could be the reason why Jesus made this the seventh Beatitude, because it is a very challenging one for all of us in wishing to achieve the title of a peacemaker.

Peacemakers are called the children of God, according to Jesus, and as we take a quick look around our chaotic world, we can clearly see being a peacemaker is now more important than ever. With the clash of people groups running away from armed conflicts, into the not so loving arms of people of other nations, along with the race for nations to capture the world's precious minerals and scarce resources, to say nothing of religious ideologies and persecutions, we all find ourselves in a cauldron of hot wars, border disputes, and internecine conflicts, all demonstrating mankind has learned very little from the thousands of years of recorded history.

Looking at more inner details through our microscope, another metric tells us more than 70 countries are experiencing a decline in political and civil rights. Indigenous people, who make up about five-percent of the populations of some 90 countries, are suffering oppression, starvation, exploitation, and a very short life. More than 800 million people worldwide are food insecure, and wonder if they will eat tomorrow. The UN Refugee Agency states some two-thirds of refugees come from many of the countries subject to the fighting mentioned above. Yes, the world is in a terrible state, yet we find Jesus telling us all to go out and be peacemakers. Clearly, if there ever was a time to be a peacemaker, it is today.

As we briskly thumb through the Beatitudes, we may get the impression peacemaking is somewhat of a passive endeavor, such as keeping our business to ourselves, and avoiding stressful situations. This could not be further from the truth, because Jesus did not avoid conflict, he actually engaged in it. He did not do so to make the situation worse, but rather to solve it. Jesus is saying a peacemaker needs to be active in the pursuit of justice, reconciliation, and most importantly, peace. There is no question, when we take this approach, it can prove to be dangerous, as in the case of Jesus when it cost him his life on the cross. When we were born, we were not given the choice of which country we would be born in, or the type of world we would like to live in. We were also not given the choice of becoming peacemakers, because as Christians we are duty bound to bring peace whenever we can.

It is worth further study to determine just what Jesus meant when he asks us to be peacemakers. So, let's see if we can narrow further what Jesus was talking about.

We must first realize being a peacemaker is not the absence of conflict, because peace in the Bible should never be confused with pacifism. It is interesting to note, we are never instructed to run from the conflict, or place our head in the sand, like an ostrich. This will not make the problem go away, but only delay the situation. You may have heard the term, "Peace at any price," which is also not a biblical command. Sometimes you cannot make everyone happy as realized by Neville Chamberlain, the British prime-minister at the beginning of World War II. He appeared to be willing to do almost anything to avoid a war, but it happened anyway. Some people try accommodating issues by acting as though everything is fine, as they gloss over important issues that need to be resolved. This is also not the role of a true peacemaker.

So, we must all ask the question, what did Jesus mean by us being peacemakers? A good working definition of a peacemaker is when we are actively involved in seeking reconciliation between the parties, and ensuring it is done in a manner pleasing to God. The word "peacemaker" is a compound word meaning peace and maker. In Hebrew, the word "peace" is "shalom," meaning peace, hello and goodbye. However, in a broader sense it relates to health, harmony, prosperity, and implies wholeness. It goes even further by suggesting a perfect form of welfare, fulfillment, tranquility, and freedom from any troubles getting in the way of contentment. So, when a Jew says, "shalom," he is wishing us peace, prosperity, and the blessedness of God. The Aaronic benediction perhaps says it best, "The Lord bless you and keep you; the Lord make his face shine upon you, and be gracious to you; the Lord lifts up his countenance upon you and gives you peace." (Numbers 6:24-27). You will find peace in the Bible is always based on justice and righteousness, because whenever you have these two virtues in mind, peace is the natural bi-product. Without them, you will find everlasting peace is not possible.

The second part of the word, peacemaker, is "make," which comes from a Greek verb meaning "do" or "to make." It is a word full of vitality, which forces action. Sometimes a peacemaker has to influence two parties to the negotiating table, and provide logical reasons as to why they should adjust their positions, in order to solve problems. Remember, Jesus never said, "Blessed are the peace wishers, or the peace lovers. He did say, however, we need to be peacemakers, because inevitably peace needs to be made. Peace generally does not come about through non-action or by chance, but rather through initiative and actions. For this reason, a peacemaker does not enjoy the luxury of being passive.

It is not just the absence of conflict motivating peacemakers, or a situation without strife. Peacemakers attempt to apply the blessedness of God on the parties, with the hope and prayer it will lead to peace. God, we find, is the author of peace, and Jesus has been anointed the supreme peacemaker! This means peacemaking is a divine work, which is why Jesus refers to peacemakers as children of God. Jesus said just before the crucifixion, "Peace I leave with you; my peace I give to you. Not as the world gives do I give to you. Let not your heart be troubled, neither let them be afraid." (John 14:27). It was the death of Jesus that gave us the possibility of peace. Even after the Resurrection, when people change, they can enjoy the full benefits of peacemaking.

Jesus tells his disciples, "Peace to you." (Luke 24:36). Jesus realized how difficult man's problem was, but rather than ignore it, he chose to address it, which required the terrible ordeal of him shedding his own blood to cleanse us of our sins, and give peace an opportunity to gain a foothold in man's corrupt world.

When people are told peacemaking is a blessing, they respond positively without realizing how hard it really is. It often takes time and a lot of spent, emotional energy, in order to make progress. Peacemaking sometimes fails, which is why Paul said, "If possible, as far as it depends on you, live peaceably with all." (Romans 12:18). Notice how Paul said, "If possible." Even Paul, with all his missionary and problem-solving experience, had to admit that peace cannot always be successful. However, Paul goes on to say if we focus "on our part," we will be doing everything expected of a Christian, which is to do our very best to get along with people. In 1 Corinthians 7:15, Paul said: ". . . God has called you to peace." This, of course, does not mean we have to agree with everything others say or do, because it is possible to disagree, agreeably. All Christians need to be "bridge builders," however.

What can we do to be successful bridge builders? We must start by taking the matter to prayer with God, who can provide us with insight into how the problem came about. We take this step automatically before engaging in peacemaking, even when we know we are 99% correct in our position. Nevertheless, we still need to make confession to God for any errors we have made, and seek his counsel on how to proceed. The passage in Matthew 5:23-26, sets a good example for this lesson.

It is important to tell the other person how you feel, which can be remembered when we quote Solomon in Proverbs 15:1-2, "A soft answer turns away wrath, but a harsh word stirs up anger." We also find Paul stating, "Let no corrupting talk come out of your mouth, but only such as is good for building up, as fits the occasion, that it may grace those who hear." (Ephesians 4:29).

Here are some simple rules to help in our peacemaking activities:

- Cooperate as much as possible

- Focus on the problem and not attacking the person. Any ad hominems are not necessary

- Clarify the problem as clearly as you can

- Isolate areas of disagreement while concentrating on areas we can agree

- Make reconciliation the main focal point rather than trying to win the debate

- A peacemaker, we must remember, is opposite to a troublemaker, who likes to pick fault and create problems

- Keep in mind we can always agree to disagree, without being disagreeable.

The good news about the Gospel message is, troublemakers can be turned into peacemakers, because they often experience internal struggles, which can be changed. And in summing up peacemaking, it is apparent we cannot be an effective peacemaker until we have found peace within ourselves. It is hard to give to others what is not real to us, because all peacemaking begins with peace in our heart. When we study all thirteen of Paul's epistles, we notice his salutation always begins with, "Grace to you and peace from God." The word "grace" always comes before the word "peace," which indicates we first need the grace of God in our lives in order to experience the peace of God. This can only happen when we come into a faithful relationship with Jesus Christ.

As mentioned, we live in very troubling times, and there is great opportunity to develop our skills as peacemakers, but being fearful and timid is not the answer. Here is a quote from 1

John 4:18: "There is no fear in love, but perfect love casts out fear. For fear has to do with punishment, and whoever fears has not been perfected in love. We love because he first loved us. If anyone says he loves God and hates his brother, he is a liar; for he who does not love his brother whom he has seen, cannot love whom he has not seen. And this commandment we have from him: whoever loves God must also love his brother." So, with every step we make towards peace, the more blessing we receive from God.

> **Blessed are those who are persecuted because of righteousness, for theirs is the Kingdom of Heaven – Matthew 5:10**

Notice Jesus' Beatitudes begin with an upwardly Godly attitude, where emphasis is placed on spiritual poverty, spiritual mourning, demonstrating meekness, while hungering after righteousness. Then it progresses to addressing human concerns with a focus on mercy, purity, and peacemaking, before ending with testing through persecution. Remember, though, the Beatitudes also provide us with a promise of a share in a divine life after this one ends.

This is true blessedness, because we have a communion with the "blessed" God. Evidence from all over the world indicates Christians suffer terrible persecution, which can cost them their livelihoods, their businesses, their families, and even their lives. Today, one in seven Christians live in a country hostile towards their faith. According to Open Doors, in reviewing their top 50 watch list as of 2020, there were 260 million Christians being persecuted for their beliefs, compared with 245 million in 2019. They also state in 2014, only North Korea was considered 'extreme," but in 2020 there will be 11 countries falling into that category. Also, the International Society for Human Rights estimates Christians are targets of 80% of all acts of religious discrimination or persecution. Clearly, the peacemakers mentioned in the last Beatitude have their work cut out for them.

Christian suffering is nothing new as it has been going on now for the past 2,000 years, with ignorance, poverty, illiteracy, and a lack of historical perspective being the prime reasons in explaining the suffering of the past. Today, however, there is less excuse because people know about the Crusades, the Inquisition, and even the holocausts in the 20th century, caused by the Turks against the Armenians, the Nazis against the Jews, Mao Zedong and Joseph Stalin against their own people, as well as the Hutus against the Tutsi, along with Pol Pot murdering half of his own population in Cambodia.

The question today is, why have we not learned the lessons of the past? The answer lies in the fact that man has placed even greater distance between himself and God. Man has become a god in his own mind, and thinks he can run the world without God. This is a mistake repeated many times in the past, and continues to this very day.

In this Beatitude, however, we find suffering is blessed because it is suffering for righteousness' sake, and we are being persecuted for doing the will of Jesus Christ. In order to hold on to the promise of this Beatitude, the persecution must be for doing his righteous will (1 Peter 3:8-17). Only then do we enjoy the Kingdom of Heaven. Those who are persecuted for righteousness' sake find themselves living a life pleasing to God, in a world that does not appreciate them. It is also important to point out persecution can be recognized in many forms, which could include violence, but it can also take more subtle forms, such as ridicule, exclusion, dismissiveness, and marginalization.

We can take satisfaction, however, in knowing the blessings of Jesus Christ can help us in a number of ways. First, we can remain resolute in knowing the Kingdom of Heaven is ours. We can also find great joy in knowing we are being identified with Jesus.

(Matthew 10:25; Acts 5:41). Lastly, we learn persecution can act as a marker as we progress towards Jesus.

It can be said persecution represents a testimonial to our union with Jesus. (Philippians 3:8-11). Here we find an example of Paul turning from the persecutor, which he once was, to the persecuted. Even though Paul lost all that was valuable to him, he was able to gain Jesus Christ, and the righteousness that came through his faith.

Jesus is saying it is necessary for us to become like him in his death, if we wish to share in his life. In other words, we are to be in union with Jesus in order to share all things that are his, which includes the rejection and persecution he experienced. Therefore, if we share in him, we will then enjoy the Kingdom of Heaven. Aided with this knowledge, we are then able to persevere with joy in our trials.

As Christians we are aware we are in this world, but not of this world. Therefore, we should be sensitive to the fact that if the world has only good things to say about us, we need to do a reality check to make sure the absence of persecution is perhaps because we are fitting into this world's value system too easily. Dietrich Bonhoeffer, the great German pastor during World War Two, commented on this issue when he said it may mean we have exchanged our discipleship for citizenship in this world. So, let's keep our eye firmly on Jesus, and look forward to an eternal life with him.

In this and the last chapter, we have discussed the teachings of Jesus Christ, with emphasis being placed on his wonderful and powerful Sermon on the Mount, and particularly his eight

Beatitudes, which are blessings to all who follow him. These Beatitudes are a form of wisdom literature that can be found in the Books of Psalms, Proverbs, and Ecclesiastes. However, when Jesus preached them, he tied godly wisdom with the prophetic reward received in God's Kingdom. Jesus teaches us a great deal when we read the four Gospels, but you will notice Jesus put the Beatitudes at the front of his teachings, in order to emphasize the spiritual characteristics, which is a discipline we need to have in order to become a citizen of the future kingdom.

At the very heart of the Sermon on the Mount we find Isaiah's theme of righteousness, mentioned earlier, which will be the marker of the Messiah's reign, and it will be emblematic of citizens in God's Kingdom. Isaiah wrote: "Righteousness shall be the belt of his waist, and faithfulness the belt of his loins." (Isaiah 11:5). We find the Bible telling us righteousness refers to an ethical and moral standard of us being upright and honorable, taking a virtuous approach to life. Jesus was also declaring to his disciples that God's righteous standards found in the Old Testament will not be upended, but rather enriched for our benefit.

The Beatitudes provide us with a pathway we can take to guide us to an eternal life. Without the Beatitudes, it would certainly be more difficult for all of us to know the mind of Jesus, who is God, and the standards he has set for us to enter the Kingdom of Heaven. It is not possible for us to do this by our own will, but only through having faith in Jesus Christ, who will then help us to navigate our way there.

Jesus taught us many life principles during his short ministry, which are "peppered" throughout the four Gospels, and further developed by Paul as he took the message of Christ to the non-Jewish populations, the Gentiles. So, in the next chapter we will discuss the many challenges and obstacles needed to be overcome and removed, in order for the Gospel to spread worldwide.

JOURNAL YOUR THOUGHTS

_____

_____

_____

_____

_____

_____

_____

_____

_____

_____

_____

_____

_____

_____

_____

_____

_____

_____

15

SPREADING THE LIGHT TO A DARK WORLD

There are many types of light: transparent, translucent, opaque etc., but Jesus said: "I am the light of the world. Whoever follows me will not walk in darkness, but will have the light of life!" –John 8:12

JESUS SHED HIS BLOOD AND DIED ON THE CROSS AT CALVARY IN ORDER to cleanse us of our sins, provided we have faith in him, and yearn for a righteous life. Before Jesus died, however, he had trained and educated his apostles to carry the torch of light to the Jewish people, and later beyond to the rest of the world. When you consider the challenges of taking the message of the Gospel to a pagan and corrupt world, it is easy for us to think Jesus would select men of education, power, and great influence. This was not the case, however. Let me take a moment to demonstrate how modern man's mindset would go about solving this challenge, by offering you a tongue-in-cheek letter from a consulting firm given the task of choosing the 12 men to serve Jesus:

To: Jesus, son of Joseph, Woodcrafters Shop, Nazareth
From: Jordan Management Consultants, Jerusalem
Subject: Staff Aptitude Evaluation

Thank you for submitting a résumé for each of the 12 men you have chosen for various management positions in your new organization. All of them have now taken our battery of tests, and we have run them through our psychology and vocational aptitude consultants.

It is the staff's opinion that most of the nominees are lacking in background, education and vocational aptitude for the type of enterprise you are undertaking. They do not possess the team concept. We recommend you continue your search for persons of experience in managerial ability and proven capacity.

Simon Peter is emotionally unstable and given to fits of temper. Andrew has absolutely no qualities of leadership. The two brothers, James and John, the sons of Zebedee, place personal interest above company loyalty. Thomas demonstrates a questioning attitude that would tend to undermine morale. We feel it is our duty to tell you that Matthew has been blacklisted from the Greater Jerusalem Better Business Bureau. James, son of Alphaeus, and Thaddeus definitely have radical leanings, and they both registered a high score on the manic-depressive scale.

One of the candidates, however, shows great potential. He is a man of ability and resourcefulness, meets people well, has a keen business mind, and has contacts in high places. He is highly motivated, ambitious and innovative. Therefore, we recommend Judas Iscariot as your controller and right-hand man. All other profiles are self-explanatory. We wish you every success with your new venture. (Source: Unknown).

Clearly, Jesus did not choose successful leaders of influence to fulfill his agenda. Instead, he chose men, mostly from the Galilee area of northern modern-day Israel, with the exception of Judas, who was from Judea. These men were obviously not picked due to their brilliant, educated minds, nor were they highly esteemed members of society. Some were single, some were married, with occupations as diverse as fishermen, a tax collector, and even a revolutionary zealot who wanted to overthrow the Roman government. For reasons we may never know, Jesus chose these men to carry the "light" of his teachings to a pagan world after he later died on the cross. Jesus selected these men to tell the world about God's great love for mankind, and that God had sent Jesus, his only begotten Son, to redeem the world. Along the way, these men would become valuable and loyal companions to Jesus, and their intimate conversations with Jesus became immensely valuable, when they later set out on their missionary journeys to spread the Gospel message.

Jesus understood these chosen men thoroughly. He had keen insight into their strengths and weaknesses, and he knew they would disappoint him by temporarily deserting him, denying him, and even in one case, betraying him. However, Jesus also knew they all, with the exception of one of them, would be filled with the Holy Spirit. He knew they would become wonderful witnesses for the Gospel, effectively communicating God's message of redemption to all those who accepted Jesus Christ as their Lord and Savior. They did so on the basis of faith alone. Remember, the original 12 tribes of Israel had already been blessed by God to be a blessing to the nations, and now these 12 Jewish men would follow in similar manner in reaching out to all mankind with the message of love and redemption by our Creator God.

These disciples, who became known as apostles, knew ahead of time they would face persecution and possibly an early death. Notwithstanding the odds against them, however, and being filled with the Holy Spirit, they were able to perform miracles, and go on to perform a monumental body of good teachings of our Lord to an ignorant, and sometimes very hostile world.

As we dig into the life of the Apostles, and the missionary work they achieved, we find the way they died is somewhat obscure, and is still debated by theologians to this day. Before profiling these 12 brave men, let me point out there is still confusion with certain theologians regarding three men named, James, and two men named, Philip. Some people also get confused with Thaddaeus and Jude, as well as Bartholomew and Nathaniel. These Apostles, including Matthias, who later replaced Judas Iscariot, (the man who would betray Jesus), became the pillars upon which we place our Christian faith. It is, therefore, important for us to know as much about these men, their accomplishments, and the sacrifices they made, in order for us, and future generations to appreciate their amazing stories.

One of the purposes served in profiling these 12 great men, is to make the gospels come alive as you later study them. So, we will attempt to profile these apostles based on the works of great Christian, and secular scholars, who have dug deep over the years to unearth and share their insights with us. This is with the understanding, of course, that some of you may wish to do your own independent research into their backgrounds. The Bible, unfortunately, only provides limited information in describing these men and their exploits, and therefore we must rely on the testimonies of early church leaders, as well as other non-biblical sources such as Flavius Josephus. However, with the sources we now have available today, we can create a limited composite that helps us sketch out a more meaningful profile of these courageous men.

Peter

Our first profile is Peter, who went by several names, including: Cephas (the "rock"), Simon Peter, Simon, and Simeon bar Jonah (Simon, son of Jonah). He lived in Capernaum, on the shores of the Sea of Galilee. He was a fisherman by trade, and had a brother named Andrew, who also became an Apostle of Christ. Peter was married but left everything to follow Jesus. Although he demonstrated traces of cowardness (Matthew 26:69-74), he went on to be both brave and solid in his convictions, especially after Pentecost. Also in Matthew, we are told that Jesus says to Peter, "And I tell you, you are Peter, and on this rock, I will build my church, and the gates of hell shall not prevail against it." (The Roman Catholic Church considers Peter to be their first pope). Peter became one of the main pillars of the Christian Church (Acts 1:15; Galatians 2:9), and is considered the main apostle to the Jews at that time (later Paul would be named as the apostle to the Gentiles). At the end of his life, Peter was a prisoner in Rome, and was executed, upside down on a cross, at his own request.

James (son of Zebedee), (James the Elder, or James the Greater, and brother of John)

There are three prominent men in the Bible with the name, James, which can create some confusion. There is James, known as James the Lesser, or James the Younger, which we expand on later. There is also James, the half-brother of Jesus, who was not one of the 12 Apostles, but was a senior church leader, and the man that wrote the wonderful Book of James. Now we come to James, the son of Zebedee, who is also known as James the Elder, or James the Greater. He was also the brother of John, (Matthew 4:18-22), and was also a fisherman and partner with Peter. (Luke 5:10). We don't know a lot about James, but the Bible mentions he became one of the leaders of the Jerusalem church, according to Galatians 2:9. We know that James and John were rebuked by Jesus for requesting God to rain fire on a Samaritan village (Luke 9:54- 55), but we also know James was very committed to Jesus, and courageous to the end (Acts 12:2). Jesus gave James and John the name, Boanerges, or "Sons of Thunder." (Mark 3:17). James was a witness at the Transfiguration, and was with Jesus at Gethsemane. He witnessed the miraculous catch of fish from the Sea of Galilee, which took place after Jesus' Resurrection. (John 21:2-7).

James preached in Judea, but some claim he became the first bishop to Spain. We do know for certain, however, that some ten-years after Christ's crucifixion, we find King Agrippa 1st ordering James to be put to death by the sword, which made him the only apostle whose death is actually recorded in the Bible. (Acts 12:2).

John (son of Zebedee)

John, the brother of James, (The Elder or Greater), was an evangelist, and the "beloved disciple," whom Jesus loved. He too, was a fisherman in partnership with his father, Peter, and his brother, James. (Matthew 4:18-21). John, preached in Jerusalem and Ephesus, and was later exiled to the Island of Patmos, a prison colony for convicts, by Emperor Titus Flavius Domitianus in 95 A.D. This is where John wrote the apocalyptic end time Book of Revelation, the last book of the New Testament, which provides us with valuable insight into the future. John's later history is somewhat obscure, but there are several reports worth mentioning. Tertullian, a theologian in North Africa, claimed at one point John was plunged into boiling water, but miraculously escaped, and later died of natural causes.

There are a number of highlights in John's life, with the most important being the production of five of the New Testament books: The Gospel of John, 1,2 and 3 John, plus the Book of Revelation.

In the second century A.D., we are told Polycrates, who was bishop of Ephesus, claimed John's tomb was at Ephesus, which remains the claim to this day. There are also verifiable notes from

Irenaeus, bishop of Lyon, circa 180 A.D., who said John wrote his Gospel and letters at Ephesus, and the Revelation at Patmos. We believe he died of natural causes around 100 A.D., the only apostle to do so.

Andrew

As the son of Jonah, and the brother of Peter, we know Andrew was born in Bethsaida, and later lived in Capernaum. (Mark 1:29). Andrew is a Greek word for Andreas, which means manly. This is an interesting choice of names considering his brother, Peter, was given an Aramaic name. He was the first apostle to follow Jesus, having been a previous disciple of John the Baptist.

The early church leaders claim Andrew preached in Scythia, Greece, Phrygia, in Turkey, Asia Minor, and Russia. He was later crucified by the Roman Consul at Patras in Greece. The cross was X shaped at his own request. Church tradition goes on to state he was killed because he had converted the Roman Consul's wife to Christianity. This resulted in his slow, tortuous death. Patras is where the image of St. Andrew's cross comes from, and since then we find that Scotland, in 1320, A.D., made Andrew their patron saint, which followed in the footsteps of Ukraine and Russia.

Philip

Another disciple born in Bethsaida is Philip, (John 1:44), and therefore may have possibly known Peter and Andrew's family. His name derives from Greek, meaning "he loved horses."

He was one of the early disciples Jesus called, and there is a good probability he could speak Greek (John 12:20, 21). He also brought Nathaniel (Bartholomew) to Jesus. Philip preached in Greece, Syria, Phrygia, and was later hung as a martyr in Hierapolis, Turkey, in 80 A.D.

One final point is not to confuse Philip the Apostle with Philip the Evangelist, who was appointed along with Stephen (the first Christian martyr), to represent two of a total of seven men given the responsibility to oversee the caring for the poor, mentioned in Acts 6. Philip the Evangelist preached and reputedly performed miracles in Samaria. He is also the Philip who baptized the eunuch, who went on to start the Ethiopian Church. Also, according to Acts 21:8-9, he lived with his four unmarried daughters, who had the gift of prophecy.

Bartholomew (Nathaniel)

Bartholomew had a Greek name, which means "son of Tomai." It appears he also went by the name of Nathaniel, derived from Hebrew, which means "God has given." Although it was not unusual for men to use two names in the First Century, there is not enough conclusive evidence to be certain they are both the same person, but many traditions, however, hold them to be one and the same. Bartholomew is not mentioned in the Gospel of John, but a man named Nathaniel is named as one of the Apostles. (John 21:1-2). We also find Nathaniel does not appear in the other Synoptic Gospels. There does seem to be good reason to believe these two names are one and the same person, and if this is the case, we know more about Bartholomew as a result.

We know Bartholomew was born and raised in Cana, near the Sea of Galilee, and was well versed in the Hebrew Scriptures. Jesus claimed Bartholomew to be an honest Israelite (John 1:47-48), and Jesus educated him on what to expect (John 1:50-51).

There are several traditions of how Bartholomew / Nathaniel died. One states he was flayed alive and beheaded after having converted the King of Armenia, but to this very day, he is still considered the patron saint of that country, and is buried in

Albanopolis, Armenia. Another tradition, from Foxe's Book of Martyrs, says he was beaten, and crucified in India.

Matthew

Matthew also went by the name, Levi, and was the son of Alpheus. (Mark 2:14). The name Matthew comes from Hebrew, meaning "Gift from God." Scripture tells us he was from Capernaum (Mark 2:1-14), and was a tax collector working for the Romans near the Galilee area. (Matthew 9:9). Tax collectors were reviled by the Jews. Even to this day, his symbol is a bag of coins, referencing his occupation before he encountered Jesus. He was sent on a mission to the Jews to preach "the Kingdom of Heaven is at hand." His great contribution was in authoring the Book of Matthew, which was written primarily for a Jewish audience. It is the first book of the New Testament, and acts as a "natural" bridge between the two testaments. It is the first of the Synoptic Gospels, although it is claimed the Book of Mark was written before it.

According to a number of stories, we are told Matthew completed missionary work in Persia (Iran), Macedonia, Syria, Parthia, Media, and Ethiopia. He was acclaimed for bringing the Gospel to kings as well as the common man. Church tradition tells us he was stabbed in the back in Ethiopia, while at the altar. He is buried in Salerno, Italy.

Thomas

Thomas, in keeping with the tradition of the time, used a number of names. He was known as Thomas, but also Didymus (Greek translation), or twin. (John 20:24). He was also known as Judas Thomas, and, of course, the well-known "Doubting Thomas," due to his inability to accept Jesus had risen after the crucifixion.

We know Thomas doubted the Resurrection of Jesus, stating he would "have to touch his wounds in order to believe." (John 20:25). This doubt, forever, cast him as not having initial faith in Jesus as God, although his later ministry proved very successful, after having affirmed Jesus as his Lord and God. (John 20:28). He witnessed the miraculous catch of fish, and ate breakfast with Jesus after the Resurrection. (John 21:2-7).

We are told Thomas traveled to India, reaching Kerala on the southwest Malabar coast about 52 A.D. It is claimed he was killed by spear in Madras (modern name, Chennai), on the eastern side of India in 72 A.D. You can visit his burial place in Santhome, Cathedral Basilica, Chennai.

James (son of Alphaeus), (James the Younger, and James the Less)

This James is the son of Alphaeus according to Mark 3:18, while also going by other names such as: "James the Younger," and "James the Less." James is the Greek name, *Iakobos*, which means "supplanter." He is also a possible brother of Matthew (Levi), the tax collector, who also happened to be the son of Alphaeus. (Mark 2:14). Bible scholars to this very day still have challenges with three men with the name, James. James the son of Alphaeus, is often confused with James, the son of Zebedee, and James, the half-brother of Jesus. Most often, however, the confusion comes with James, the son of Zebedee.

Scripture tells us James, son of Alphaeus, was selected as one of Christ's Apostles, (Matthew 10:3; Acts 1:13), and he was sent on a mission to the Jews to preach the "Kingdom of Heaven is at hand."

We do not have a clear picture of where James ministered outside of Jerusalem, but we are made aware of the sad ending to his life. According to Foxe's Book of Martyrs, James was, at age 94, beaten and stoned by the Jews, and finally had his brains dashed out with a fuller's club. The other tradition states he was mar-tyred by crucifixion at Ostrakine, in Lower Egypt, where he had preached the Gospel.

Thaddaeus (The Apostle with many names)

Attempting to identify this Apostle can be confusing, because he went by a number of names. In Matthew 10:3, he is mentioned as Thaddaeus, (a surname for Lebbaeus). However, he also went by the names of Judas, the son of James, (Luke 6:16), Jude, and of course, Lebbaeus. In Mark 3:18, he is identified as Thaddaeus, and we also know both the names of Thaddaeus and Lebbaeus are Aramaic names, meaning "beloved," or "dear heart" or "heart of courage." It is possible the surname, Thaddaeus, was used in order to distinguish his other name, Judas, the son of James, from the more infamous, Judas Iscariot. (See John 14:22).

Some argue there are two or more people represented by the above names, but most Bible theologians are in unity these various names refer to the same person. We know little about Thaddaeus' early life, other than the likelihood he was born in the Galilee area, where one tradition says he was born to a Jew-ish family in Paneas, while another tradition states his mother was a cousin of Mary, mother of Jesus. This would make him a possible blood relative of Jesus.

We learn Thaddaeus was taught the Gospel from Jesus. De-spite much persecution, Thaddaeus was found to be very loyal to Jesus. Like many of the other apostles, he did abandon Jesus dur-ing his trial, but later became a strong proponent in spreading the light of the Gospel, where tradition tells us he founded a church in Edessa, and was crucified there as a martyr. Another legend states he was executed by an axe or club. Later, his remains were brought to Rome and placed in St. Peter's Basilica. It is said his bones are interred in the same tomb as Simon the Zealot.

Simon the Zealot

Simon the Zealot is a name used to distinguish him from Simon Peter. Sources do confirm he was part of the uprising of the Jews against the Romans in 6 A.D., concerning the Census of Quirinius, which led to the Jewish independent movement. This movement developed into a fourth philosophy that distinguished these freedom fighters from the Sadducees, Pharisees, and Essenes. Some say, but it is doubtful, that Simon may have been instrumental in the major Jewish uprisings between the years 66 – 73 A.D., which resulted in the destruction of Jerusalem, numerous losses of life, and destruction of the Temple.

Simon was listed as a Zealot in Matthew 10:4; Mark 3:18; Luke 6:15, and Acts 1:13. He is also listed as one of Christ's apostles. The name, Simon, is derived from the Hebrew name, Shimon, meaning "hearing." He is also referred to as Simon the Cananaean, which derives from the Aramaic word, "zealous one."

Simon's missionary work is difficult to track as various sources advise us he ministered in Edessa, Greece, Egypt, as well as joining Thaddaeus in Persia. According to the non-canonical Apocryphal Book of Acts of Simon and Jude, we find it stating Simon was martyred by being cut in half by a saw, longitudinally. His symbols include a cross and a saw, a fish lance, and an oar.

Another source states he died peacefully at Edessa, but this is not confirmed, he is buried in St. Peter's Basilica at the Vatican.

Judas Iscariot

Last of the 12 apostles is Judas Iscariot, who was the treasurer and also a thief. (John 12:5-6). He was also referred to as Judas, the son of Simon, and "Judas the Betrayer." Although he had been chosen by Jesus as one of the 12 apostles, (Matthew 10:4), he was later referred to by Jesus as the devil. (John 6:70-71).

Judas criticized Mary for anointing Jesus with expensive perfume, (John 12:4-8), and denied he was the one who would betray Jesus during the Last Supper (Matthew 26:23-25). We know the devil entered his heart at the Last Supper, (John 13:2), and he later betrayed Jesus for 30 pieces of silver, (Matthew 26:14-16).

Later in the story, we find Judas suffering great remorse and agony for what he had done. So, he threw the silver coins, (blood money), back into the Temple, and then went out and hanged himself. The priests used the silver coins to purchase the Potter's Field, which fulfilled prophecy. (Zechariah 11:12-13).

It is hard for any of us today to imagine what Judas Iscariot did, but it does serve as a reminder that not all who claim to follow Jesus are faithful to him, and his goals. Some scholars have suggested Judas was a member of the Zealots, known as Sicarii, who were dagger bearing assassins.

Summary

After the demise of Judas Iscariot, the remaining 11 apostles chose Matthias to replace Judas, which then brought the total number of apostles to 13. We are also made aware later on, that Paul and Barnabas were named apostles. (Acts 14:14). Also, James, the brother of Jesus, was later named an apostle. (Galatians 1:19 – see footnote). Some Christian churches even name Mark and Luke as apostolic, due to being authors of two of the Gospels.

The word, apostle, and the word, disciple, are often interchanged, but there is a difference. A disciple is considered a student, whereas an apostle is a messenger charged with the responsibility of promoting the Gospel to the known world. Also, an apostle can be a disciple, but a disciple is not an apostle.

It is also fitting to mention one female in this prestigious group of apostles. Her name was Mary Magdalene, who is mentioned 12 times in the Gospels, which is more times than most of the apostles. She was a witness to one of the most iconic moments in Jesus' ministry, being the first person to see Jesus after the Resurrection. Perhaps this is the reason she has been called the "Apostle to the Apostles." It should also be mentioned there is no evidence she was a prostitute in Scripture. Apparently, in 591 A.D., Pope Gregory 1st got her confused with another Mary from Bethany. His identification of her as prostitute lasted until 1969, when the Catholic Church finally admitted their mistake, and redeemed her name. It is sad to think someone's good name would be maligned and tarnished for some 1400 years!

We must realize there are many traditions, urban legends, folk stories, and the writings of early church leaders, causing us to rethink our knowledge regarding the intimate details of these great apostles' lives. Scientific analysis of relics is often inadequate, only confirming bones are of the right gender, and time period. We are encouraged, however, in knowing advances in testing and technology, together with the discovery of still unknown manuscripts, which we continue to frequently identify, will move us closer to identifying the missing parts of the puzzle. Deuteronomy 29:29 is where we find God saying, "The secret things belong to the Lord our God, but the things that are revealed belong to us and to our children forever." There is no question we know far more about the biblical past today than we did 100 years ago, and we have every reason to believe the trend will continue for all God's truth seekers.

In the meantime, how do we then best understand these great individuals if the reach of science is limited? With reference to most early Christians, we have to depend on legend and historical accounts, while also acknowledging the great power these men still exert over our lives to this very day, some 2000 years removed from their great work for the Lord.

Perhaps Paul summed up the lives of these apostles best, when he wrote in 1 Corinthians 4:9-13:

> "For I think that God has exhibited us apostles as last of all, like men sentenced to death, because we have become a spectacle to the world, to angels, and to men. We are fools for Christ's sake, but we are wise in Christ. We are weak, but we are strong. You are held in honor, but we in disrepute. To the present hour we hunger and thirst, we are poorly dressed and buffeted and homeless, and we labor, working with our own hands. When reviled, we bless, when persecuted, we endure; when slandered, we entreat. We have become and are still, like the scum of the world, the refuse of all things."

This abbreviated undertaking, in attempting to profile the work of these great saintly men, cannot do proper justice to their magnificent accomplishments in providing our post-Christian world with the much-needed light of God we so desperately need. These men, with the aid of the Holy Spirit, despite tremendous and overwhelming odds from both Judaizers (Jewish converts who wanted to continue with the obeyance of the old law), and great opposition from the oppressive pagan societies they ministered to, were sent out by Jesus. He charged them to take nothing for the journey except a staff – no bread, no bag, no money in their belts – but to wear sandals and not put on an extra tunic. (Mark 6:8). This approach strengthened their faith journey, and with the uplifting power of Jesus, they were able to lay a foundation the Christian Church has resided on for the last two millennia, and will continue into the future, because Jesus said:

> "And I tell you, you are Peter, and on this rock I will build my church, and the gates of hell shall not prevail against it." (Matthew 16:18).

It seems rather incredible when you think back to those trying and dangerous times, that just a few men, many of whom lacked any type of formal education or leadership experience, could achieve what they did. Without money to promote any type of sophisticated marketing and advertising campaigns, aided only with the support of the Holy Spirit, we learn that by the third century, there were more than three million converts to Christianity. By the 4th century, the number had risen to some 30 million converts, and the Roman government also converted to the faith. Today, there are in excess of two billion people who adhere to the faith of Christianity.

Christians will continue to witness persecution while living in this world, even more so in many other areas outside of the United States. The effects of living in our post-Christian nation are becoming more prevalent with each passing day. Christians, however, can take deep satisfaction in knowing the rest of the story, which tells us we win in the end, because we have faith and trust in Jesus as Savior, which will help and guide us through our transition in this life, into a life of eternity on the other side of physical death.

16

St. Paul and His Missionary Journeys

Perhaps the greatest individual persecutor of the early Christian Church, we find Jesus saying to him, "Saul, Saul, (later Paul), why are you persecuting me?" "Who are you, Lord?" I am Jesus, whom you are persecuting." –Acts 9:4

IMAGINE FOR A MOMENT A MAN WHO WAS ATTACKED BY MURDEROUS mobs, beaten, stoned, and left for dead, starved, betrayed by friends, shipwrecked, imprisoned, and finally executed by beheading, all in order to serve the very thing he had previously tried to destroy – Christianity! His name was Saul, who was also called Paul, a common tradition in Jewish culture at that time, which I mentioned earlier. For the purpose of clarity, we will use the name, Paul, noting the term, "Saul, who was Paul," is not mentioned until chapter 13:9 in the Book of Acts.

Paul's background

Paul was born into a prominent family in Tarsus, in modern-day Turkey. His father was an official and a Roman citizen. This allowed Paul to receive an excellent education, resulting in him excelling in several languages, including Greek. Paul's Roman citizenship, coupled to his knowledge of the Greek language, would serve him well later in life, as he spoke about Jesus to the Hellenistic (Greek) communities throughout the known world. He became a Pharisee, and traveled to Jerusalem to receive tutelage from Gamaliel, one of the great Jewish teachers of the time. Paul later became a zealous Pharisee himself, causing him to think all Jews must keep every one of the traditions of Judaism. He became well respected by his people, but he also became very legalistic in the interpretation of his faith, and therefore he applied little grace. At one point, Pharisees plotted to kill Jesus because he condemned them for being too self-righteous and hypocritical. (Matthew 23). Paul's thinking was in tune with these Pharisees, and he ended up hating Christians.

In Acts 7:58-59, we find the priests casting out, and stoning the first Christian martyr, Stephen.

During this event, Paul appears on the scene as a historic figure. The Bible clearly states those who took part in the stoning, laid their clothes at the feet of a young man named Saul (Paul), who was in agreement with this punishment. This is the man who would prey so intently upon the early Church. Then, beginning in Acts 8:1, it says Paul had approved the execution of Stephen, because Paul himself was part of a great persecution against the Christians, causing many to escape to other lands. Paul continued to ravage the church through a dragnet, causing him and other Jews to search Christian homes, and throw them in prison. He became the fear of Christians, and his mania towards anyone who was Christian caused him to be full of hatefulness.

Now, before we think about standing in judgment of Paul, I believe it important to understand the world in which he lived at the time. Raised as a zealot Jew, and rising to a position of prominence and leadership, he saw Christians as enemies to his faith. Paul, being of pure Jewish lineage, had honored the tribe of Benjamin from whom he came, and as a Pharisee he upheld the law's precepts with precision and zeal. In his mind, Christians were negatively influencing his religion, and corrupting God's law.

It is now easier to see how Paul viewed this impossible Messiah, whom he thought was born out of wedlock, and who attracted a vagabond group of mostly uneducated men of low status. These men had no credentials to esteem themselves, and they cavorted with obvious sinners. He heard Jesus had healed people, performed miracles, but at the same time violated the Sabbath, and ignored other sacred Jewish laws. Paul was not happy with the fact Jesus had defied the high Jewish council, the Sanhedrin, and Jesus also defamed the Pharisees by referring to them as "whitewashed tombs", who tried to demonstrate an outward appearance of respectability, while being full of hypocrisy in the way they lived their personal lives.

Paul was incensed that Jesus had discarded God's sacrificial system, by telling everyone he was the only person to relieve people of their sins. Jesus had made the admonition Jerusalem would not become the seat of a new Messianic empire, but instead would be destroyed, and the Jewish Temple burned to the ground. On top of all this, Paul knew Jesus had failed to deliver the Jews their long-awaited emancipation from the yoke of the Roman Empire. Instead, Jesus ended his life on a "tree," between two thieves, and thus was accursed by God according to Old Testament law (Deuteronomy 21:23).

Dangerous religious times

To put matters into even greater perspective, we need to realize this was a dangerous time for religion in general. Men were often beaten and killed for practicing the wrong religion, not accepting a religion, or dying through ignorance of some religious principle. Vestiges of the many ancient cults and secret societies still existed. With the rise of Hellenism in the 4th century B.C., the world was exposed to the Greek pantheon, consisting of 12 gods known as the Olympians, because they resided on Mount Olympus. The gods' names were: 1) Zeus, king of all kings, and the god of sky and thunder. 2) Hera, the Queen of the gods, and the wife/sister of Zeus. 3) Poseidon, the god of the sea, storms, and earthquakes. 4) Demeter, the god of the harvest. 5) Athene, the god of wisdom, courage, and inspiration. 6) Ares, the god of war. 7) Aphrodite, the goddess of sexual love and beauty. 8) Apollon (Apollo), the god of healing and medicine. 9) Hephaestus, the blacksmith god. 10) Dionysus, the god of wine. 11) Artemis, the goddess of the hunt, and 12) Hermes, the god of travel, trade, and who also acted as a messenger between man and the other gods.

Later, when the Romans ruled the world, they introduced their own gods, of which the three main ones were: Jupiter, the equivalent of the Greek god, Zeus; Juno, who was queen of the gods, and Minerva, the god of wisdom, and strategic warfare. Some of the Roman emperors also claimed to be God himself. Add to all this the high rate of illiteracy among the people, coupled to all forms of superstition, and it becomes much easier to understand the mindset of Paul, who was attempting to protect the one religion, his own, that he thought was the purest form of love for God.

With this background clearly in mind, we can now see how Paul, in his fury, went to the high priest and was given permission to travel to Damascus to round up any members of *The Way,* as the new Christian movement was called at the time. He intended to seize them in the Damascus synagogues and bring them back in chains to Jerusalem to stand trial. (Note the early Christian church members used synagogues, because many Christians were converted Jews, and there were no physical church buildings at the time).

What happened next, is perhaps one of the greatest conversions to Christianity the world has ever known. It serves as an example to all who have sinned, no matter how badly, that it is never too late to seek redemption, by having their sins washed away by the sacrificial blood of Christ.

Paul's conversion

Damascus was an ancient city even in Paul's time. It is mentioned in the tablets of Tell el-Amarna from Egypt, as being among the cities that Thutmose III ruled. Over the centuries, Egyptians, Israelites, Chaldeans, Syrians, and Persians had all been masters of Damascus, until 333 B.C., when Alexander the Great conquered Syria, which reigned in the Hellenistic period of Greek language and culture. By 33 A.D. we find Paul and his entourage on the road to Damascus when, suddenly, a very strong light strikes Paul to the ground. Paul then hears the voice of Jesus who calls Paul by his former name, and says: "Saul, Saul, why are you persecuting me?" Paul stammers and responds, "Who are you, Lord?" "I am Jesus, whom you are persecuting. Now get up and stand on your feet. I have appeared to you to appoint you as a servant and as a witness of what you have seen of me and what I will show you. I will rescue you from your own people and from the Gentiles. I am sending you to them to open their eyes and turn them from darkness to light, and from the power of Satan to God, so that they may receive forgiveness of sins and a place among those who are sanctified by faith in me."

Paul got up, his eyes were open, but he could not see. With help from his comrades, he arrived at the house of Judas on the Straight Road, in Damascus, where Ananias, who had been commanded by Jesus, found Paul three days after the event. Ananias, full of the Holy Spirit, later laid his hands on the blind eyes of Paul, which removed the scales from his eyes, and he could now see again. Paul immediately converted to Christianity and was baptized in the name of Christ. He then began to preach with strength and passion, claiming Jesus was the true Messiah.

It is of no surprise to learn, those who had previously known Paul as a persecutor and a tyrant of Christians, were now angry and furious with him due to his conversion. They wanted to kill him, but his disciples lowered him down over the walls of Damascus in a basket, where he escaped to safety.

There are 27 books in the New Testament, (which are mentioned in a later chapter), and Paul is credited with authoring 13 of them. One book, Hebrews, whom scholars claim has an unidentified author, may possibly have been written by Paul, but there is controversy on this point. Nonetheless, it is easy to see why Paul was named the "Apostle to the Gentiles," which was his main focus besides addressing the Christian faith to his own Jewish brothers and sisters.

A Book, a letter, or an epistle?

Before we go further, it is important to note the Bible often uses the word book, letter, and epistle interchangeably, especially in the New Testament writings. So, to eliminate any confusion, a brief explanation is required. As you read the Bible and other Christian writings, you will often come across these three terms. A book, according the KJV dictionary, is a general name given for offering literary composition, printed, and composite bound; a volume. It is a name given to any number of written sheets when bound or sewed together. The Bible is often referred to as having 66 books. However, the word, *letter,* and epistle are also used quite often. Some people say a letter and an epistle are the same. However, there is a difference, and they are not always interchangeable. A letter, for instance, can be a form of written communication that can be personal, for pleasure, or for business. However, a letter does not always include teaching. On the other hand, an epistle is a form of letter, but a very special form of letter. An epistle is doctrinal in nature, teaching us about God's truth. Therefore, the New Testament letters are really epistles. We can conclude; therefore, all epistles are letters, but not all letters are epistles. Hopefully, this will clear up any later confusion when you come across these terms, which we freely use interchangeably.

Spreading the Gospel to a pagan world

After Paul's conversion, it is claimed he spent some time in Arabia and Syria before traveling to Jerusalem. It appears those years were spent learning about Christ, and strengthening his ardor for the mighty task that lay ahead. During his three major missionary journeys, which we will discuss momentarily, we find Paul being beaten with rods three times, whipped with 39 lashes five times, starved, attacked by angry mobs, imprisoned, betrayed by friends, stoned, and left for dead, while also receiving numerous death threats. Nonetheless, Paul's high education, his facility with several languages, coupled to his zealous nature, along with being filled with the Holy Spirit, would later contribute to creating in him the necessary confidence, will, and strength, to stand for Jesus Christ at every opportunity, no matter the odds.

Paul knew, as he later mentioned in 2 Timothy 3:12, "Indeed, all who desire to live a godly life in Christ Jesus will be persecuted." Although a man of extraordinary gifts and abilities, we find Paul later repeatedly inferring that he is merely a "slave of Jesus Christ." He tells us he is a farmer working in God's field. (1 Corinthians 3:5-9). Paul was a strong, driven person, long before he became a Christian. Yet when Jesus chose him to preach the gospel throughout the world, Paul was very much aware he could not rely on his own abilities to face the murderous mobs, the thousands of miles of travel, and many other hardships. So, Paul prayed for strength, and the courage and confidence he would need, so he could be effective in getting people to listen to the

Lord's message and be saved. He asked for opportunities to reach the non-believers, and the necessary safety he would need. Paul asked others to pray for him, and join him in this mighty struggle to cast light into a dark world. He was grateful for their support and demonstrated love. Paul also knew he was weak and needed God's power, (2 Corinthians 12:9, Acts 9:15, Ephesians 6:20, and Philippians 1:19). As Paul later commented in Philippians 4:13, "I can do all things through Christ who strengthens me."

The successful missionary journeys of Paul

By now, Paul is in his mid-forties, and ready to embark on the first of his great, historic missionary journeys. Over the next 11 years or so, Paul covered some 10,000 miles, and built 14 churches by the time he had finished his third missionary journey about 57 A.D. Remember, there were no planes, trains, or automobiles in those days, but thanks to the great Roman road system, travelers at that time were able to cover large geographical areas even on foot. Some theologians say Paul completed a fourth missionary journey to Spain, which is not verified. However, he did complete another journey when he traveled to Rome, where he was eventually executed.

First missionary journey

To learn more about this first missionary journey I refer you to the Book of Acts, chapters 13:4 – 14:28. I have also provided a map outlining his 1400-mile journey, from about 46 A.D. to 49 A.D., and the principal cities and towns he visited. (See Exhibit "B"). The journey, as you look at the map, began in Antioch in Syria, where Paul then moves through Cyprus, after crossing the sea, before journeying to Turkey, and returning to Antioch. It appears he wrote the epistle, Galatians, towards the end of his journey at Antioch.

Takeaway lessons of Paul's first journey

In this journey, Paul demonstrates suffering and hardship are part of the call to follow Jesus Christ. Today, we often wonder why we have to suffer and experience trouble in our lives, but in John 16:33, Jesus warns, "I have said these things to you, that in me you may have peace. In the world you will have tribulation. But take heart; I have overcome the world." Jesus is saying peace is possible for those who endure, because suffering is part of the journey uniting our hearts closer to the crucifixion of Jesus. This journey teaches us worshiping and fasting help to open our hearts and ears to hear the call of The Holy Spirit. Paul shows us the importance of teamwork in working for the Kingdom of God, and nowhere in the Bible does God affirm the idea of working independently, concerning spiritual matters. Paul never went out alone, and there are many instances of biblical characters working together for greater effectiveness. We find praying and partnering between churches helps the work of the Lord to move forward.

Second missionary journey

Paul's second journey began about 49 A.D. until 51 A.D. and covered about 2800 miles. It began again in Antioch, Syria, and covered parts of Turkey and Greece, before Paul returned to Antioch, which can be more clearly seen on the attached map. (See Exhibit "B"). The details of Paul's journey can be traced through Acts, chapters 15:36 - 18:22. Paul wanted to return to the field, in order to reinforce the churches he and Barnabas had planted on their first missionary journey.

His objective was twofold. First, he wanted to explain the letter that had been sent to the churches from Jerusalem concerning circumcision, and secondly to strengthen the faith of young Christians, some of whom were being corrupted by zealous Jews into breaking away from the new faith.

Take away lessons of Paul's second journey

Overcoming objections to this new faith had become almost an everyday experience for Paul and his companion, Barnabas. Although neither were troublemakers, or difficult people, we find Paul mentioning that to some we were like the aroma of life, but to others the aroma of death. Even with the best communication skills in preaching the gospel, they often ran into misunderstandings. In Lystra, for instance, the enthusiasm they received led the people to treat them like pagan gods who had come in human form. People develop a "worldview" at an early age, which was even more difficult to change due to the high-level of illiteracy at that time. Paul also came to realize that although it is important to evangelize, it is also essential to encourage and strengthen people's faith through a renewing of their minds. We also learn elders are being trained to manage the new churches and shepherd the flock, thus creating a model for future church leadership.

Third missionary journey

In this third journey, which also began in Antioch, Syria, Paul was accompanied by Timothy, Luke, and others, and covered some 2700 miles through the regions of Galatia, Phrygia, and Ephesus in modern day Turkey. They then traveled on to Macedonia, Greece, and Lebanon, before finishing in Jerusalem. In Acts 18:23 – 21:16, you will experience Paul's journey, which is illustrated on the enclosed map. (Exhibit "B").

Take away lessons from Paul's third journey

It has now become quite evident no one is outside of God's reach, as clearly demonstrated by Paul himself. Pagan people were coming to Christ after having been involved in horrible crimes, and

God was forgiving them their sins as they listened to Paul, and committed their lives to Jesus Christ. Paul also demonstrated that our achievements do not define us. The other apostles were mainly from ordinary backgrounds, with little education compared to the scholarly Paul. Yet we find Paul saying in Philippians 3:7-11, "But whatever gain I had, I counted it as loss for the sake of Christ. Indeed, I count everything as loss because of the surpassing worth of knowing Christ Jesus my Lord. For his sake I have suffered the loss of all things and count them as rubbish, in order that I may gain Christ and be found in him not having a righteousness of my own that comes from the law, but that which comes through faith in Christ, the righteousness from God that depends on faith – that I may know him and the power of his resurrection, and may share in his sufferings, becoming like him in his death, that by any means possible I may attain the resurrection from the dead."

Lastly, this journey tells us the importance of understanding contentment, when Paul once again says in Philippians 4:11-13:

> "Not that I am speaking of being in need, for I have learned in whatever situation I am in to be content. I know how to be brought low, and I know how to abound. In any and every circumstance, I have learned the secret of facing plenty and hunger, abundance and need. I can do all things through him who strengthens me."

Summarizing Paul's life

Paul's ministry can be divided into three parts, based on approximate dates, because no one can pin-point the dates exactly. From about 33 – 47 A.D., Paul was experiencing a period of personal growth and discipleship, (See Acts 9 – 12). Then, from 48 – 57 A.D., he completed his three missionary journeys where he planted 14 churches (see Acts 13 – 21). Finally, from 58 – 62, he spent much of his time consolidating and strengthening churches, (Acts 22 – 28). It was also during this time he completed a fourth journey ending in Rome, where he was eventually beheaded by Emperor Nero. Part of Paul's life is further documented in Galatians 1 and 2, 2 Corinthians 11 and 12.

At this point, it benefits us to take pause for a moment and try to imagine if the Book of Acts had never been written, and was not part of the Bible. We would find ourselves reading the four gospels, and then suddenly finding Paul writing to Christians in Rome! It would cause us to wonder who Paul was, and how on earth did the gospels travel from Jerusalem to Rome? It is fortunate for us that Luke, the physician, wrote the wonderful book of The *Acts of the Apostles,* which helps to answer these and other questions. The book goes on to inform us of how this young, infant, and emerging Christian faith, was able to rise from the very backwater of the Roman Empire, and then go on to spread the light of Christ throughout the known world.

The great and inspiring story of how the gospel was spread from Jerusalem to Rome, is quite remarkable when you stop and think about it. This new faith did not have much to promote itself. It had no money to advertise, and very few educated and proven leaders. Furthermore, it had no technology to accelerate God's message through faster transportation, or the Internet. On top of these obstacles, there were numerous challenges to overcome. The faith had the task of telling God's truth to an unregenerate, hostile, and quite often illiterate world. This environment caused its new converts to be subject to much hate and persecution. We call the book "The Acts of the Apostles," but some theologians have referred to this book as "The History of the Acts of the Holy Spirit," because the book refers to the outpouring of the Holy Spirit. This divine intervention is the main ingredient causing the Christian faith to grow after the crucifixion of Christ. The

12 apostles did their job admirably in promoting the Great Commission of Christ, and many paid with their lives as I mentioned. But the Holy Spirit played a significant role in communicating, through these great men, the true Gospel of Jesus.

It must be pointed out, however, that Paul, with the aid of the Holy Spirit, stands out as an apostle who conveyed the gospel to the greater Gentile nations. The richness of his theology, and the wise advice he provides to church leaders, is unsurpassed in Scripture, with the exception of Jesus himself. Paul's heart is open for all to see, as demonstrated from his brilliant penmanship. In terms of understanding the Scripture message, and its insights into the Gospel, there is no clearer writings than those of Paul. He promotes the Gospel like no other, especially salvation by grace coming through faith alone in Jesus Christ. Paul provides us with clear instructions on how we should live our life in the Spirit, and to free ourselves from sin as we grow closer to Christ. It is through Paul we learn the true meaning of Christian liberty, to be free in Christ, and free from the bondage of sin. We learn most clearly, we are justified by grace, not works, but we also grow in spiritual maturity, through our faith in Jesus, and our dependence on the Holy Spirit.

Paul provides us with 13 epistles in the New Testament, which are gems in providing many answers about wisdom, and life after this one ends. All are well worth your time to read, because the spiritual growth and wisdom coming from their mastery is unsurpassed in value. Of the Pauline epistles, nine are addressed to Gentile churches: Galatia, Thessalonica (2), Corinth (2), Rome, Colossae, Ephesus, and Philippi, with four written to individuals: Timothy (2), Philemon and Titus. A list of the epistles, along with the approximate dates they were written, who they were written to, and from where they were written, are mentioned on the next page for your review.

Overview of Paul's 13 Epistles:

Epistle	Written to	Date	From	Main Theme
GALATIANS	Church at Galatia	49 A.D.	Antioch, Syria	Freedom through faith in Christ alone
1 THESSALONIANS	Church at Thessalonica	51 A.D.	Corinth	Addressing new Christian issues
2 THESSALONIANS	Church at Thessalonica	51 A.D.	Corinth	Teaching perseverance until the return of Christ
1 CORINTHIANS	Church at Corinth	56 A.D.	Ephesus	Solving problems that had arisen in the Church
2 CORINTHIANS	Church at Corinth	56 A.D.	Macedonia	Paul's authority verses the authority of false teachers
ROMANS	Church at Rome	57 A.D.	Corinth	Addressing salvation and the Righteousness
EPHESIANS	Church at Ephesus	61 A.D.	Rome	The Church as the body of Christ
COLOSSIANS	Church at Colossae	61 A.D.	Rome	Everything centers around our Lord Jesus Christ
PHILEMON	At Colossae	61 A.D.	Rome	Addresses the brothers
PHILIPPIANS	Church at Philippi	62 A.D.	Rome	Think about positive things and seek joy at all times
1 TIMOTHY	Church at Ephesus	62 A.D.	Macedonia	Managing the Church and its leadership
TITUS	Church at Crete	63 A.D.	Corinth	Teaching how to live in Faith at all times
2 TIMOTHY	Church at Ephesus	67 A.D.	Rome	The last words of Paul

17

GOD'S GREAT RESET #7 - PART ONE

The Bible tells us that God says, "I know the plans I have for you, plans for welfare and not for evil, to give you a future and a hope!" –Jeremiah 29:11

Understanding The Future

SO FAR, WE HAVE DISCUSSED SIX OF GOD'S GREAT RESETS, CHANGING the course of history for mankind, and all of them have become a reality. The seventh Great Reset, however, is about the future. Our understanding of the future is based on truthful evidence found in the Bible, and no other place. Christians have no reason to doubt Jesus, and other prophets who have predicted the future, because we are confident it will all come true. Fortunately, believers who are alive today are able to greatly benefit from the knowledge gained from God's first six Great Resets, and the revelatory nature of the unfolding wisdom of the Bible. This fact alone, represents a "goldmine" of opportunities allowing believers to learn more about the future, as God allows them to see more clearly through the future corridors of time. In this way, God reveals his purpose for his children. He does this in order for them to be kept safe by having the opportunity to choose what is good and true (Amos 3:7).

If we believe the words of the Bible, then we have to accept the fact its contents are the true Word of God. As such, we need to be aware about 25% of the Bible was prophetic when it was first written, and there are over 1,000 Bible passages of prophecies, of which more than one-half have literally, and verifiably, already come true. Jesus himself warned his disciples in his Olivet Discourse, there would be many deceivers, and false christs, who will lead the people astray, which is a major reason why we need to be fully informed about what Scripture says about the future. If we are the generation charged with identifying the signs of the times, then we need to prepare ourselves for what to expect, so we are not deceived. Knowledge of end times provides us with certainty of God's wonderful plan for our lives, and this is certainly not the time in man's history to be ignorant of future events.

We need to know more about prophecy, not less!

The more we dig into the Bible, and study its great mysteries, the more we come to realize God is here to help us, providing we obey him, and follow his instructions for our lives. You see, when we study Scripture, we come to the knowledge of knowing God gives us history in advance. You will find, for instance, God has previously given us a number of insights to know his plan for our lives, and our future. These include God communicating with us by:

— writing his divine law on nature (Psalm 19:1)

— inducing it on man's conscience (Romans 2:15)

— etching it physically on tablets of stone (Exodus 24:12)

— making his Word become flesh in Jesus (John 1:14)

- providing man with the Holy Scriptures (Romans 15:4)

- placing his law on our hearts and minds (Hebrews 8:10)

- and, using Christians as his living epistles (2 Corinthians 3:2; Romans 1:19-20).

All of the above passages provide man with insight into God's mind, and what he expects from all of us in planning our lives forward.

Some prophecy can be a little difficult to understand, which causes Christians to disagree with how the "roadmap" into the future will eventually work out. However, there are a number of important future topics where all Christians can basically agree. They include the Second Coming of Christ; the resurrection of the dead; the future activities of the dead, which include the Judgment Seat of Christ (Bema Judgment) for Christians only, and the Great White Throne Judgment, for non-believers. There is also general agreement in an eventual new Heaven and new Earth at the end of time. All of these topics and more, will soon be detailed.

There are, however, a number of topics where good Christian theologians disagree, including the Rapture, its timing, and a 1,000-year Millennial time period. Much of the differences have to do with hermeneutics, which is the study of the principles of interpretation. Part of the challenge in attempting to understand the future, is the fact many important biblical doctrines are not determined from a single verse, but are derived from a combination of several Bible verses, which are all needed to help harmonize into an overall conclusion. You will find, for instance, some truths, such as the deity of Christ, are directly stated, whereas the doctrine of the Trinity (explained earlier), and the incarnate nature of Christ, are an end product of harmonizing a number of Bible passages that tie into these subjects.

So, it is important to realize, as we approach this subject of the future, we do so with the understanding that although there may be disagreement in some quarters, none of these issues will in any way affect a Christian from being saved. Honest disagreement is healthy as we study this fascinating subject, because none of us truly have a 100% comprehensive overview of all the action points taking place in the future, and the exact order in which they play out. God does, however, due to his revelatory unfolding story, continue to provide truth seekers with further insights into what will happen as we move forward in faith and prayer. Beyond the veil, however, I am confident we will all then know the answers we have been yearning to know.

Author's approach

In this chapter and the next, the approach I am taking is to be as faithful to the biblical text as possible, using a literal interpretation of future events, including what Jesus has to say about the end times. This position of taking a literal interpretation, involves using an approach based on using actual words in their ordinary meaning, and not stretching words beyond the facts. In other words, a literal interpretation of the words in the Bible, means explaining them in the original sense, according to normal and customary usage of the Bible language. This means using normal rules of grammar; using historical events consistent with historical settings of the passages, and using contextual interpretation. Some theologians once uttered what has become the "Golden Rule" of interpretation. So, if we find ourselves trying to decipher what an author said, we simply take the position if the plain sense of Scripture makes common sense, seek no other sense. Some theologians have gone further by adding, "Otherwise it becomes nonsense!"

The above approach represents the beliefs of a consensus of many Christian scholars and theologians, who have devoted their entire lives to understanding what God's plan is for all of us. It appears the majority view today is to accept the Bible stories as historically accurate, and should be interpreted literally, but with some spiritual truths being revealed through the common literary mechanisms of allegory, parable, simile, metaphor, hyperbole, irony, poetic, and figurative language. In summary, the majority of Bible text is meant to be understood by the vast majority of our population, and for people in other countries when it is translated into their own local language.

With these points in mind, the paradigm I will be using is a futurist, premillennial viewpoint. This approach appears to fit best in applying the consistent, literal interpretation of the entire Bible, which logically leads to a pre-tribulation approach. This means the next great prophetic event will be the Rapture, when Jesus will come in the air for his saints. This dramatic event will be followed by a seven-year tribulation period, leading into a 1,000-year millennium kingdom, which will be theocratic, ruled by Jesus Christ himself (explained later). My approach, incidentally, is supported by many of our nationally acclaimed pastors, who have many years of research and prayer devoted to "peeling" away the layers of mystery surrounding this amazing subject. These scholars include: Billy Graham, Thomas Ice, Robert Jeffress, Charles Stanley, David Jeremiah, Tony Evans, Renald Showers, John Walvoord, Charles Ryrie, Dwight Pentecost, Charles Swindoll, John MacArthur, Tim LaHaye, Erwin Lutzer, Mark Hitchcock, John Hagee, Ron Rhodes, Chuck Smith, and Greg Laurie. Forgive me for not mentioning them all.

Disclaimer

In moving forward, it is important to point out this subject of the future, often referred to as eschatology, or the end times, is a subject of great popular interest, and consequently volumes have been written to explain its many facets over the centuries. My focus in this book, however, is for the reader to develop a better understanding of the Bible, which is the main theme. Therefore, due to space limitations, I will only be discussing a summary overview of this topic, which, at the very least, I will provide you with a starting "template" upon which you can then build your own future scenario as God leads you. Be aware, I am making good use of Ockham's Razor Principle, that attempts to slash away at complex explanations, in order to simplify the process, and minimize space.

One final point. Due to differences between very well-intentioned Bible scholars, it is important, as we begin our studies, to realize the pitfalls of being too dogmatic in the position we take. Rather, it is best to take a humble, loving, student-like approach. In this way, by minimizing ourselves, and maximizing our Creator, we can gain greater insights into this remarkable subject called eschatology. This is the truth seekers way, as God leads us.

A few controversial issues

As we begin our review of eschatology, it is perhaps important to take a quick overview of certain perspectives and theories put forward over the years. In this way, we can then easily compare the differences as we etch out our own "roadmap" in greater detail. God understands our ignorance and limitations, but by committing our whole heart and mind into the ultimate position we end up taking, we are confident the Lord will inspire and lead us to a position giving us peace on this subject. Be aware, any confusion you experience reviewing these topics will be cleared up later. With this point in mind, we will review the three basic approaches to eschatology – postmillennialism, amillennialism, and premillennialism.

Postmillennialism

This term simply means the Second Coming of Jesus Christ will occur after the 1,000 millennial time period, which is discussed later.

Amillennialism

This approach denies an earthly millennium of universal righteousness and peace, and it will neither precede nor follow the Second Advent of Jesus Christ. Some say, the 'a' in front of the word, means 'no,' there is no millennial time period. Some, however, say there is a millennial, and we are already living in it. Others believe the millennium is a spiritual concept. In summary, amillennialism advocates believe up until the end, there will be a parallel development of both good and evil - God's kingdom and Satan's.

Premillennialism

This is the position I am taking. Simply put, this version states the Second Coming of Christ will occur prior to the millennium, which will witness the establishment of Jesus Christ's kingdom on this earth for 1,000 years. There will be several occasions when resurrections and judgments take place, and eternity will begin after the 1,000-year period ends. Please note that within premillennialism, there are differing views as to when the Rapture takes place.

The timing of the Rapture

According to many, the Rapture is the next great event on the prophetic calendar. However, there are differing opinions as to when it takes place. The Rapture, it should be pointed out, can fit into any of the above eschatological positions just mentioned. Some Premillennialists state the Rapture event will take place prior to the seven-year tribulation period, while others state it will take place at the midpoint, or the end of the tribulation period. This subject will be discussed in more detail shortly.

The importance of taking a position

Notwithstanding differences in our view of the future, I believe it important to adopt some overall faith system surrounding future events in order to eliminate the mental "fog," and inject some clarity into a deeper understanding of what to expect, even if we don't know all the answers clearly. Ducking our head in the sand like the proverbial ostrich, does not make the issue go away. By tackling the subject of end times head-on, we begin to catalog events more clearly, even while knowing others may have a different interpretation. However, the more we dig into our study of the future, and take our questions to God in prayer, the more progress we make in our spiritual walk. None of us will have the complete future picture this side of the veil, but at least we will have a lot better understanding going forward. Lewis Carroll, the author of *Alice in Wonderland,* once said: "If Alice did not know where she was going, then she had already arrived!" Knowledge dispels fear, and the more we learn about the future, the more confidence we have, and the less fear moving forward with our lives.

Understanding signs of the times

I mentioned previously in Deuteronomy 29:29, that God does reveal his secrets to his followers. God has withheld many secrets from mankind until such time as the season is right for him to know them. Consequently, we have far more biblical knowledge available to us today than the people in the Old Testament. Today, for instance, God is providing us with "signs of the times," pointing to the end times. It appears God is sharing his story in advance. Therefore, if we are dutiful students of God's Word, our wisdom on these matters will grow as we further develop our spiritual nature.

Man's prior attempts to forecast the future

Attempting to predict the future has been a controversial subject for centuries. In 999 A.D., for instance, people who studied the Apocrypha predicted the end of the world in 1000, and the Last Judgment would take place in Jerusalem. Hundreds of thousands perished from sickness and starvation on their journey to Jerusalem, but in the end nothing happened. A German bookbinder, named Hans Nut, claimed the world would come to an end in 1528. In 1843, Pastor William Miller, predicted Jesus would return on March 21, 1843, and then again on March 21, 1844. Even the founder of the Mormon Church, Joseph Smith, predicted the coming of Jesus before the end of 1891. Prognosticators abound, but no man knows the true answer as to when Jesus will return.

What did Jesus teach us about the end times?

The return of Jesus is referred to as his Second Coming. These two words together are not mentioned in the Bible, but the event itself is mentioned more than 300 times in the New Testament. Here are a number of biblical quotes you can refer to in establishing the Second Coming of Jesus, and predictions of future events: Matthew 19:28; 23:39; 24:1-51 – Mark 13:24-37 – Luke 12:35-48; 21:25-28 – Romans 11:25-27 – 1 Corinthians 11:26; 15:15-58 – 1 Thessalonians 4:13-18 – 2 Thessalonians 1:7-10 – 2 Peter 3:10-12 – Revelation 16:15; 19:11-21.

Some signs to consider

Before explaining the next big prophetic event, known as the Rapture (see below), we can gain great insight into what will happen prior to the Rapture itself by a careful reading of Jesus's Olivet Discourse, found in Chapter 24 of Matthew. In these passages we find the apostles asking Jesus about the signs of his coming, and the end of the age. Jesus' answer is very direct, and extremely instructive, when he tells them to be shrewd observers of the times. Our take-away is, we should all be looking for earth and sky signs, famines, pestilence, earthquakes, and signs in the heavens that will increase. It appears these things will begin in an embryonic form, and then, just like birth pains, steadily increase.

In another Bible passage we are given further insight into the last days, when in 2 Timothy 3:1-5, it says the following:

> "But understand this, that in the last days there will come times of difficulty. For people will be lovers of self, lovers of money, proud, arrogant, abusive, disobedient to their parents, ungrateful, unholy, heartless, unappeasable, slanderous, without self-control, brutal, not loving good, treacherous, reckless, swollen with conceit, lovers of pleasure rather than lovers of God, having the appearance of godliness, but denying its power. Avoid such people..."

Do the above words sound familiar when comparing them to our current society? Someone once gave us some sage advice when they told us to be forewarned is to be forearmed!

The Rapture

Although the beginning of the end-times began after the crucifixion of Jesus, some theologians believe the re-birth of Israel in 1948, after more than 1900 years, is perhaps the most updated beginning of the end times, which many of us have been living in all of our lives. This incredible story ties into Ezekiel 37, in the famous "valley of dry bones" vision. In it Ezekiel describes an end-times reconstitution of the nation of Israel in terms of reversal of the death and decay of a body. The result will be Israel's national conversion at the end of the tribulation in preparation for the millennial reign with Jesus, their reconnected Messiah.

So, as the end times signs begin to escalate, the Bible tells us the next great biblical event for all Christians to be waiting for is known as the Rapture, a word not mentioned in the Bible. However, the word is a proper use of the event. The word, *rapture,* is the experience of being carried away, and our English word comes from a Latin word, *rapio,* which simply means to snatch or seize, in relation to a type of ecstasy of the Spirit, or actual removal from one place to another. Put plainly, it means the carrying away of the church from earth to heaven. The Greek word, *harpazo,* which means to snatch away, is used in 1 Thessalonians 4:17, translated "caught up." Other examples of a Rapture event can be found in Acts 8:39, 2 Corinthians 12:2-4, which should leave no doubt we are talking about removing people from earth to heaven.

The Rapture is a glorious event whereby Christ comes to resurrect and raise the dead in Christ being immediately followed by all living Christians, who are also transformed into their resurrected bodies. Both groups will be caught up in the air to meet Christ, who will then take them to heaven, thus avoiding the terror to come. (John 14:1-3; 1 Corinthians 15:51-54, and 1 Thessalonians 4:13-17). This means anyone still alive at the time, may escape natural death. Suddenly, in a twinkling of an eye, (about 1/17TH of a second), we could be with Christ in our immortal bodies. Even if we do die before the Rapture comes, we will still be uplifted into the air with Christ, but before living Christians, who are also lifted up.

The Rapture and its aftermath

Once the Rapture happens, the universal body of believers in Christ, dating from Pentecost, (the date for the beginning of the Christian church, 50 days after the crucifixion of Jesus), and all through the church age (which we are currently in), right up until the Rapture takes place, will all be caught up in the air to be with Christ (see previous Bible passages). Try to imagine for a moment millions of Christians suddenly, without notice, raptured out of this world. Christians from all over the world, many who are brilliant leaders, scientists, and people with specialized knowledge in managing our technological economies – all disappear quickly with no time for the world to make contingency plans to keep the supply chains going. Then contemplate the havoc to follow.

In 2 Thessalonians 2, we find Paul explaining the mystery of lawlessness is already at work, but being restrained, but by whom? The Bible does not specifically state, but it is a reasonable conclusion to figure only God has the power to restrain Satan, and therefore it is believed the Holy Spirit is the restrainer as mentioned in Genesis 6:3. Once the church is removed, so will the Holy Spirit be partially removed, thus making way for the lawless one (the Antichrist), to do much damage to those people left behind. However, the Holy Spirit will still be on earth, but in a more limited way as in the Old Testament.

The bridegroom and his bride

Those who believe in the Rapture taking place prior to the tribulation, are further encouraged by Bible passages referring to Jesus being the bridegroom, and the church being the bride, as mentioned previously. Both Old and New Testaments cover this subject, thus making it somewhat inconceivable that Jesus would allow the church (his bride), to suffer through the seven-year tribulation period. This is a significant point considering his very words in Revelation 3:10:

> **"Because you have kept my word about patient endurance, I will keep you from the hour of trial that is coming on the whole world, to try those who dwell on the earth. I am coming soon."**

John 3:29 portrays Christ as a bridegroom and the church as his bride (see also Revelation 19:7). This concept appears to be rooted in Jewish wedding tradition, which took place in three phases: 1) The marriage had to be legally approved by the bride and groom's parents, followed by the groom going to prepare a place to live in his parent's home. 2) The groom then comes to claim the bride. 3) Finally, the marriage supper takes place, which lasts for several days. This Old Testament marriage concept helps us clearly see all three phases taking place in Jesus' relationship with his church, which is the bride of Christ.

Another lens through which to analyze Jewish marriage tradition, is by paralleling the Rapture and Jesus' Second Coming, by looking at three additional ways of viewing the concept: 1) Believers come to salvation during the church age (Pentecost to the Rapture), which enables them to become part of the bride of Christ. During this time, Christ is in heaven preparing a place for his bride in his Father's house. 2) Secondly, the bridegroom (Jesus), will then come and claim his bride (the church) at the Rapture, and take her to heaven, where he has prepared a place for her (John 14:1-3). We find the actual marriage takes place in heaven sometime after the Judgments, and prior to the Second Coming. (Revelation 19:6 -16) There is also a Marriage Supper of the Lamb, which takes place on earth at the end of the tribulation period, or at the beginning of the 1,000-year Millennial Kingdom, (explained later). See Matthew 22:1-14. Additional chronology for these two events will be shown shortly in summary fashion.

Digging even further into traditional Jewish marriages, we also find the groom often paid a dowry to sanctify the marriage contract. Jesus did this when he paid the ultimate price with his life, and the shedding of his blood for his church (1 Corinthians 6:19-20). And, just as a Jewish bride is set apart and sanctified while waiting for her groom, so too is the church as it is sanctified and set apart for Christ (The bridegroom). (See 1 Corinthians 1:2; Ephesians 5:25-27; Hebrews 10:10; 13:12). And finally, just as the Jewish bride was unable to know the exact time her groom would come for her, so too the church does not know the exact time when Jesus will arrive. We do know, however, as mentioned earlier, it could happen at any time, in the twinkling of an eye. (1 Corinthian 15:51-52).

I tie the above passages together in order to show how wonderful Old Testament traditions of Jewish marriage relate to Jesus marrying the church, and later holding a great supper at the end of the tribulation period, or just at the beginning of the Millennial Kingdom. These passages also help us see more clearly how ancient Jewish marriage tradition is used by Jesus Christ, whose earthly family was Jewish. By taking his bride (the church), Jesus then entered into both a marriage ceremony and later a marriage supper. These passages also underscore the reasons why we need to know about the Old Testament in order to fully understand the New Testament. They go together like a hand in a glove.

Bible passages that differentiate the Rapture from the Second Coming of Christ

To further reinforce the fact the Rapture and the Second Coming are two separate events, you will find a number of Bible passages that support this view.

This following list is by no means exhaustive, but it clearly shows a huge difference between the two events:

The church Rapture	Jesus' Second Coming
Rapture is a mystery (1 Cor. 15:51)	No mystery. Happens at end of tribulation
Rapture not mentioned in Old Testament	Mentioned in both Testaments (Jude 14)
Occurs prior to the tribulation	Occurs after tribulation (Rev. 19:11-16)
No signs or prophecies must be fulfilled prior to event (1 Cor. 15:50-53; 1 Thess. 4:16)	Many signs must be fulfilled first (Mt.24:29-3; Rev. 6-19)
Event is imminent (1 Cor. 1:7; Jas 5:8)	Takes place after the seven-year tribulation, So, it is not imminent (Mt. 24:29-31)
A pretribulation event occurring before the tribulation begins	A post tribulation event occurring after the tribulation ends. (Rev. 19:11-16)
Christ comes FOR his church (Jn. 14:1-2; 1 Thess. 4:16-17)	Christ comes WITH his church (Rev. 19:14)
Christ does not come to earth. He comes in "the air." (1Thess. 4:16-17)	Christ returns to earth. (Zech. 14:4; Mt. 25:31)
Christ's appearance not visible to people on Earth (1 Cor. 15:52; 1Thess. 4:16-17)	Christ is visible to entire world (Mt. 24:30; Rev. 1:7)
Christ takes believers to heaven (Jn. 14:2-3; 1 Thess. 4:17)	New believers stay on earth and enter the Messianic Kingdom with Christ ((Mt. 25:34).
The Rapture removes believers from earth	The Second Coming removes unbelievers from Earth
Believers receive a glorified body, getting ready for eternity (1Cor. 15:50-53)	Believers who survive the tribulation remain in their natural bodies (Isa. 65:20; Mt. 25:31-34)
No Godly judgments affect the earth	Much judgment afflicts the earth (Rev. 6-19)
Believers are rewarded after Rapture (1 Cor. 3:11-15; Rev. 19:7-9)	All nations are judged after the tribulation (Ezek. 20:34-35; Mt. 25:32)
Satan not mentioned at the Rapture	Satan is bound for 1,000 years (Rev. 20:1-3)
Rapture is a message of hope	The Second Coming is a message of judgment

We now have a number of clues from the Bible indicating the Rapture will take place before the seven-year tribulation period, which happens before the 1,000 Millennial Kingdom begins.

As mentioned, Jesus said in Revelation 3:10, the church in Philadelphia will be kept from the hour of trial that is coming. Also, it is insightful to note none of the Old Testament passages on the tribulation ever mentions the church. (See Deuteronomy 4:29-30; Jeremiah 30:4-11; Daniel 8:24-27; 12:1-2). Note also the New Testament makes no mention of the church during the tribulation, which should indicate the church, and its believing followers, have already been raptured before the tribulation begins. (1 Thessalonians 1:9-10; 5:4-9; 2 Thessalonians 2:1-11.

In summarizing the Rapture event, it appears safe to say the Rapture of the church is best placed prior to the tribulation period, because this view is most consistent with a literal interpretation of biblical prophecy, and a view held by a majority of renown Christian scholars.

The resurrection of glorified Christians

Bible readers have plenty of evidence to know Christ was resurrected physically from the dead. (See the Gospels of Matthew 28:1-15; Mark 16:1-11; Luke 24:1-12, and John 20:1-18). Also review: (1 Corinthians 15:1-7; Colossians 1:18, and Revelation 1:5, 18). The Bible tells us numerous witnesses stepped forward to attest to the bodily resurrection of Christ. (See Acts 2:32; 3:15; 1 Corinthians 15:3-8, and John 20:24-29). These testimonials serve to give us confidence of our own resurrection after we die. Jesus also said, "I am the resurrection and the life. Whoever believes in me, though he dies, yet shall he live, and everyone who lives and believes in me shall never die." This statement of Jesus was quoted in John 11:25-26. Jesus certainly proved his ability to bring back the dead, when he raised Lazarus from his grave.

The Bema Judgment

The Bema Judgment, known as the Judgment Seat of Christ, which follows the Rapture, is mentioned in Romans 14:8-10, and 1 Corinthians 3:11-15; 9:24-27. This will be a time when the lives of believers are audited by Christ. All deeds done while in our earthly body will be examined, along with all personal motives and intents of the heart. They will all be weighed, and then given rewards, or possibly lose rewards. It is important to point out, however, this life examination will not affect whether a believer is saved or not. All believers in Jesus Christ will be saved irrespective of the dispensing of rewards.

The apostle, Paul, discussed the Judgment in this fashion: "Now if anyone builds on the foundation with gold, silver, precious stones, wood, hay, straw – each one's work will become manifest, for the Day will disclose it, because it will be revealed by fire, and the fire will test what sort of work each one has done. If the work that anyone has built on the foundation survives, he will receive a reward. If anyone's work is burned up, he will suffer loss, though he himself will be saved, but only as through fire." (1 Corinthians 3:1-12).

Paul's reference to these materials appears to be based on combustibility, because precious metals and stones do not burn, whereas wood, hay, and straw burn quite easily. It can certainly be inferred that gold, silver, and stones, represent the power of the Holy Spirit, based on right motivated deeds coupled to Godly obedience. On the other hand, wood, hay, and straw, represent perishable things such as acts of sin, carnal behavior, prideful motives, and self-centered ambition.

The judgment of Christians will focus on their gifts, talents, opportunities, and responsibilities, they experience during their earthly life. Actions will be judged, thoughts will be judged, and every word we have ever spoken will be judged, according to

Matthew 12:35-37. We also know careless words can do great damage according to James 3:1-12. **So, believers will not be judged for their sins, but for their works!** In other words, what they did **with their spiritual gifts** while on earth.

Crowns awarded

At the Bema Judgment, Scripture describes the rewards we receive as crowns to be worn for the glory of God. Five are mentioned:

- **The Crown of Life,** mentioned in James 1:12, and Revelation 2:10. This crown is given to those Christians who are able to persevere under stress and trial, and endure the suffering associated with temptation. All Christians are given eternal life, so here it is referring to a special enjoyment of life based on faithfulness in overcoming the hardships of life.

- **The Crown of Glory,** is addressed in 1 Peter 5:4, and is given to those who are faithful, and sacrificially communicate God's Word to the people. It addresses elders exercising oversight of their flock, not under any compulsion but by willingly serving God.

- **The Incorruptible Crown,** (also referred to as the **Victor's Crown or Crown of Mastery)** is given to those people who demonstrate temperance and self-control and run the race of life successfully mastering the sins of the body, having tamed it under control. See 1 Corinthians 9:24-27.

- **The Crown of Righteousness,** discussed in 2 Timothy 4:8, and is given to those who long for the Second Coming of Christ. Note that all Christians receive the righteousness of Christ, because without it we would not be able to enter

Heaven. This crown is for a special righteousness because of a love for Christ.

— **The Crown of Rejoicing** is confirmed in 1 Thessalonians 2:19-20, and Philippians 4:1. It is a crown given to those who witness to non-believers. Paul is a great example of this crown.

Other Awards

The Bible provides us with a number of descriptions of rewards that Christians will receive. For instance, the Book of Revelation provides the following special privileges to overcomers:

— Rev. 2:7: "I will give the victor the right to eat from the tree of life, which is in God's paradise."

— Rev. 2:11: "The victor will never be harmed by the second death."

— Rev. 2:17: "I will give the victor some of the hidden manna. I will also give him a white stone, and on the stone a new name is inscribed that no one knows except the one who receives it.

— Rev. 2:26: "The one who is victorious and keeps my works to the end: I will give him authority over nations.

— Rev. 3:12: "The one who conquers, I will make him a pillar in the temple of my God, and he will never go out again. I will write on him the name of my God and the name of the city of my God – the new Jerusalem, which comes down out of Heaven from my God – and my new name."

A major war against Israel

Now I want to briefly discuss a side-bar story that you may wish to independently research for yourself, due to the uncertainty of the timing of the event. Some scholars believe this event takes place prior to the Rapture, while others think it happens after the Rapture.

I had mentioned earlier that the State of Israel was reborn in May 1948, after almost 1900 years of the Jews being scattered all over the world. It is interesting to note some 2600 years ago, where we find the Old Testament prophet, Ezekiel, making the prophecy the Jews would be regathered from the nations of the world, and resume living in their land in the end times. Ezekiel 36-37). Then, in chapter 38, Ezekiel went on to predict an all-out future assault against Israel from a massive military force made up of a number of nations.

The invading forces would include: Rosh, (possibly modern-day Russia), Magog, which possibly includes the stan countries of Kazakhstan, Kyrgyzstan, Turkmenistan, Tajikistan, and Uzbekistan; Meshech and Tubal, (referring to the area south of the Black and Caspian Seas, which would be modern day Turkey); Persia, (modern-day Iran); Ethiopia, (which would include modern day Sudan); Put, (encompassing modern day Libya, Tunisia and Morocco). The name, Gomer, is also a reference to Turkey, and the name, Beth-Togarmah, apparently refers to both Turkey, and possibly Azerbaijan.

Fortunately for Israel, these massive invading forces will not succeed, due to the divine intervention of God. The Bible tells us God will inject a four-fold judgment against these forces, which will include: 1) an earthquake, 2) the various forces will fight and kill each other. 3) God will incite judgment with plague and bloodshed, and 4) God will reign down torrential rain, hailstones, fire and burning sulfur (Ezekiel 38:21-22).

In Ezekiel 38 -39, it graphically describes the end of the invading forces and their allies. It states seven-months will be required to bury the dead from the conflict (Ezekiel 39:11-15) and the defeated army's weapons will provide enough fuel for Israel for seven-years (Ezekiel 39:9, 10). It appears inconceivable the Israelites would be burning military fuel during the Millennium period. Therefore, it is reasonable to assume, given only a seven-year timetable from the time of the Rapture to the Second Coming of Jesus Christ, that this war will take place before the Rapture. This would provide sufficient time to conclude the seven-years of fuel burning by the mid-point of the tribulation, a time when Antichrist breaks his peace agreement with Israel. Matthew 24:15-21 discusses the fleeing of the Jews from Israel about this time.

The above outline appears to have merit, but due to timing and other issues, I recommend the reader do their own research on this subject matter.

The Book of Daniel

In order to appreciate the connectivity of the Old and New Testaments concerning the future, and especially in light of the details of the future shared in the next chapter concerning the Book of Revelation, I think it important to provide a somewhat abbreviated summary of Daniel's great prophetic book.

Doctor Harry Ironside called Daniel 9:24-27, "the greatest-of-all-time prophecies." Sir Edward Denny described it as, "the backbone of prophecy." It might be fair to say that the Book of Revelation is but a more detailed, expansive narration of Daniel's book regarding the future end times. But before getting into the ninth chapter, I need to provide a little further background.

Daniel and his friends were deported from Jerusalem in 605 B.C., to the court of King Nebuchadnezzar of Babylon, before the destruction of Jerusalem and the Temple. In the book we later find the king worrying about a dream, which none of his wise men could decipher, but Daniel did. It resulted in one of the most amazing prophecies in the Bible. The king had seen a very large statue in his dream, which Daniel interpreted its head of gold as the Kingdom of Babylon; its chest and arms of silver, represented the Medo-Persians; its belly and thighs of bronze were identified as Greece, and it had legs of iron, with feet partly of iron and partly of baked clay, representing the Roman Empire. In the king's dream, a giant rock was hurled at the statue, striking it at its feet and breaking the iron and clay into pieces, along with the destruction of the whole statue (Daniel 2:32-35).

Amazingly, in the later panorama of history, these great military powers were all defeated in succession. The Babylonians (gold) were defeated by the Medo-Persians, (silver) in 539 B.C.; The Persians crushed by the Greeks (bronze), in 449 B.C.; and the Greeks by the Romans in 146 B.C; The Roman Empire (legs of iron and clay) split into two in 330 A.D., with the western part in Rome being defeated in 476 A.D. by German barbarians. The eastern empire, with its capital in Constantinople (Istanbul), was defeated by the Ottoman Turks in 1453 A.D. You may want to revisit the first two chapters of this book, to refresh your memory on the details of these great empires and their later demise. The main point is, of course, that all of Daniel's prediction came true, which provides us with much confidence that his next great prophecy, much of which has already been proven, will also transpire in the future, just as he describes it.

Daniel's 70-Week Prophecy

Daniel accurately predicted another great future prophecy. In just four verses, (9:24-27), he provides prophetic clues encompassing thousands of years of human history. This prophecy predicts the time from when the order went out to restore and rebuild Jerusalem, up until the coming of the anointed one, Jesus Christ, resulting in his crucifixion. (A total of 483 years). We are then told that Jerusalem and the temple will be destroyed (which happened in 70 A.D. when General Titus of the Roman army, besieged and destroyed it all, just as Jesus had predicted some 40 years earlier). There is then a parenthetical period of time, which has been going on now for almost 2,000-years since Christ's crucifixion, known as the Age of the Church, or the Age of the Gentiles. We do not know how much time will transpire before the Rapture, the next great event on the prophetic calendar, but when it does happen, the church, with all its believers will be ushered up to meet Jesus in the air. All remaining people left on earth will experience the seven-year tribulation period, explained in the next chapter.

If you are interested in knowing further details regarding how theologians, engineers and mathematicians have calculated the timeline from when the 70-week prediction began, to the time of Jesus' triumphant entrance into Jerusalem on Palm Sunday, his ultimate crucifixion, and the explanation of the Church Age leading to the final seven-year tribulation, you may find the below sources of great value. In all fairness to these great Christians who have attempted to define Daniel's timeline, you will find that although they use different methods with the use of solar, lunar, and prophetic calendars, they all come remarkably close to each other in figuring out that Jesus' triumphant entrance into Jerusalem took place somewhere between 30 and 33 A.D. Even the great Christian mathematician and scientist, Isaac Newton finished his exhaustive calculations to predict a time of entrance into Jerusalem between 30 and 33 A.D. Finally, we have accurate knowledge of historical characters that were in Jerusalem during Jesus' triumphant entrance leading to his crucifixion. They would include: Pontius Pilate, the Roman governor at that time (26 – 36 A.D.); King Herod Antipas (4 B.C. – 37 A.D.), and the high priest of the Sanhedrin, Caiaphas, the one who plotted the murder of Jesus (18 – 36 A.D.).

Sources:

- Alva J. McClain, Th.M., D.D.; – Daniel's Prophecy of the Weeks

- Rev. Clarence Larkin – Dispensational Truth or God's Plan and Purpose in the Ages

- Don C. Olsen, PhD, CEO Global FIA Inc., – Was Jesus' arrival accurately predicted in the Bible?

- Harold W. Hoehner – Chronological Aspects of the Life of Christ.

A preview of the Book of Revelation

In the next chapter we will conclude our view into the future, by reciting some of the remaining highlights of the last book in the Bible, The Revelation. Authored by Jesus Christ himself, and given to his angels to describe to John, the Apostle, so that he could communicate its contents to the seven churches, and to the world. This event happened on the Island of Patmos, in approximately 96 A.D., in the eastern Mediterranean. This is where John was imprisoned by the Roman Emperor Domitian. John had left Jerusalem some 30 years earlier to preach in Ephesus before his imprisonment. This is the same apostle John who gave us the Gospel of John, and 1 John, 2 John, and 3 John.

The Revelation provides a rich, detailed account of much of what happens in the future, but unfortunately, many people are confused by some of the book's symbolism. However, by taking a literal approach to reading it, and temporarily suspending for the moment any figurative or symbolic speech, it becomes much easier to penetrate its meaning, especially as you make a project of it, and pray to God for guidance. Also, looking through another lens, we know while God's inspiration did not eliminate human authorship and literary style, it did guarantee us what these humans wrote was true and trustworthy. We should also treat history as history, poetry as poetry, hyperbole as hyperbole, metaphor as metaphor, and any generalization and approximations for what they are.

Eventually the pieces of the puzzle will come together, thus allowing you to teach others. Please also remember in the first chapter of Revelation, it states:

> **"Blessed is the one who reads aloud the words of this prophecy, and blessed are those who hear and who keep what is written in it, for the time is near."**

In other words, God wants us to read this apocalyptic end times book, and he blesses us for doing so. It should now be obvious to all of us that prophecy is very important to God, and it is interesting to note there are three times more prophecies concerning the Second Coming of Jesus Christ, than the prophecies of his First Coming.

The Book of Revelation (Greek, *apocalypses*) is an unveiling of Jesus, as the reader is allowed to delve into the unknown and unseen spiritual forces operating behind the scenes in history, but with Jesus controlling the events and outcome. By simply focusing on the books of Daniel, Isaiah, Ezekiel, Zechariah, and Jesus' Olivet Discourse in Matthew 24, along with some of Paul's writings, we can see, through a series of symbolic visions, which help us tie these Old Testament prophecies, along with Jesus' discourse, into a divine prediction of the future, as well as a better understanding of current affairs. Other books can be studied later to further clarify our understanding of future events.

Revelation is divided into three-major divisions: 1) It refers to time, which is, and time which is to come: 2) It then discusses the relationship of the seven-churches to the tribulation, and to the kingdom: 3) Next comes Jesus' high offices of the High Priest,

Bridegroom, and King-Judge. Jesus is the central theme of Revelation, in which the book moves forward towards completing its goal, and the ultimate consummation bringing about the covenanted kingdom.

These three major divisions are important to discuss in an overall understanding of the book. John was commanded to write about three classes of things: 1) Things past, which John had seen. 2) The present, such as the existence of the churches, the temple had been destroyed, and the Jews being dispersed. 3) Issues about the future, which fall into a series of six sevens, coupled with five parenthetical passages, thus making the church division into seven sevens. The six sevens are the seven seals, the seven trumpets, the seven personages, the seven bowls, the seven dooms, and the seven new things. The parenthetical passages are a) The Jewish remnants and the tribulation saints: b) the angel, the little book, the two witnesses, and the 144,000 Jewish witnesses: c) the Lamb, the remnant, and the everlasting Gospel: d) it then leads up to the gathering of the kings at the Great Battle of Armageddon (the last battle): e) the four Hallelujahs are sung in heaven. All are discussed in the next chapter.

Incidentally, the number seven is mentioned more than 50 times in Revelation, and almost 700 times in the total Scriptures. Obviously, this number has symbolic meaning beyond being a mere number, and is often thought of as completeness, where man is referred to as six (incomplete), and God is seven (complete).

By taking the above passages, and looking backward as well as forward, they show us the results of what has been accomplished, and go on to speak of results yet to come, as if they had already happened. For instance, they show the Lamb and remnant as seen prophetically on Mount Zion, although they are not there until chapter 20. You will also notice there is no mention of the church in this book, after chapter three, until chapter nineteen, which is another indicator to support the belief the church, and all believers, are taken out by the Rapture, and therefore avoid the horrors to come, known as Jacob's Troubles.

At the First Coming of Jesus, he was referred to as a sacrificial lamb, because he gave his own life on the cross to wash the sins of all believers. John the Baptist had it right when he said, "Behold, the Lamb of God, who will take away the sin of the world." (John 1:29). In the Book of Revelation, however, we find Jesus as a warrior king, who comes with a sword to destroy all those who oppose God. He came as a sacrificial lamb 2000 years ago, but as a warrior-king at his Second Coming. This adds great significance to some of his last words on the cross - "It is finished!" (See also Revelation 16:17, where the seventh angel poured out his bowl into the air, and a loud voiced came out of the temple, from the throne, saying, "It is done!").

Journal Your Thoughts

_____

_____

_____

_____

_____

_____

_____

_____

_____

_____

_____

_____

_____

_____

_____

_____

_____

_____

_____

18

God's Great Reset #7 - Part Two

"And I am sure of this, that he who began a good work in you, will bring it to completion at the day of Jesus Christ." Philippians 1:6

Understanding the Future (Continued)

IN BRIEFLY RECAPPING THE LAST CHAPTER, WE DISCUSSED THE RAPTURE AND its aftermath. I believe this subject is well worth pausing for a moment to consider further the horrible consequences for all those poor souls who are left behind on earth to face the wrath that descends upon them. Millions of believers will suddenly no longer be around, and the world will be without some very brilliant and talented people, many of whom make a considerable impact on the inter-connectivity of our world economy, where goods and services are transported from one country to another in unprecedented numbers, unheard of in all man's history. Think about these issues as we move forward with the story, by imagining such things as supply-chain challenges, tremendous economic disruption, leading to pestilence, famine, huge increases in crime, and much death.

Meanwhile the Bible tells us believers in Jesus Christ, who have been physically raptured to be with Christ, will avoid all the horrors of this time. This is significant! Those same believers will then be judged at the Bema Judgment, mentioned in chapter seventeen.

Some Bible scholars believe somewhere prior to the beginning of the tribulation, but after the Rapture experience, we are told of a major war in Ezekiel 37-38, (mentioned in the last chapter), whereby Russia and many Moslem nations attack Israel, but fail due to divine intervention. The Jews burn the invading army's military equipment for seven-years (Ezekiel 39:8-10), which many theologians claim ends at the midpoint of the tribulation.

The Seven-Year Tribulation Period Begins

In chapters six of the Book of Revelation, it provides us with details of the beginning of the seven-year tribulation period, also mentioned in the Old Testament by Daniel in chapter 9:24-27.

Please bear in mind at the outset, that this great book flows somewhat chronologically, such as the first six chapters, for instance. However, other chapters, do not necessarily do so. There are also scenes that take place in heaven, and others on earth. For this reason, I mention at the end of this chapter a flow chart separating the two types of events.

Bible scholars who specialize in end times eschatology, however, generally believe the beginning of the seven-year event takes places in chapter six, with a midpoint at the end of chapter eleven, leading into chapter 12. The last half of the tribulation period, known as the Great Tribulation, begins in chapters thirteen and fourteen. This allows us to slot certain events into the first or second half of the tribulation period, thus providing us with some sense of chronology without pinpointing the exact timing of events.

The first half of the tribulation period

Beginning in Rev. 6, we find the Lamb (Jesus) opening the first seal of the scroll (see below), and six of the seven Seal Judgments are released, with, the seventh Seal Judgment not being released until later in Rev. 8. These Seals are followed by Seven Trumpet Judgments, (Rev. 8), which also take place during the first half of the tribulation. Meanwhile, before detailing the impact of the Seven Seals and Seven Trumpets, it is important to introduce the Antichrist.

The rise of the Antichrist

Sometime after the Rapture, we are told the Antichrist comes onto the world stage. He brokers a seven-year peace covenant with Israel, which allows them to rebuild their Temple. Unfortunately for Israel, Antichrist breaks the agreement after three-and-one-half years, which also represents a trigger point for the second half of the tribulation, known as the Great Tribulation.

The apostle, Paul, cited Antichrist as a "man of lawlessness." (2 Thessalonians 2:3, 8-9). Paul goes on to tell us a time will come when a specific person will gain world power in the future tribulation period. (See also 1 John 2:18, and Revelation 11:7; 13:1-10). Antichrist will ultimately lead the world in total rebellion against God. (2 Thessalonians 2:3-10). He is currently being restrained by the Holy Spirit, but once the Rapture is complete, and all Christians are removed from earth, the Antichrist will begin his reign of terror. Antichrist will demonstrate his intellect (Daniel 8:23), trade (Daniel 11:43); war (Revelation 6:2), articulation of speech (Daniel 11:36), and he will be a master of politics (Revelation 17:11-13). More on the Antichrist later.

New Jewish temple built

Bible history tells us two Jewish temples have been built and rebuilt. King David wanted to build the first temple, but God would not allow him due to his warrior and warlike status. So, it was built by his son, Solomon, about 957 B.C. (1 Kings 6:1-38; 2 Chronicles 3-4). This temple was later destroyed by the Babylonian King Nebuchadnezzar, in 586 B.C. Later, a second temple was built, known as Zerubbabel's temple, completed about 515 B.C., and lasted about 420 years. Then, in 19 B.C., King Herod, began renovating and adding to the temple, which was completed in 64 A.D. This temple was later destroyed by the Romans in 70 A.D, along with most of Jerusalem.

Scripture now reveals a third tribulation temple will be built during the first half, or three and one half-years, of the tribulation period. However, at the midpoint of the tribulation we find Antichrist breaking the seven-year peace agreement with the Jews. Antichrist then goes on to desecrate the temple by erecting an image of himself, and forcing people to worship him or be killed. This event is mentioned by the prophet Daniel, in chapter 11:31-35, and we also find Jesus referring to Daniel's prophecy in Matthew 24:15-16. (See also Rev. 13). Finally, a fourth temple will be built, referred to as the Millennial Temple, which is discussed in detail in Ezekiel 40, and it will be the center from which our worship of Jesus Christ will be focused for 1,000-years. As Israel fulfills her national calling, the glory of the Lord will return to the temple (Ezekiel 43:1-5).

Seven Seal Judgments

The inhabitants of planet earth have experienced many cruel times throughout history, including natural disasters, famine, and millions upon millions of people who have died due to man's inhumanity to man, resulting in countless wars and bloodshed. Nothing, however, has ever come close to what will happen to mankind during the seven-year tribulation period.

Just prior to the first half of the Tribulation (Rev. 5), we find Christ holding a sealed scroll. It contains Christ's title deed to the earth by right of creation and redemption. We find the judgments inside this scroll are divided into three groups: Seal judgments, found in (6: 1-17; 8:1), Trumpet judgments (8:7-9:21; 11:15), and Bowl judgments (16:1-19:21), with an interlude between each set.

At this point it is of interest to compare the parallel of the Seal judgments to the havoc mentioned by Christ in Matthew 24 (Christ's Olivet Discourse), predicted some 2,000 years ago. For instance:

— Matthew 24:5 mentions false christs as does Revelation 6:1-2;

— Matthew 24:6-7 war is discussed, as mentioned in Revelation 6:3-4;

— Matthew 24:7-9 talks about death, which is mentioned in Revelation 6-8;

— Matthew 24:9-10 discusses martyrdom, also found in Revelation 6:9-11;

— Matthew 24:7 refers to earthquakes, which is discussed in Revelation 6:12.

The seven seals are released chronologically, and cover the first quarter of the seven-year tribulation period. In other words, six seal judgments are dispensed first, with the seventh judgment releasing the seven trumpets, which are released in the second quarter of the first half of the tribulation, ending at the midpoint. This is followed by the seven bowl judgments, which take place in the second half of the tribulation.

The Seven Seal Judgments are unsealed and released to cause much pain and suffering in the world. Seven seals appear to be in line with first century tradition of Roman law, whereby a last will and testament required seven seals, as mentioned in the wills of Caesar Augustus and Vespasian, for instance.

The first four seal judgments are known as the *Four Horsemen of the Apocalypse.* They appear to present a picture of man's inhumanity, causing terrible suffering. How many times in history has man been given false hope of peace, only to be followed by war, famine, and death?

The Lamb of God (Jesus) opened the **First Seal**. (Rev. 6:1-2). There is then the sound of thunder roaring throughout heaven, and a Rider on a White Horse appears with a bow and a crown. Many believe the rider is the Antichrist, as Jesus Christ does not appear on a white horse until much later in Revelation 19:11. The Antichrist has a bow in his hand and goes to conquer and become the ruler of the "The federated kingdoms" of a revived Roman Empire. This also proves Antichrist comes at the beginning of the tribulation, and not in the middle as some have suggested.

A **Second Seal** is opened (Rev. 6:3,4), and the Rider on a Red Horse appears, (red being a symbol of war), who has the power to take peace away from the earth. Red is the color of blood, symbolizing the "sword" of war. The time is prophesied by Christ in Matthew 24:6, 7. These wars will probably produce the "Ten Federated Kingdoms," of which the Antichrist will become their leader. Considering upwards of 200 million people lost their lives in wars during the 20th century, and so far in this century the bloodletting continues, it would be hard to imagine how matters could get any worse, but they do.

The Third Seal is opened (Rev. 6:5, 6), and the Rider on a Black Horse appears, (black being a symbol of famine), holding a pair of scales in his hands. Here the meaning is clear, as many able-bodied men are drafted for war, there is no one to till the fields, and famine results. This is prophesied by Jesus in Matthew 24:7. The monetary description indicates normal purchasing power will be reduced to one-eighth. Today, partly due to the impact of Covid-19, there has been a great increase in the number of people around the world who are facing severe food insecurity, with figures exceeding 800 million people. As bad as these figures are, they will be dwarfed by the results of the opening of the Third Seal.

Seal Four is then opened, (Rev. 6:7, 8), representing a pale horse, and its rider's name was Death, and Hades followed him. The Greek word used by Paul for death is, *Thanatos,* and *Hades* is used to describe Hell. They were given authority over a fourth of the earth, to kill with sword, famine, pestilence, and by wild beasts of the earth.

When the **Fifth Seal** is opened (Rev. 6-11), we find John seeing the "souls of martyrs" under the altar. They represent the martyrs who were killed due to standing on the word of their testimony of Christ, and who loved their life unto death during the tribulation. (Rev. 12:11). Matthew 24:9-13 tells us after the Rapture, a great persecution takes place, and it is the "souls" of the martyrs of this persecution that John saw under the altar.

With the opening of **Seal Six** (Rev. 6:12-17), there is a tremendous earthquake. The National Earthquake Information Center states there are some 20,000 earthquakes each year around the world, or about 55 per day. None, however, will have the impact of an earthquake taking place when this Sixth Seal is broken. These changes are so terrible, men will call upon the mountains and rocks to fall and hide them from the wrath of the Lamb.

The 144,000 Jewish Witnesses

In Rev. 7 we are told four angels are given the power to harm earth and sea, but are told, "Do not harm the earth and the sea or the trees, until (see 7:3), we have sealed the servants of our God on their foreheads." The number of the sealed was 144,000 from every tribe of the sons of Israel. (Also see Rev. 14:1-5). These sealed sons of Israel came from 12,000 of each of the 12 tribes of Israel. Many Christian scholars believe that in order to understand this portion of Scripture, it is important to remember God had originally chosen the Jews to be his witnesses to the world. They were to be God's representatives to the Gentiles, but they failed in their duties. This was especially true due to the Jewish people not realizing Jesus Christ was their Messiah.

So, it appears fitting that these future 144,000 male Jews, who have become believers in Jesus after the rapture event, will finally fulfill God's original plan, and many millions of people will be saved at this time. (Revelation 7:9-14).

God's two witnesses

During the first half of the tribulation period, God will also bring to the forefront, two prophetic witnesses, (Rev. 11), many of whom believe to be Moses and Elijah, who will attest to the true God, and consequently many more souls will be saved. Two witnesses were required in the Old Testament era to solidify testimony (Deuteronomy 17:6; 19:15). This idea was also confirmed in the New Testament (Matthew 18:16; John 8:17, and Hebrews 10:28). God stated these two witnesses, shall prophesy for 1260 days, (3.5 years), wearing nothing but sackcloth. Then, their miraculous work will end with execution by Antichrist. It is said both witnesses will lie in the street for three and a half days, while the people gaze at their dead bodies and refuse to let them be placed in a tomb. The people will rejoice and make merry. Then a loud voice shouts, "Come up here." The two witnesses arose, and were ushered into heaven while their enemies watched them. For many centuries, most readers of the Bible could never have comprehended people all over the world witnessing such an event, but now we all know better, don't we?

Seventh Seal

At the breaking of the **Seventh Seal**, there is silence in heaven for about a half-hour, (Rev. 8.1), which is a period of preparation for greater calamities to come. The silence is so ominous, its very nature is a harbinger of the tremendous difficulties that will soon come upon the earth. This silence is significant in two ways: 1) It is completely the opposite of the normal sound pattern of Heaven, and 2), it provides time for Jesus to advise his angelic followers what is about to happen. Then, after the silence ends, seven angels, in succession, sound seven trumpets.

Seven Trumpet Judgments

The seven angels who had seven trumpets now prepared to blow them. In the ancient world trumpets were used to signal a special event. Many of these trumpet judgments are similar to the ten plagues administered against the Egyptians (Exodus 7-11).

After the **First Trumpet** sound, (Rev. 8:7), there is hail and fire mingled with blood cast upon the earth. It causes a third of the trees, and all green grass to be burned up. This fulfills the prophecy of Joel. (2:30, 31). It is also a reminder of the judgment against Sodom and Gomorrah (Genesis 18:16-19:28).

With the sound of the **Second Trumpet**, (Rev. 8:8), a burning mountain, perhaps a meteor, drops into the sea, and will destroy one-third of the creatures of the sea. It will destroy a third part of the ships, and the blood of the destroyed will discolor a third part of the sea. Scripture, when referring to the "sea," refers to the Mediterranean.

When the **Third Trumpet** sounds, (Rev. 8:10), a great burning star called "Wormwood," which means "bitter," falls from Heaven and poisons the streams of fresh water. Wormwood is used in the manufacture of Absinthe, which is an intoxicating beverage used in France, but is also poisonous. The prophet Jeremiah refers to this time. (Jer. 9:13-15).

When the **Fourth Trumpet** is sounded, (Rev. 8:12), a third part of the sun, moon and stars will be smitten, and their light diminished by a third. Jesus spoke of this in Luke 21:25-26. An angel will then fly across Heaven announcing, "Three Woes," followed by the sounding of the three trumpets yet to sound. This parallels the ninth plague in Egypt (Exodus 10:21-23). We now have an angelic announcement to the earth concerning the three remaining trumpet judgments.

The **Fifth Trumpet** sounds, which is also the First Woe, (Rev. 9:1), and it causes a star to fall from Heaven to the Earth, with a key to the bottomless pit. It will not be a real star, but rather an angel who will look like a star, who was given the key. He will not be a fallen angel, nor even Satan himself, as some suppose. This angel will, however, be the same angel who will bind Satan and cast him into the bottomless pit, (also called the Abyss), for 1,000 years. (Rev. 20:1-3).

The angel opened the shaft of the bottomless pit, and from the shaft rose smoke like the smoke of a great furnace, and from the smoke came locusts upon the earth. (Rev. 9). In appearance they were a combination of a horse, man, woman, lion, and scorpion. Locusts typically feed on vegetation, but these locusts will be prohibited from hurting the grass or the trees, or any green thing. They will only be permitted to afflict men for five months, but only those who do not have the "seal of God," written on their foreheads. It appears this vast army of scorpion locusts could be a large army of demons, who will be liberated from the bottomless pit. They shall torment men to the point they will want to die, but death will flee from them. These scorpion locusts have a king who is identified by the Hebrew word, Abaddon, Apollyon in Greek, meaning "destroyer." Scripture appears to identify two types of demons, those who are free in the spiritual realm, who invade the bodies of people, and those who are confined in dark, gloomy dungeons awaiting the judgment. (2 Peter 2:4).

The bottomless pit

Parenthetically, the bottomless pit, (the Abyss), is not Hell or Hades, but has been explained by theologians as the bottom of a great gulf in Hades, that separates the place of torment from the place of comfort. Jesus described it as "the place of the dead." (Luke 16:19-31; Jude 6). The bottomless pit is always seen as a holding place for those whose ultimate abode will be the lake of fire. In a way, it serves like a country jail, acting as a temporary location for prisoners, before they are relocated to a state or federal penitentiary - a final destination.

After the sound of the **Sixth Trumpet**, (the Second Woe), (Rev. 9:13-14), there is a voice from the Golden Altar, which commands the trumpeter to release four angels, who are specially created for this moment in history, and are bound at the great River Euphrates. These are evil angels as noted by the fact they are bound, and are the leaders of an army of 200,000,000 infernal cavalry. They are not, as some believe, 200 million from China and Southeast Asia, because they are clearly demonic. This army, therefore, will not be made up of ordinary men and horses, for the horses will have the body of a horse, the head of a lion, a tail like a serpent, with the head of a serpent at its end. They will breathe out fire, brimstone, and smoke, which will kill a third of mankind, and the sting from their serpent tails will inject great pain. Scripture tells us supernatural armies are not unknown, as exemplified by 2 Kings 6:13-17. Also, we understand when Jesus returns, he will bring with him a supernatural army from Heaven, so it is reasonable to assume Satan also has an army. Needless to say, this invasion of scorpion demons will not cause men to repent.

Another interval

Between the Sixth and Seventh Trumpet, there is an interval, similar to the interval between the Sixth and Seventh Seals. This is when a mighty angel will descend from Heaven with a "Little Book" open in his hand. (See Rev. 10). He will place his right foot on the sea, and his left foot on the earth, and then lifting up his hand to heaven, he swears there is no more time. Although Christ takes formal possession of the earth, the earth will not be fully secured until he comes again on the Mount of Olives, at the close of the tribulation.

With the blowing of the **Seventh Trumpet** (The Third Woe), which is not mentioned until Rev. 11:15, there are loud voices in Heaven saying, "The kingdom of the world has become the kingdom of our Lord and of his Christ, and he shall reign forever and ever." This takes place in Heaven, and afterwards there is another waiting, or intermittent period, which provides us with additional detail of what will take place during the rest of the tribulation period. Some events include the persecution of God's children (Rev. 12), additional power given to Antichrist, as well as the False Prophet (Rev. 13). There is also a heavenly vision (Rev. 14), as well as an introduction to the last part of the tribulation (beginning in Rev. 15). This heavenly scene announces the great events coming to earth, and because it is so awesome, it is referred to as "The Great Tribulation," the last three-and-one-half years that are left to conclude this horrible nightmare for mankind!

The Midpoint of the Tribulation

At the halfway point in the tribulation period, (the end of the first 42 months or 1260 days), generally described in Rev. chapters 11 and 12, we are told there is a war in Heaven, and Michael, the arc-angel, defeats the forces of Satan (the great red dragon), who is thrown down to earth along with his fallen angels (referred to as stars, but actually are demons). In his wrath, Satan pursues the pregnant woman (Israel), in order to kill her child (Jesus Christ), in an attempt to thwart God's plan of salvation. However, God intervenes by snatching the woman's child up to God's throne and allowing the woman to flee to the desert for her safety for a time, times, and half a time (referring to 1260 days or three-and-one-half years). See notes in Rev. 12:6, 14; Daniel 7:25; 9:25, 12:7, and 12:12).

The Last Half of the Tribulation

The last three-and-one-half years of the seven-year tribulation, is known as the Great Tribulation, whereas the full seven-years is simply referred to as the tribulation period. It begins during the midpoint mentioned above, in Revelation 12, where Satan loses the war in Heaven, and he and his fallen angels are thrown to earth, and no longer have access to Heaven. This is the time Satan makes wholesale war on both Jews and believers. The wrath caused by the Seven Bowls, mentioned shortly, is unlike anything man has ever experienced.

Jerusalem abandoned

As a result of the Antichrist attacking the woman (Israel), we are told the Jews flee from Jerusalem (Matthew 24). We are also told in Daniel 11:41, that the Antichrist invades Israel, and many other countries, but Edom, Moab, and Ammon will be delivered from his hand. It is worth noting that each of these three places are all east of the Jordan River, which is where three of the six Jewish ancient cities of refuge were located. Note also that in Isaiah 62, and Isaiah 63:1-6, where it says Jesus (during the Lord's

Day of Revenge), shall come from Bozrah to rescue the Jews at Zion. Mt. Zion is the later name for Mt. Moriah, located inside the old walls at the Temple Mount. Calvary (Latin) and Golgotha (Greek), are the same and are located outside the old walls.

Now this is where it gets even more interesting. Bozrah today is a ruined archaeological site, which does not appear to be the place to protect a large number of Jews. However, Petra, located a little further south, is located inside a mountain, which contains a perennial water supply. The entrance to gain access to the inside is very narrow (a siq), and it is easily defensible as the Roman Empire discovered before they finally ousted the Nabataeans in 106 A. D. In having traveled extensively through the southern part of Jordan, including Petra, it appears easy today to make the case that Petra, rather than Bozrah, is where the Jews will flee to, but Jesus will depart from Bozrah when he rescues Israel (Zion), according to Isaiah 63:1-6. Some scholars also think that Petra could be the seventh ancient city of refuge, thus making the perfect number seven, for completion. As scholars continue to research this subject we may get closer to God's plan in the future, but for the moment this is part of the puzzle we are working with.

The Two Beasts

In the beginning of Rev. 13, we are told of a beast rising out of the sea, (the Antichrist). Satan now indwells Antichrist and gives him his own power, his throne, and authority to target and destroy both the Jews and the followers of Christ. Antichrist appears to be slain, but is resurrected, which is somewhat similar to the resurrection of our dear Lord, Jesus. This causes the people to praise and follow him in worshiping the dragon.

Then a second beast rises from the earth (The False Prophet), and it is allowed to exercise all the authority of the first beast in its presence. The False Prophet then makes the earth, and its inhabitants worship the firsts beast (Antichrist), whose mortal wound had been healed.

The Antichrist and the False Prophet are two distinctly separate individuals who work towards achieving a common goal. Their roles and relationship typify the ancient world, of a relationship between a ruler (Antichrist), and the high priest (False Prophet).

Rev. 13:15 tells us the beast (Antichrist), will kill anyone who does not worship him. Vs. 16 continues: "And it causes all, both small and great, both rich and poor, both free and slave, to be marked on the right hand or the forehead, so that no one can buy or sell unless he has the mark, that is, the name of the beast or the number of its name. This calls for wisdom: let the one who has understanding calculate the number of the beast, for it is the number of a man, and his number is 666." Matthew 24 tells us believers will be put to death during this time if they do not have the mark of the beast.

Origins of the mark of the beast

Where did the number 666 come from? Three reasons are given. In Scripture, the number of man is six, because he was created on the sixth day. Secondly, Hebrew language superlatives are expressed by repeating the same word or phrase three times, which is considered the apex, or highest point. Thirdly, both Hebrew and Greek letters also stand for numbers, thus making it possible to add a numerical value for every name. Antichrist's name may add up to 666 in either Greek or Hebrew. However, no matter how much people seek to understand this number, and try to identify the Antichrist (Adolf Hitler, Josef Stalin etc.,), it is without profit or biblical significance. Dr. John Walvoord states it this way:

"In the book of Revelation, the number "7" is one of the most significant numbers indicating perfection. Accordingly, there are seven seals, seven trumpets, seven bowls, seven wraths of God, seven thunders, etc. This beast (Antichrist), claims to be God, and if that were the case, he should be 777. This passage, in effect, says, no, you are only 666. You are short of deity even though you were originally created in the image and likeness of God."[1]

During the tribulation we find Satan attempting to exalt his man, Antichrist, as a substitute Messiah. This is where the Holy Trinity is defied by the Satanic trinity of Satan, exalting himself as God; Antichrist substituting for Christ, and the False Prophet attempting to replace the Holy Spirit of God.

In our technological age, where so many aspects of our economy are controlled by computers, it does not take much imagination to think about the Internet being shut down, or our credit cards not being accepted when we try to purchase food. It seems clear to me, since the mid-90s, our economy has moved closer and closer to a state where all the supplies and necessities of life are being controlled by technically driven supply chains that can be cut-off at a moments' notice. So, the reality of what the Bible tells us about the future, where a powerful entity limits our access to survival items, is not that far-fetched. If we don't have the proper access code, 666, we could easily be cut-off from our survival needs. Yes, our study of the Bible certainly does call for wisdom.

The Lamb and the 144,000

Rev. 14 mentions Jesus (the Lamb) on Mount Zion, with 144,000 who had his name and his Father's name written on their foreheads. It is interesting to parallel the above seal with the fact

---

1   Prophecy Knowledge Handbook, p 587.

that during this time period, many of the world's population will be forced by Antichrist to accept the "mark of the beast." (Rev. 13:14-18). As our economic system heads towards a digital form of currency, controlled by a central government, it does not take too much imagination to see when the levers of power are in few hands, the majority are at their mercy.

The abomination of desolation

I mentioned earlier, at the half-point mark in the tribulation period, Antichrist breaks his peace agreement with Israel, which was a seven-year covenant brokered at the beginning of the tribulation, as mentioned in the previous chapter.

Antichrist goes on to commit the abomination of desolation in the Jewish Temple, which is mentioned in the Book of Daniel 9, 11, and 12. It is believed Antiochus Epiphanes IV, (175 – 164 B.C.), was the one who originally desecrated the Jewish Temple, set up the god Zeus, abolished circumcision, profaned the Sabbath, and offered pigs as a sacrifice in the temple. Another abomination took place by the Romans in 70 A.D., when they destroyed Jerusalem, killing more than one million Jews, and tearing down the Temple, (a prediction made by Jesus some 40 years before).

So, in Matthew 24:15-21, where we find Jesus referring to Daniel and the abomination of desolation, he is talking about a future event, whereby the Antichrist sets up an image of himself inside the Jewish Temple. In Matthew 24, we find Jesus giving strong credibility to Daniel's prophecy regarding this abomination of desolation in the Temple.

It is now plain to see the difference between the Holy Trinity and the Satanic trinity, and how Satan tries to imitate God:

Holy Trinity | Satanic Trinity

God the Father | Satan – the nemesis of God

Jesus Christ | Antichrist – antithesis of Jesus

Holy Spirit | False Prophet – Imitating the Holy Spirit

Man's profound trinity is based on, Me, Myself, and I – an incurable state without the acceptance of our Lord Jesus Christ!

A parallel to the Great Tribulation

Before moving into the Bowl Judgments, I will quickly mention a visit I made some time ago, to the infamous Nazi death camp in Poland, known as Auschwitz - Birkenau, (A-B), because there is an interesting parallel between A-B and the Great Tribulation. This is the place where some 1.2 million Jewish men, women and children were murdered. Also, many gypsies, Polish and Russian prisoners of war, prisoners of conscience, and various religious faiths, were also murdered. A-B was comprised of three camps, and 36 sub-camps, built just outside of Oswiecim. It was built on a remote 40 square kilometer site. This is where it gets interesting. Auschwitz was opened on September 3rd, 1941, and was closed on January 27, 1945, due to the oncoming Russian and allied armies. This time period just happens to be 42 months, or three-and-one-half years, the same time period of the Great Tribulation! Unfortunately, this is where the parallel ends, because what happens during the Great Tribulation, causes the slaughter in A-B to pale in comparison. All in all, the tribulation will consume one out of every two people on earth, after those believers who have been raptured. This is mentioned in Revelation 6 and 9, where a fourth and then a third of mankind will die, respectively.

The Seven Bowls of God's Wrath

In Rev. 16 we hear a loud voice from the temple telling the seven angels to pour out on earth the seven bowls of the wrath of

God. This third series of seven judgments, when compared to the seven seal and trumpet judgments, are much more severe. The angels who administer these bowl judgments pour out every last drop of God's wrath. (Rev 16).

So, the first angel went out and poured the **First Bowl** on the earth, causing harmful and painful sores on those who wore the mark of the beast, and worshiped his image. An angel then poured out the **Second Bowl** into the sea, causing it to become like the blood of a corpse. It caused every living thing in the sea to die, and the stench and disease from this event will be unimaginable. Another angel then poured out the **Third Bowl** into the rivers and springs of water, turning them into blood. This third bowl judgment is God's answer to the martyrs' prayer to be avenged (Rev. 6:10). The next angel poured out the **Fourth Bowl** on the sun, causing it to scorch people with fire. They cursed the name of God, and did not repent. Then the **Fifth Bowl** was poured out by an angel, who poured it onto the throne of the beast, causing its kingdom to plunge into darkness.

As the people gnawed their tongues with anguish, they did not repent. Then an angel poured out the **Sixth Bowl** into the great River Euphrates, causing its water to dry up, which prepared the way for the kings of the East to do battle at Armageddon. At this point, it appears God is baiting Antichrist into his trap, before the Second Coming of Christ. We are told John saw out of the mouths of the dragon (Satan), the beast (Antichrist), and the False Prophet, three unclean spirits like frogs, who were demonic figures. They go abroad to assemble the kings of the whole world to combine them for battle on the great day of God the Almighty.

Armageddon

The word, Armageddon, is only used once in the Bible (Rev. 16:16), but the battle, or campaign, is described in Daniel 11:40-

45; Joel 3:9-17, and Zechariah 14:1-5. It will take place in the final days of the tribulation, as we are told the kings of the world will be gathered together "for the war of the great day of God, the Almighty." According to the Bible, there will be great armies from the East and the West, who will gather together to do battle. Threats will be made to the power of Antichrist from the South, and he will also move to the east before finally turning his forces toward Jerusalem to subdue and destroy it.

Armageddon represents a series of battles that take place in the land of Israel, which includes: (1) the Plains of Esdraelon (aka the Valley of Jezreel), which is about 20 miles long and 14 miles wide. It includes Tel Megiddo. This is where the Antichrist and his armies will eventually meet their maker. (2) The Valley of Jehoshaphat, also known as the Kidron Valley, which runs between the City of Jerusalem and the Mount of Olives, is the other area of conflict. Incidentally, the real actual last battle that takes place in the Bible happens at the end of the 1,000-year Millennium period, when Satan is released, and tries once more to win, but loses again. (Rev. 20:7-11).

The Battle of Armageddon begins near Tel Megiddo, (about 60 miles north of modern-day Jerusalem), which is the remains of an ancient fort that was built to protect the Via Maris, an ancient trade route, connecting Egypt with Syria and other countries in the north. This helps explain why Tel Megiddo was destroyed and rebuilt some 27 times over the centuries.

Tel Megiddo is the site where Barak fought the Canaanites (Judges 4:15); King Saul perished in battle against the Philistines (1 Samuel 31:8), and where the Israeli King Josiah, was killed by Pharaoh Necho (2 Chronicles 35:22). There is an amazing prophecy made by the prophet Joel, who lived about 920 B.C., (although we are not totally certain of the exact date). This is what he said:

"For behold, for in those days and at that time, when I restore the fortunes of Judah and Jerusalem, I will gather all the nations and bring them down to the Valley of Jehoshaphat, and I will enter into judgment with them there, on behalf of my people and my heritage Israel, because they have scattered them among the nations and have divided up my land." (Joel 3:1-2).

Considering all the other biblical evidence we have already gathered and verified, concerning the future Battle of Armageddon, this is an amazing prediction made almost 3,000 years ago!

When Napoleon visited Megiddo in the early 19th century, he pondered there could not be a better place anywhere in the world for the last great battle to take place. Having visited the place myself, I cannot help but agree. This great battle concludes Jesus' judgment against Israel, and makes a final judgment on those people who persecuted Israel. (Imagine as Jesus was growing up in Nazareth, and contemplating this last battle of the future, that it was within only 15 miles from where he grew up!

At the end of Rev. 16, the **Seventh Bowl** is released, as an angel poured out his bowl into the air, and a loud voice came out of the temple saying, "It is done." This parallels Jesus saying on the cross, "It is finished!" This event is followed by flashes of lightning, rumblings, and a great earthquake, far more eruptive than any since man came to earth. This earthquake will cause Jerusalem to be split into three-sections, thus preparing the way for millennial changes after the Second Coming. This is also about the time Babylon is suddenly destroyed.

Rejoicing in Heaven at the Second Coming

Rev. 19 begins with rejoicing in Heaven, and the Second Coming of Jesus Christ, "Hallelujah, for the avenging of the blood of the saints." Then, in Rev. 19:11, a rider on a white horse appears, (Jesus Christ), who is called faithful and true, and in righteousness judges and makes war. From his mouth came a sharp sword, with which to strike down the nations, so he will then rule them with a rod of iron. An angel then called to the birds saying, "Come, gather for the great supper of God, to eat the flesh of kings." Then John saw the beast and the kings of the earth with their armies gathered to make war against him, who is sitting on the white horse. And the beast was captured and with it the False Prophet, and they were thrown alive into the lake of fire. And the rest were slain by the sword coming from the mouth of him who was sitting on the horse, and all the birds were gorged with flesh.

The marriage supper of the Lamb

In Rev. 19:6, we are told the marriage of the Lamb has come, and his bride (the church), has made herself ready, clothed with fine linen, bright and pure. Rev. 19:9 goes on to say blessed are those who are invited to the marriage supper of the Lamb. We should all want to receive this invitation to an eternal life with Jesus Christ.

The Millennium

Rev. 20 goes on to describe an angel coming down from Heaven with the keys to the bottomless pit. He has a great chain, and he seizes Satan, and binds him for 1,000 years by throwing him into the pit, and sealing it so he cannot deceive the nations any longer. Then the souls of those who had been beheaded for having a testimony of Jesus and the word of God, who had not received the mark of the beast (tribulation saints), came to life, and reigned with Christ for 1,000 years, along with Old Testament saints. All those who had accepted Jesus during the church age up to the

Rapture, will also reign with Jesus during the Millennium. The rest of the dead do not come alive until the 1,000 years ends. This is known as the first resurrection.

The Old Testament prophet, Isaiah, provides us with some of the most descriptive details of what the Lord says about the Millennial period:

"For behold, I create new heavens and a new earth, and the former things shall not be remembered or come into mind. But be glad and rejoice forever in that which I create: for behold, I create Jerusalem to be a joy, and her people to be a gladness. I will rejoice in Jerusalem and be glad in my people; no more shall be heard in it the sound of weeping and the cry of distress. No more shall there be in it an infant who lives but a few days, or an old man who does not fill out his days, for the young man shall die a hundred years old, and the sinner a hundred years old shall be accursed. They shall build houses and inhabit them; they shall plant vineyards and eat their fruit. They shall not build and another inhabit; they shall not plant and another eat; for like the days of a tree shall the days of my people be, and my chosen shall long enjoy the work of their hands. They shall not labor in vain or bear children for calamity, for they shall be the offspring of the blessed of the Lord, and their descendants with them. Before they call, I will answer; while they are yet speaking, I will hear. The wolf and the lamb shall graze together; the lion shall eat straw like the ox, and dust shall be the serpent's food. They shall not hurt or destroy in all my holy mountain," says the Lord. (Isaiah 65:17-25).

Other Bible verses describing the Millennial include: Zechariah 14:8, 16-21; Ezekiel, chapters 40 – 48, where the new temple, and conditions for worshiping during the Millennial, are mentioned.

Then, with the ending of the 1,000-year period, Satan is released for a little while, where he once again will try to deceive the nations. It is hard to imagine the number of Satan's army being like the sand of the sea, but that did not prevent them being defeated by Christ. It states Satan will then be thrown into the lake of fire and sulfur, where the beast and the False Prophet were, and they will all be tormented day and night forever and ever.

A quick recap of the major events of the Millennium period include:

1. Binding of Satan for 1,000 years (Rev. 20:1-3)

2. The ultimate restoration of Israel, including regeneration (Jeremiah 31:31-34; Deuteronomy 30:1-10; Isaiah 11:11-12:6; Matthew 24:31)

3. Possession of the land of Israel (Ezekiel 20:42-44; 36:28-38)

4. The Davidic Throne re-established (2 Samuel 7:11-16; 1 Chronicles 17:10-14; Jeremiah 33:17-26)

5. Jesus Christ rules righteously (Isaiah 2:3,4; 11:2-5)

6. Satan is released from bondage to produce one more rebellion against Christ at the end of the Millennium period (Rev. 20:7-10)

7. The Great White Throne Judgment takes place (see below)

The Great White Throne Judgment

This is the judgment for the unbelieving dead at the end of the Millennium (Rev. 20:11). All who experience this judgment are there because they have rejected Jesus Christ during their lifetimes. John describes this terrible judgment by stating he saw the dead, great, and small, standing before the throne, and books were opened. Before we discuss the books, it is important to understand that people are judged by their works. These books will contain the secrets of men (Romans 2:16), because we find that all things are naked and opened before the eyes of God (Hebrews 4:13). Remember, the subconscious mind retains all our thoughts and experiences, and can be recalled into the conscious mind under certain circumstances. When facing death, for instance, people have often commented they saw their whole life flash before their eyes. God, we find, keeps a record of all of our words and deeds.

The Book of Life

The first book to be opened was the Book of Life, which is mentioned a number of times in the Bible (Exodus 32:33; Psalm 69:28; Daniel 12:1; Luke 10:20; Philippians 4:3; Revelation 3:5; 17:8; 20:12; 20:15; 21:27; 22:18). It was common in ancient times for a ruler to record the names of those under his control or domain. The book appears to be a list of the elect, since Scripture tells us the names were "written from the foundation of the world." (Rev. 17:8). This is where the dead were judged by what was written in the books, according to what they had done. The sea gave up the dead, and Death and Hades gave up the dead who were in them, and they were judged, each one of them, according to what they had done. Then Death and Hades were thrown into the lake of fire. And if anyone's name was not found written in the Book of Life, he was thrown into the lake of fire. This is the second death.

The Book of Life is actually two books. One is called "the Book of Life," and the other is called, "the Lamb's Book of Life." The Book of Life contains the names of all living people. Although the Old Testament does not call it by that name, it does discuss a book in which names are recorded. The Lamb's Book of Life is a book belonging to Jesus Christ. This book contains the names of all those who have received his gift of eternal life (Rev. 13:8). In Rev. 21:27 it states the only people who will enter the Holy City are "those names written in the Lamb's Book of Life." We find two differences between these two books: (1) the Book of Life seems to contain the names of all living people, whereas the Lamb's Book of Life includes only the names of those who have called on the Lamb for their salvation. (2) It is possible for a person's name to be erased from the Book of Life (See Exodus 32:33). On the other hand, it is not the case with names contained in the Lamb's Book of Life. (Rev. 3:5).

The Bible tells us there are three reasons explaining why a person's name can be erased from the Book of Life: (1) sinning against Almighty God (2) not being draped in righteousness through the new birth of being born again in Christ, and (3) misusing the words of this prophecy. Remember, we can never enjoy an eternal life unless we are born again in Jesus Christ. Jeremiah 17:9 tells us the heart is deceitful above all things, and desperately sick; who can understand it?" Also, in Genesis 8:21, we find God saying: ". . . for the intention of man's heart is evil from his youth." So, it is really up to each one of us, based on our free choice, to accept or reject Christ as our Lord and Savior. Remember, God is a loving and gracious God, and does not want any of us to perish, but to come to repentance (2 Peter 3:9).

> If anyone's name is not written in the Book of
> Life, he was thrown into the lake of fire!

The New Heaven, New Earth, New Jerusalem

John then saw a new Heaven and a New Earth, (Rev. 21), for the first Heaven and Earth had passed away, and the sea was no more. He then saw the holy city of Jerusalem coming down from God in Heaven, prepared as a bride prepared for her husband.

Rev. 21:10-27 describes the new holy City of Jerusalem as being 12,000 stadia, in length, width and height. A stadia is 607 feet in length, which translates the size of this city into 1380 miles in length. Because it is also 1380 miles in width, it further translates into almost two million square miles, about the size of modern-day India, or 40 times the area of England, 20 times greater than New Zealand, or 10 times the area of France. Incredibly, the Bible goes on to say this new city will be 12,000 stadia in height also. By allowing 12 feet between stories, this city could easily contain more than 600,000 stories, stretching well above our atmosphere. It will be a city unlike anything ever built in the history of man, and will be a place where believers get to live forever.

God now dwells with man, and they are his people. **God wipes away every tear from their eyes, and death shall be no more, neither shall there be mourning, nor crying, nor pain anymore, for the former things have passed away.** (This is what believers have to look forward to!). And he who sits on the throne says, **"Behold, I am making all things new." And he said to me, "It is done. I am the Alpha and the Omega, the beginning and the end."** (Rev. 21:4-6)

Jesus goes on to say those who have conquered receive this heritage, but as for the cowardly, the faithless, the detestable, as for murderers, the sexually immoral, sorcerers, idolaters, and all liars, their portion will be in the lake that burns with fire and sulfur, the second death.

Bible Numerology

It is interesting how students of Bible numerology string together certain numbers attesting to divine authorship. For example, the number one stands for unity; two for union; three for the Trinity; four for the number of the earth (north, south, east, west); five serves as a divisional number, as in the example of the five wise and five foolish virgins; six represents the number of man, because mankind seems to revolve around this number (man is created on the sixth day; Antichrist uses 666, man's number, and man shall toil for six days and rest on the seventh). Seven is the number of completeness, or perfection. It is God's number. God instructed Solomon to build a temple with seven steps to its throne; God also created seven days for his divine calendar, and in Rev. 21 and 22, we find God creating seven new things: 1) a new Heaven 2) a new Earth 3) a New Jerusalem 4) new things 5) a new paradise 6) a new place for God's throne, and 7) a new source of light. God goes on to use 12 as a government or administrative number; this explains why we find multiples of 12 in the universe of God. For instance, there are 24 thrones around the altar; 144,000 Messianic Christians, and in Rev. 21 there are 12 gates, 12 angels, the names of 12 tribes, 12 foundations, 12,000 stadia, and the names of the 12 apostles.

The River of Life

Rev. 22 opens with an angel who shows John the river of the water of life flowing from the throne of God and of the Lamb, through the middle of the street in the city, and on either side of the river, there is the tree of life with its 12 kinds of fruit. They will see his face, and his name will be on their foreheads. Night will be no more, as God will be their light, and they will reign forever and ever.

Jesus is coming

And Jesus said, "And behold, I am coming soon. Blessed is the one who keeps the words of the prophecy of this book." Jesus goes on to say, "Do not seal the words of the prophecy of this book, for the time is near. Let the evildoer still do evil, and the filthy still be filthy, and the righteous still do right, and the holy still be holy. Behold, I am coming soon, bringing my recompense with me, to repay each one for what he has done. I am the Alpha and the Omega, the first and the last, the beginning and the end."

This is a sober warning for every human being born on this earth!

Summary

During the last two chapters we have covered a lot of ground, despite my effort to simplify and condense the material as much as possible, and I think we all agree none of us will have the complete picture of the future until we travel beyond the veil. This incomplete picture of the future allows Christian theologians to debate and hold different positions, especially with reference to the chronology of how it all plays out. Nonetheless, it is my belief all Christians need to remain united, and not allow our differences to affect our relationships as we continue forward in developing and refining our faith walk into the future. Remember the old Christian admonition, "In essentials Unity, in non-essentials Liberty, and in all other things, Charity!"

So, because of the importance of the information mentioned in these last two chapters, I thought it beneficial to provide you on the next few pages, as best as possible, a summary overview of these future events, realizing that not every scholar will necessarily agree on all points.

Below, aided by many Christian scholars who appear to agree with the format, I have provided a design format separating actions taking place in Heaven from those taking place on Earth, during the seven-year tribulation period. Also, the tribulation period is split into four separate segments: the first half, the midpoint, the second half, and action that takes place beyond the tribulation period. This should clarify your overall picture in "connecting" some of the dots of how the future could come together. Its purpose is to serve as a spiritual "roadmap," allowing you to use it as a foundation upon which to build your own framework through prayer and study. As a fellow truth seeker, I wish you well on your spiritual quest.

Possible Biblical Overview of Future Events

Scenes Taking Place in Heaven:

1. The next great prophetic event will be the Rapture of the Christian Church. (1 Thessalonians 4:13-18; 1 Corinthians 15:51-58; Revelation 3:10).

2. Later, the Judgment Seat of Christ (the Bema Judgment), for Christians only, takes place. (Romans 14:10; 1 Corinthians 3:9-15; 4:1-5; 9:24-27; 2 Corinthians 5:10).

3. Christ (the Lamb) receives the Seven-Sealed Scroll (Rev. 5).

4. The Fifth Seal shows souls under the altar, those souls who had been slain for the Word of God, and for the witness they had borne. (Rev. 6:9).

5. There is a war in heaven, which Satan loses and is cast out of heaven (Rev. 12:7-9).

6. The Marriage of the Lamb (Christ), which is for Christians only, takes place (2 Corinthians 11:2; Revelation 19:6-8).

7. The Marriage Supper of the Lamb (Rev. 19.6). (In Heaven or on earth is still debated).

Events That Take Place on Earth

Sometime around the tribulation period, it is possible Ezekiel's War breaks out, as Gog and his allies invade Israel. This evil coalition is defeated by the intervention of God. (Daniel 11:45; Ezekiel 38-39). Review this war in chapter seventeen.

The seven-year tribulation begins sometime after the Rapture, which is divided into three segments, and then the period beyond the tribulation.

The first three-and-one-half years:

1.   Antichrist is released on to earth and signs a seven-year covenantal agreement with Israel, which provides Israel with peace (Daniel 9:27).

2.   The Jewish Temple is rebuilt (Revelation 11:1-2).

3.   A Ten Nation Federation is established, similar to the Old Roman Empire. This group of ten is mentioned in: (Daniel 2:40-44; 7:7; Revelation 17:12).

4.   The Seven Seal Judgments are opened and released (Revelation 6; 8:1).

5.   The Seven Trumpets are released. (Rev. 8).

6.   144,000 Messianic Jewish men start their world-wide evangelistic mission (Rev. 7, 14).

7.   God's two chosen witnesses start their three-and-one-half year evangelistic ministry. (Revelation 11:2-3).

The midpoint of the tribulation:

1.   There is a war in heaven between the arc-angel Michael, and Satan, and Satan and his army lose the war, and are cast down to earth. Satan then starts to war with the woman (Israel). (Revelation 12:7-13). His chief proxies for waging the war are the two beasts, the Antichrist and the False prophet, mentioned in Revelation 13.

2.   Israel's peace agreement is broken by the Antichrist, as his forces attack Israel. (Daniel 9:27; 11:40-41).

The last three-and-one-half years of the tribulation:

1.   This half of the tribulation is called the Great Tribulation, because Satan realizes he has little time left to accomplish his goals, and increases the intensity and persecution of God's people. (Daniel 7:25; Revelation 12:12; 13:15; 20:4).

2.   During this time, we are told Antichrist blasphemes God. He uses the false prophet to perform many signs and wonders to impress the people. This is done to entice the people to worship the Antichrist. (Revelation 13:5, 11-15).

3.   The two witnesses are killed by the Antichrist, and their bodies lie in the street for the world to see for three-and-one-half days, before God miraculously resurrects them back to life. The people of the world are in awe as they see the two witnesses ascend to heaven. (Rev. 11:7-12).

4.   With the full support of Satan, the Antichrist is allowed to totally dominate the world both religiously, economically, and politically. (Revelation 13:4-5, 15-18).

5.   During this time the faithful flee from Jerusalem to possibly Petra or Bozrah on the east side of the Jordan River, where they will receive protection during the rest of the tribulation period. (Matthew 24:16-20; Revelation 12:15-17. See also Isaiah 63:1-6).

6.   At some point we are told Antichrist appears to suffer a mortal wound, but later recovers. (Rev. 13:3, 17:8; Daniel 11:45).

7.   Sometime after allegedly rising from the dead, the Antichrist manages to consolidate political control over the ten kings of the united Roman Empire. Later, we are told three of the kings are slain by the Antichrist, while the remainder submit to his rule. (Daniel 7:24; Revelation 17:12-13).

8.   Antichrist commits the abomination of desolation inside the rebuilt temple. (Daniel 9:27; 12:11; Matthew 24:15; 2 Thessalonians 2:4; Revelation 13:5-6).

9.   666, the mark of the beast is implemented, and the False Prophet won't allow anyone to buy or sell without the mark. (Revelation 13:16-18).

10. The ten kings, led by the Antichrist, destroy the religious system, and then proceed to set-up their own religion and economy in the city. (Revelation 17:16-17).

11. Antichrist travels from North Africa to finish the job of annihilating the Jews. (Daniel 11:44).

12. The third set of seven great plagues takes place, called the Seven Bowl Judgments.

13. The Seven Bowl Judgments are poured out in rapid succession. (Revelation 16).

14. The commercial system is destroyed. (Revelation 18).

Jesus Christ returns to the Mount of Olives where he slays the enemies of God, all throughout the Holy Land (Zechariah 14:1-4).

Beyond the tribulation period

1.   We are told of a short interval of time. (Daniel 12:12).

2.   The Antichrist and the False Prophet are cast into the lake of fire. (Revelation 19:20-21).

3.   The scattered elect is regathered. (Matthew 24:31).

4.   The Jews remove the abomination of desolation from their temple. (Daniel 12:11).

5.   Then those who survive the tribulation, are also judged. (Matthew 25:31-46).

6.   Satan is thrown into the bottomless pit (the abyss). (Revelation 20:1-3).

7.   Old Testament saints and tribulation saints are resurrected and rewarded. (Daniel 12:1-3; Isaiah 26:19; Revelation 20:4).

8.   Christ begins his 1,000-year reign on earth. (Revelation 20: 4-6).

9.   At the end of the 1,000-year Millennium period, Satan is released one last time, and revolts against God. He gathers a large army, but is defeated once again. (Revelation 20:7-10).

10. The lost souls are finally judged at the Great White Throne Judgment. (Rev. 20:11-15).

11. Destruction comes to the present Earth and Heaven. (Matthew 24:35; 2 Peter 3:3-12; Revelation 21:1).

12. A New Heaven, a New Earth, and a New Jerusalem are created. (Isaiah 65: 17; 66:22; 2 Peter 3:13; Revelation 21:1).

13. Christians are blessed to live on into eternity with the Lord Jesus Christ. (Rev. 21, 22).

If you wish to pursue this subject further, you will find numerous sources available to assist you in your goal. Meanwhile, it is important to stress the importance of prayer so you can be led by the Holy Spirit, and not to rely on your own understanding. (Proverbs 3:5-6).

Other constructs that have been developed in an attempt to simplify the 22 chapters of Revelation are also worth mentioning. For instance, Pastor Robert J. Morgan takes all of the chapters and identifies them according to whether the events within each chapter take place on earth or in heaven. In doing so, it is amazing to see how the story line moves from heaven to earth, back to heaven, and then again to earth, all through the complete book. We are very grateful to Pastor Morgan for bringing this structure to our attention, as we are always looking for easier ways to interpret this wonderful and fascinating book. Here is his overview:

On Earth: The Apostle John on the Island of Patmos (Revelation 1-11)

In Heaven: The Glorified Christ (Revelation 1:12-20)

On Earth: The seven churches (Revelation 2:1-3; 22)

In Heaven: The Throne at the beginning of the tribulation (Revelation 4:1-5;14)

On Earth: The Seven Seals (Revelation 6:1-7:8)

In Heaven: The Great Multitude (Revelation 7:9-8:5)

On Earth: The Seven Trumpets (Revelation 8:6-11:14)

In Heaven: Thunderous praise around the Throne (Revelation 11:15-19)

On Earth: The Anti-Trinity (Revelation 12:1-13:18)

In Heaven: The Lamb is Worshiped (Revelation 14:1-5)

On Earth: Angels of Judgment, Bowls of Wrath, and collapse of Babylon (Revelation 14:6-18:24)

In Heaven: The Hallelujah Chorus (Revelation 19:1-16)

On Earth: The Return of Christ and its aftermath (Revelation 19:17-20:15)

In Heaven: Eternity begins (Revelation 21:1-22:21)

Man's final destiny:

Before ending this chapter on future events, it seems appropriate to mention the final destiny of all people who have been born on this earth, and where they will reside after death. The Holy Scriptures discuss two distinct resurrections – for the just and the unjust. All Bible believers agree there will be a resurrection of both believers and non-believers.

Space does not allow me to discuss those who believe we are all resurrected at the same time, as some people think. The case for separate resurrections can be established through a reading of 1 Corinthians 15:20-23, and Rev. 20:4-5. Also, Paul discusses, "For as in Adam all die, so also in Christ shall all be made alive. But each in his own order: Christ the first fruits, then at his coming those who belong to Christ." (1 Corinthians 22-23).

Order of Resurrection

1. Jesus Christ Resurrected first (1 Corinthians 15:20, 23; Acts 26:23; Colossians 1:18)

2. Rapture of the Church - includes both Jewish and Gentile believers. (1 Thessalonians 4:16; 1 Corinthians 15:51-58)

3. Tribulation Saints (Revelation 20:4-6)

4. Old Testament Saints (Daniel 12:1-2)

5. Great White Throne (Revelation 20:11-15)

Jesus Christ was the first to come back from the dead, and never to die again. "But now Christ is risen from the dead, and has become the first fruit of those who have fallen asleep . . . But each in his own order. Christ the first fruit, afterward those who are Christ's at his coming." (1 Corinthians 15:20, 23). See also Acts 26:23; Colossians 1:18.

The Rapture of the Church, includes the bodies of believers, both Gentiles and Jews, who are dead, and those who are alive, will all be changed. "For the Lord himself shall descend from Heaven with a shout, with the voice of an archangel, and with the trumpet of God. And the dead in Christ will rise first (1 Thessalonians 4:16). Also, we find in 1 Corinthians 15:51-58, those believers who are alive will be raised up and given imperishable, immortal bodies.

The Tribulation Saints, are those who were not raptured, and entered the seven-year tribulation period, but later converted, and were then killed during the tribulation. They will be raised up at the Second Coming of Christ at the end of the tribulation. See Revelation 20:4-6.

Old Testament Saints, are those righteous people who died before the time of Christ, will be raised at Christ's Second Coming. See Daniel 12:1-2. At this point, every righteous believer, from the time of Adam until Jesus' Second Coming will have all been resurrected.

The Great White Throne Judgment, will take place 1,000-years after Christ's Second Coming.

This judgment is mainly for unbelievers (Revelation 20:11-15), which will include all the unbelieving dead who have ever lived. At this time, they will be resurrected, judged, found guilty, and cast into the lake of fire, forever.

In summing up the future destiny of mankind, we find some Christians believe only one resurrection takes place at the end, but I believe Scripture speaks of more than one resurrection. The first resurrection will be for believers, and the second resurrection will be for non-believers, of which both are separated in time. There has now been some 1,990-years (2022), since the Resurrection of Christ (32 A.D.), to the present, and even more time when we add the future time of the Rapture. With the Rapture and resurrection of the Church, there will then be a resurrection of the tribulation saints (those who died for Christ during the tribulation period). They too will be raised to be with Christ at his Second Coming. And at that time, Old Testament Saints will also be raised to be with Christ. Then, after the 1,000-year reign of Christ (The Millennium), the last resurrection of the unrighteous dead takes place (which also includes those who accepted the mark of the beast during the tribulation). It is known as the Great White Throne Judgment, and once this last judgment is rendered, there will be no more resurrections.

Are you ready to take your rightful place with your name in the Lamb's book of life, and spend your conscious life in eternity with the Lord, Jesus Christ?

19

The New Testament in Less Than 30-Minutes

"A thousand times over, the death knell of the Bible has been sounded, the funeral session formed, the inscription cut on the tombstone, and the committal read out loud. But somehow the corpse never stays put!" (Unknown).

L ET'S START BY TAKING A BRIEF MOMENT FOR YOU TO PULL OUT YOUR Bible, and then place your finger between the Old Testament and the New Testament. It is easy to then see how much larger the Old Testament is compared with the New Testament. For example, there are more than 23,000 verses in the Protestant Bible's Old Testament, whereas there are less than 8,000 verses in the New Testament, which means only one-third of the Bible is dedicated to the Christian portion of the Bible, the New Testament. You see, while the Old Testament was written by about 40 authors over a 1000-year time span, (approximately the 15th century B.C. to the 5th century B.C.), the New Christian Testament was written by nine authors, (assuming Paul did not write the Book of Hebrews) and were written in less than 50 years.

Upon further review we find both Testaments are divided into four-parts. The Old Testament has:

1. the Law, (known as the Torah), consisting of the first five books: Genesis through to Deuteronomy;

2. the Historical books, which reprinted Israel's story of conquest of Canaan, through to the destruction of Jerusalem, and later leading to its rebuilding;

3. we then have the Writings, which include the Psalms, wisdom literature, and faith Reflections;

4. the fourth category covers the Prophets, who were ordained by God to inspire the people to remain faithful to him. They also warned of the consequences of not obeying God, while offering hope for those that do endure.

We also find in the New Testament four-parts or categories:

1. We start with the four Gospels of Matthew, Mark, Luke, and John. They include biographical information on the teachings and wisdom of Jesus, coupled to an understanding of his commands, and the introduction of a New Covenant. We can now see more clearly a parallel between the books of the Torah, which provide the Law and Israel's definitive story, when we compared them to the Gospels telling the story of Christianity, and the following of a new law;

2. With the Old Testament historical books, we see another parallel with the Book of Acts of the Apostles, telling the history of the early Christian church. The book covers the period from the Resurrection of Jesus Christ, to approximately 65 A.D., where we find Paul under house arrest in Rome awaiting execution. Although the story covers a much shorter time period, it is similar to the historical books of the Hebrew Bible (the Tanakh), in the telling of background history;

3. Old Testament Writings composed of wisdom and faith reflections can be compared with the writings of the apostles, as they conveyed their Christian wisdom to the world;

4.   The New Testament ends with the future being forecast in the Revelation. This prophetic material can easily be dovetailed into the prophecies spoken of by the Old Testament Prophets.

An important take-away is the comparison of the four sections of the New Testament, when compared with the four sections of the Old Testament, which once again demonstrate the need for a good understanding of the Old Jewish Testament.

New Testament Book (Letter, Epistle) Overview

The books of the New Testament can be divided into four main categories:

1.   First are the four Gospels: **Matthew, Mark, Luke, and John.** The Gospel literally means: "Good News," which refers to the life, wisdom teachings, crucifixion, and resurrection of Jesus of Nazareth. Matthew, Mark, and Luke, are referred to as the synoptic gospels, meaning "at one look." This term is used because each of the three books tell a similar story differing only in some additions, some omissions, a special emphasis, and the overall message the author is attempting to communicate. Although John is a Gospel, it has been placed separately from the synoptics because it is so different. Instead of cataloging the facts of Jesus' life, as the synoptics do, we find John focusing more on the mystery of Jesus as the Son of God. These four books are generally placed first in the New Testament canon. Most scholars state Mark's Gospel was written first, and John's was last, covering a timespan between approximately the mid to late 50s and 70, up until the 90s A.D.

2.   The second category includes only one book: **The Acts of the Apostles**, written by Luke, who also gave us one of the above gospels. The Gospel of Luke and the Acts of the Apostles were originally written as one book, but later separated. Acts provides the reader with the formation and challenges facing

this young, fledgling faith. It tells us where the twelve apostles, and their missionaries, were sent out in the world to promote the New Covenant of Christ, as they spread out from Jerusalem. Peter concentrated on converting his fellow Jews, while Paul's mission was to convert the Gentile populations. The reader is provided with a chronological, rich, and detailed account of the history these men experienced in taking the message of Christ to pagan societies and shedding the light of Christ into some very dark places.

3.   The third category includes the **Pauline Letters**, which make up about half of the New Testament writings. By the end of the second century, the Christian communities had solidified and attributed 14 letters to Paul, which included Hebrews. However, this book was later subtracted from the list and given to an unknown writer. Paul's letters to the churches are mentioned first and arranged from longest to shortest. His letters to individuals came next and were also arranged from longest to shortest. His letters included: Romans, 1 Corinthians, 2 Corinthians, Galatians, Ephesians, Philippians, Colossians, 1 Thessalonians, 2 Thessalonians, 1 Timothy, 2 Timothy, Titus, and Philemon. Certain dates for some of these letters are still disputed, but the general consensus is that they began to be written in the early 50s, making them the oldest existing Christian texts, with the exception of the Book of James possibly written in the late 40s.

4.   The fourth category includes seven of the New Testament letters, which are conveyed to all Christians. They are known as the **General Letters**, and are also referred to as **Catholic** or **Universal**, because they are meant for all the churches. The word *catholic* is not meant to associate them with the Catholic Church, but only to reference their universal scope. They are all generally understood to have been written after the Pauline letters, except James. These letters, along with the approximate dates and places from where they were written were: James (40-

45 A.D.), possibly from Palestine; 1 Peter (62-63), from Rome; 2 Peter (64-67) from Rome; Jude (mid 60s) unknown; 1 John (85-95) Ephesus; 2 John (85-95) Ephesus; 3 John (85-95) Ephesus. The last letter in the New Testament was the apocalyptic Book of the Revelation, also written down by John.

Some scholars classify the Book of Revelation in a separate category due to its apocalyptic view of future events, which we discussed in the last two chapters.

Summary of the Gospels:

The Gospel according to Matthew

This book was traditionally written in the late 50s or early 60s, and by the second century A.D., this Gospel had been placed at the beginning of the New Testament. This was because it was thought to be the first Gospel to be written, and because its emphasis was on a Jewish audience, concerning subjects related to Judaism. Therefore, it made a good "bridge" between the two testaments. We now know, however, the Gospel of Mark was the first Gospel to be written.

Matthew wrote this account in order to demonstrate the messianic identity of Jesus, who was to be a blessing to the nation through his inheritance of the Davidic kingship (Genesis 12:1-3. Matthew 1:1). Matthew also wanted his Gospel to serve as an evangelical tool, aimed at converting his fellow Jews to accept Jesus as their long-awaited Messiah.

Matthew is arranged in seven-parts: (1) An introduction telling of Jesus' miraculous birth. and the origin of his ministry. (2) The Sermon on the Mount, introducing the basic elements of the Christian message. (3) The Mission Sermon, given to empower and encourage Jesus's apostles to make the point that more missionaries are necessary. (4) The Sermon in Parables, concerning

Jesus' concern the people are not understanding or accepting his message. (5) The Sermon on the Church responds to the challenge of establishing a lasting legacy of Christians going forward. (6) The End Times, or eschatological Sermon, (Olivet Discourse), where Jesus discusses the end of the world, all leading to the near-term certainty he will be crucified. (7) Matthew concludes by providing an account of the Last Supper, followed by Jesus' trial, and execution.

The Gospel according to Mark

Although Mark was not an eyewitness to Jesus, or a disciple, he nonetheless was widely accepted by the early church fathers, based on widespread evidence then available. It has also been confirmed Peter passed on to John Mark, (Mark), reports on the works and deeds of Jesus. Church tradition dates this book to the mid to late 50s from Rome, and therefore was written before both Matthew, and Luke.

For many years, the Gospel of Mark was the least popular of the Gospels, due to its dull prose in writing about the life of Jesus, compared to the more sophisticated prose of Matthew and Luke, when they wrote about the same subject. Mark for some reason, leaves out the account of Jesus' birth, the famous Sermon on the Mount, and a number of the most well-known parables. Later, Mark's Gospel became more popular when it came to light his gospel was the first one to be written, and it was a primary source of information for both Matthew and Luke. Also, because Jesus, or his original disciples, left no writings for posterity, it caused Mark's Gospel to be the closest writing to an original source of Jesus' life that exists. As a result, today the Gospel of Mark has been elevated to one of the most important books in the New Testament.

The main purpose of Mark's Gospel is to present and defend Jesus' universal call to discipleship, which he returns to several times. It can be divided into two sections: (1) From 1:1 – 8:26, it concerns itself with the Galilee mission of Jesus, starting with John the Baptist's prophecy proclaiming the coming of the Messiah. (2) Then, from 8:27 – 16:20, it tells the story of Jesus' prediction regarding his own suffering, leading to the crucifixion and resurrection.

Some bibles divide Mark's Gospel into three sections: (1) Chapters 1:1-8:26 – discussing Jesus' Galilean ministry, with an account of his amazing deeds. (2) Chapter 8:27-10:52 – Jesus' discussions with his disciples centered around suffering. (3) 11:1-16:8 – covers controversies, Jesus' passion, his death, the empty tomb, and the expected Parousia (Second Coming) in Galilee. Some theologians claim this gospel was written over a seven-year period from Rome.

We also know that Mark's Gospel, which is the shortest of the four gospels, is written in a direct, simple, but fast paced narrative, providing vivid, descriptive details, but only providing four of Jesus' parables, out of the 38 mentioned in the overall gospels. There is also a constant theme stating the end of the world is coming shortly, (Mark 13), which became difficult for early Christians to understand when it did not happen.

The Gospel according to Luke

From what we can gather, the final editors of the New Testament decided to separate the Gospel of Luke from the Acts of the Apostles, which was originally written in a single-two volume work. Luke's Gospel provides us with knowledge regarding Jesus' birth, his ministry, and culminating in his trial, death, and resurrection. Then, in the second volume, in The Acts of the Apostles, Luke provides us with much detail of the new Christian church's early history, and the many challenges in spreading the gospel along the way. It moves from the resurrection of Jesus to a time when Paul traveled on his missionary journeys to the pagan, Gentile nations of the known world, to minister the gospel. Luke attempts to rely on eyewitnesses of Jesus and the early disciples, because it appears he was not an eyewitness himself. Luke's Gospel appears to have been written between 75 and 85 A.D., in the general time frame of Matthew's Gospel. Luke also appears to have relied on Mark's Gospel as well as other stories circulated orally during his lifetime. Also, Luke's command of Greek, indicates a man who was cultivated, and well educated.

Unlike the Gospel of Matthew, which was directed towards a Jewish audience, we find Luke's Gospel being addressed to a Gentile audience, and he appeared to have a number of goals in mind: (1) He wanted to assure his readers of the truth of what they had been taught. (2) He also wanted his audience to understand why the Jews rejection of Jesus was all part of God's plan to adopt Gentiles into the kingdom of God. He made the point Christianity was not a new religion, but rather the fulfillment of the religion of Abraham, Isaac, and Jacob. (3) Luke also wanted to clarify Jesus' end time teachings, by conveying the fact the return of Jesus would not come immediately, but rather there would be a period of time between his resurrection and his return. (4) Luke encouraged his readers not to fear Rome, by emphasizing when Rome did persecute, it was more likely due to an error or ignorance, and once enlightened, the persecution stopped. (Note that there were ten Roman persecutions, some say eleven, against Christians, beginning with Nero in 64 A.D., and culminated intermittently with Diocletian in 310 A.D.).

The Gospel according to John

After reading the synoptic gospels of Matthew, Mark, and Luke, (the synoptics), you may be surprised from the very first verse, how different John's gospel is compared to the others. The first verse says, "In the beginning was the Word, and the Word was with God, and the Word was God." Here we can see this gospel is going to be different in its approach to Jesus' story. Instead of writing a biography of Jesus' life, there is an attempt to communicate the spiritual aspect of Jesus, which John wrote much later than the synoptics, probably later than 70 A.D. The evidence of an exact date is marginal at best. Another fact seems to separate John's gospel from the others, is that about 90% of the material in John's gospel is not found in the other three gospels. Although many of the stories found in John are different than the synoptic telling of the same stories, we find John's stories are consistent. The way Jesus speaks is perhaps what makes John's gospel so different.

Instead of focusing on what Jesus said and did, John's focus is applied more to simplifying who Jesus is, and the meaning of his life. We find John repeatedly identifying Jesus with God, and this is clear in the use of the seven "I am" verses. The synoptics tend to surround Jesus with a lot of mystery, as to who he is. John, however, gets right to the point in his opening verse, and then follows up with his "seven I am" verses, clearly identifying who Jesus is, when he says:

John 6:35: I am the bread of life

"I am the Bread of Life. whoever comes to me shall not hunger, and whoever believes in me shall never thirst." As the living bread, Jesus gave the people more than physical bread to curb their hunger, he also gave them nourishment for their hearts.

John 8:12: I am the light of the world

"I am the Light of the World. Whoever follows me will not walk in darkness but will have the light of life." Jesus is the light, and there is no darkness in him. Therefore, Christians ask that Jesus shine in their hearts, shine in their minds, and shine in their whole hearts.

John 10:7-10: I am the door

"I am the door of the sheep. All who came before me are thieves and robbers, but the sheep did not listen to them. I am the door. If anyone enters by me, he will be saved and will go in and out and find pasture. The thief comes only to steal and kill and destroy. I came that they may have life and have it abundantly." We are constantly having to choose which way to go in life, and the Bible is direct in telling us the road is not always easy, for it says: "Enter through the narrow gate. For the gate is wide and the way is easy that leads to destruction, and those who enter by it are many. For the gate is narrow and the way is hard that leads to life, and those who find it are few." (Matthew 7:13-14).

John 10:11-14: I am the good shepherd

"I am the good shepherd. The good shepherd lays down his life for the sheep." Many farmers hire a worker who does not own the sheep. So, when the wolf comes, he abandons the sheep, allowing the wolf to scatter them. A good shepherd, however, protects the sheep because he knows his sheep and they know him. In 2015 in Turkey, a number of shepherds neglected their sheep, and some 1500 walked off the side of a cliff. 450 died, but their dead bodies cushioned the others who were saved with some injuries. It is a stark reminder that Jesus never neglects his sheep!

John 11:25: I am the resurrection and the life

"I am the resurrection and the life. Whoever believes in me, though he die, yet shall he live, and everyone who lives and believes in me shall never die." To Christians, this is perhaps the most valuable verse of them all, in knowing we will have a place with Jesus forever.

John 14:5: I am the way and the truth and the life

"I am the way, and the truth, and the life. No one comes to the Father except through me." The more we read about Jesus, the more we know he is the truth. He said: "For this purpose I was born and for this purpose I have come into the world – to bear witness to the truth." Jesus is the truth!

John 15:1-5: I am the vine

"I am the true vine, and my Father is the vinedresser. Every branch in me that does not bear fruit he takes away, and every branch that does bear fruit he prunes, that it may bear more fruit." Jesus is saying no branch can bear fruit by itself; it must remain in the vine. We must be part of the body of Jesus Christ in order to fully develop the fruit displayed by our actions.

Chapter 20 ends by providing the purpose of John's Gospel. It says: "Now Jesus did many other signs in the presence of the disciples, which are not written in this book, but these are written so that you may believe that Jesus is the Christ, the Son of God, and that by believing you may have life in his name." (John 20:30-31).

Summarizing the Theology of the New Testament

The message of the New Testament cannot be separated from the Old Testament, because we read in the Old Testament God will save his people, beginning with the promise the seed of the woman would triumph over the seed of the serpent (Genesis 3:15). God's saving promises were further developed through the Old

Testament covenants he made with his people, along with a New Covenant he promised. This would give his Spirit to his people, by writing his law on their hearts, in order for them to obey his will. (Jeremiah 31:31-34; Ezekiel 36:26-27).

It is clear by the time John the Baptist arrived, God's saving promises had not yet been achieved. The Romans still held the Jews under their yoke, and a Davidic king did not rule the land. Meanwhile, the people were still living in sin, and not righteousness. It was John the Baptist, who called on the people to repent from their sins, in order to pave the way for the Messiah.

Jesus represented the fulfillment of what John was prophesying, by announcing the imminent arrival of the kingdom of God (Mark 1:15). This was another way of saying the Old Testament promises made by God were about to be ratified. Surprisingly to many, the Kingdom of God came in a different, most unexpected way. The Jews were hoping when Messiah came, all their enemies would be destroyed, and a new covenant would be installed. What they did not realize, however, was the kingdom was in the person of Jesus himself, and the ministry he was communicating to the people (Luke 17:20-21). The Jews wondered why their enemies had not been annihilated, and the Messiah did not appear to arrive with the power they expected. The Kingdom of God was more like a small mustard seed, growing eventually into a huge tree that would spread over the entire earth (today, Christianity has the greatest following of the major world religions). What was happening, is the fact the kingdom had arrived, and was already present in Jesus, but it was not yet present in its entirety. It appeared like it was here, but not quite yet.

We find there is a focus on the promise of the kingdom in the Synoptic Gospels, and we find John saying something similar when he discusses an eternal life. John's gospel is unique in that those who believe in the Son of God, already enjoy the life of the coming age right now. This is because anyone who has put their faith in Jesus has already passed from death into life. (John 5:24-25), for he is the resurrection and the life (John 11:25). Jesus' resurrection also signifies the age to come has arrived, and now is the day of salvation. We can also say an outpouring of the Holy Spirit has been fulfilled. (Acts 2:16-21; Romans 8:9-16; Ephesians 1:13-14). This is all wonderful news, but we have to also accept the reality Jesus had been raised from the dead, but believers were still waiting for their own resurrected bodies, and in the meantime were still battling against sin until the final day of redemption (Romans 8:10-13, 23; 1 Corinthians 15:12-34; 1 Peter 2:11). While Jesus still controls the power at the right hand of God, we find here on earth all things have not yet been fully subjected to him (Hebrews 2:5-9).

So, who is Jesus? We find in the New Testament he is the new and better Moses by stating God's Word as the sovereign interpreter of the Mosaic Law. (Matthew 5:17-48; Hebrews 3:1-6). We find the Law and the Prophets look forward to him and find their fulfillment in him. (Matthew 5:17). Jesus brings grace into believers' hearts and minds, for he is the true wisdom of God, by fulfilling and also transcending wisdom passages from the Old Testament (Colossians 2:1-3).

In the Gospels, we find Jesus often mentioned as a prophet, because he is the final prophet who had been predicted by Moses. (Deuteronomy 18:18-19; Acts 3:22-23; 7:37). The overwhelming evidence of Jesus' miracles, the feeding and healing of many, coupled to his power over demons, all demonstrate the promises of the kingdom all reside, and are fulfilled in him. (Matthew 12:28). His actions also tell us Jesus shares God's authority and is therefore divine himself. (Matthew 10:32-33; 1 Corinthians 16:21-24). Scripture goes on to tell us Jesus is the image of God. (Colossians 1:15; Hebrews 1:3). Although Jesus is equal to God, he temporarily surrendered some of the privileges of his deity by clothing himself in humanity, in order to save us. (Philippians 2:6-8).

Christians recognize the deity of Jesus by memorializing a meal, whereby the eating of the bread, and the drinking from the cup, symbolize the fact Jesus sacrificed his blood, and his life, for the remission of our sins. We gain redemption through the shed blood of Jesus Christ. The significance of Jesus' death on the cross helps us better understand the new creation, what the adoption means, and what it means to have our sins forgiven. The cross also explains the need for justification, reconciliation, sanctification, and the final glorification when we are with him once again.

In its simplest terms, the concept of **Justification** is the act by which God moves a willing person from a state of sin (injustice) to the state of grace (justice), which is accomplished by having faith in Jesus Christ as Lord and Savior of their life. Justification is not based on works, but faith. (See Romans chapters 4 and 5). From God's perspective, when he looks at a new believer it is as if he had never sinned. Justification literally saves us from the penalty of Hell!

Sanctification is the concept of proper functioning. When someone is sanctified, it simply means to set a person apart for the use of its designer i.e., God. A written agreement is sanctified when you sign the agreement pledging to fulfill certain promises. Or, a marriage is sanctified through the wedding vows. So, in spiritual terms, a person is "sanctified" when they live a life according to God's purpose. (See Romans, chapters 6-7). In practical terms, sanctification means God is saving us from the power of sin. We get a new body, and we will be with God in Heaven forever.

Finally, **Glorification** deals with the final perfection that happens to believers at death. (See Romans, chapter 8). While reading the book of Romans, you may also wish to read about salvation for Israel (chapters 9-10), and salvation for Gentiles (chapter 11).

The New Testament ends with the apocalyptic description of the coming end times, magnificently detailed in the last book, the Book of the Revelation, which we have discussed in the last two chapters. In many respects it is good for all of us to know what will happen in the future before it actually happens. In this way, God is providing his people with ample opportunity to change the course direction of their lives, by understanding, accepting, and living by the spiritual rules that God has provided us, as contained in the Bible.

In its simplest form, the New Testament tells us we can receive the free gift Jesus Christ offers us, when he redeems his followers from the guilt and bondage of sin, that we are all born into. It is also made clear a person's response to Jesus will lock-in their final destiny, which is one of two choices. Of all life's major decisions, this particular decision is the most important of them all. So, please, if you have not done so already, make your choice for Christ, but do it now before the Rapture comes, or before your life expires in this earthly dimension. Afterwards it will be too late.

Journal Your Thoughts

_____

_____

_____

_____

_____

_____

_____

_____

_____

_____

_____

_____

_____

_____

_____

_____

_____

_____

_____

20

GETTING THE MOST OUT OF THE BIBLE

"God wrote a book, and that reality blows me away every time I stop to think about it. Pages and pages of God. His thoughts, His words, His heart. Right there, just a few inches away. I can carry it with me wherever I go. Read it whenever I want. Reading the Bible is one of the most important things we can ever do. It's more valuable than anything we own, sweeter than anything we have ever eaten. It is literally more important than breathing." –John Piper

WE HAVE JUST SPENT THE MAJORITY OF THIS BOOK OUTLINING AN overview of the Bible, in an attempt to distill its numerous size (more than 2500 pages, and over a million words including notes in the ESV version), into this book with approximately just over 100,000 words. The main purpose in doing so, is to provide a condensed and more simplified overview of Bible content, in order to demonstrate the rich and valuable wisdom to be gained, while at the same time respecting the fact that three of the biggest excuses for not reading the Bible, are the claim of not having enough time, not understanding it, and not respecting its value. Hopefully, this book has made some strides towards simplifying and overcoming these obstacles.

We all know the best way to eat an elephant is "one piece at a time," which is nothing more than a simple way of stating when we are faced with a large task, which will consume a lot of our time to complete, the best way is to systematically break it down into smaller, more manageable sizes. In this way, we can make limited progress while actually seeing the gains we are making towards the goal. An old corporate aphorism says: "If you can't measure it, you can't manage it!" We each need to develop our own system of Bible study, based on our lifestyle considerations, which will allow us to see the progress we are making. Just a few chapters a day, for instance, can get you through the Bible in about a year. Here are some facts you need to know:

Wrapping our Arms around Holy Scripture

The average reading speed is about 240 words per minute for non-fiction, which means 13 of the Old Testament books can be read easily in less than 30-minutes. Some 18 books can be read in less than one-hour, with some in less than five-minutes! The remaining books (from shortest to longest), can be read in 85 minutes for the shorter ones, and up to 330 minutes for the longer ones (about the time to read an average novel, but with a lot more practical wisdom to dispense).

In the New Testament, almost half of the 27 books can be read in less than half-an-hour, and 23 can be read in less than 20-minutes. Only eight involve more than one-hour to read. In totality, the whole Bible can be conveniently read in less than 100 hours, depending on your reading speed. We are discussing here isolating just a couple of weeks out of your life, which can easily be accomplished by utilizing better time management awareness. For starters, simply cut down on your TV viewing, and spend less time on the Internet or your cellphone. It's all about setting priorities. I can attest that making this one simple adjustment to your lifestyle, will pay off in very special ways, far exceeding any value you gain from TV or the Internet. It will certainly change the trajectory of your life going forward, in a very positive way. The value is too incalculable to estimate, but you need to determine this fact for yourself, as no one can do it for you.

One of the beautiful things about the Bible is the fact that although its 66 books were written by some 40 different authors under divine guidance, these authors did not know each other due to the total timeline from the completion of the first book to the last, which was spread over some 1500 plus years! Yet, notwithstanding this huge diversity of authors, their different locations, and time periods, the Bible is able to consistently maintain a major theme permeating itself through all its books.

Also, when you read any given biblical book, you can learn valuable wisdom from it, without having read the other books. In other words, it is possible to departmentalize your approach and still gain much value. Naturally, if you do read it from beginning to end, it would be a wiser choice in grasping the big picture of what God wants to tell you. In part, this is what I have attempted to do with this book.

One of the main reasons for the apparent seamless continuity of the Bible, is the fact it is primarily about God's overall redemptive plan to save mankind for a future beyond this life. Dr. Charles Stanley sums it up well when he explains from the very first book, Genesis, all through to the last book, Revelation, you find the redemptive story of man being played out over the centuries. The Bible is not about man seeking God, but rather God seeking to find man!

Authenticating the Bible

The Bible tells us God has poured out his heart in love for mankind, to show us the error of our ways, and to provide a better option in renavigating our lives for a course correction. Time and again, he has acted as Father over his children, showing us his paternal character in wanting to protect us from our own sinful ways. This was further demonstrated when God allowed his only begotten Son, Jesus Christ, to be sacrificed, as an atonement for our sins. This very act has served as a sort of escape clause, which has given us all a unique opportunity to get out of this life of sin, and allows us to live guilt free, as we live out our life, and into the next one. All God asks is we make the decision to accept Jesus Christ as Lord and Savior, while we are still alive in this life, because there are no second chances after it ends.

In doing a reality check, I am not naïve in believing everyone who is reading this book, or even the Bible for that matter, is now firmly convinced, and is ready to join the family of Jesus Christ. Some, I am sure, may still have doubts. Therefore, it would appear befitting to provide such readers with additional information on the truthfulness of the Bible, because it is the only book inspired by God himself.

Archaeological evidence to support the Bible

Modern man has access to two historical evidences helping him prove God is the Creator of all things, and that he has a plan for all men's lives: (1) The Bible, and (2) archaeological sites scattered throughout the Middle East, where the ruined cities of ancient people once lived, with their strange cultures, languages, and religions. Upon further study, this evidence proves undeniably, the authenticity of the Bible, and the people who lived during the Bible time period.

All Western nations have access to the first evidence, the Bible itself, and at this time in the history of mankind, the Bible is available to a large proportion of the world's population. Unfortunately, many people are metaphorically starving at a banquet, where they are given full access to all the nourishing "soul food" they could possibly consume, and without charge. Yet, many do

not have the appetite for it, which is one of the major mysteries in our modern world. The fact this is so, however, does not
for one moment dimmish the truthfulness, or the immense value,
the Bible provides us.

With reference to the second piece of evidence, modern
readers now share the benefits of thousands of hours of great
scholars digging through ancient sites, particularly throughout
the 19th and 20th centuries, that have provided us with a treasure
trove of authentic material to support the truth of the Bible. If the
Bible claims to be the inspired Word of God, it becomes important to some people that all Scriptural records be tested against
archeological findings, located where biblical drama was actually carried out. To date, there is not one case of any archeological
artifacts disproving any statements made in Holy Scripture!

This author has identified more than 100 archaeological sites
over the years, proving the truthfulness of the Bible, which can
easily be corroborated if one desires to investigate them. Some
include: the Behistun Inscription, the Tell el-Amarna Tablets, Ab-
salom's Pillar, Babylon, the Rosetta Stone, Beersheba, Bethany,
Bethsaida, Caesarea, Calvary (Golgotha), Garden Tomb (Gordon's
Calvary), Cana, Capernaum, Corinth, Dead Sea Scrolls, Colossae,
Ephesus, En Gedi, Gethsemane, Jacob's Well, Jericho, Jerusalem,
Masada, Mari, Lystra, Megiddo, Nineveh, Nazareth, Petra, Shiloh,
Shechem, Tyre, Ur, and Thessalonica, to name just a few. If you
want material evidence to believe the Bible, there is ample to satisfy the need of the most cynical minds. The monumental amount
of archaeological evidence should be enough to convince the most
skeptical mind of the truthfulness of the Bible, but there is more.

Evidence from historical documents

Many skeptics have no problem believing the existence and authenticity of classical documents, but use a different standard in

disavowing Scriptural documents. Fortunately for Christians, the evidence, once again, is overwhelmingly in favor of God's book, the Bible. Below is a list showing the name of the author, the date the document was written, the estimated date of its earliest copy, the approximate time span between the original document and the copy, and finally the number of copies in circulation, coupled to the independent accuracy of the copies.

Pastor Andrew Archibald wrote this about Bible manuscripts compared to classical writings: "None of the original manuscripts of the Bible have been preserved. Shall we therefore reject this book? As well, we might throw away the works of Homer, who flourished from eight to nine hundred years before Christ, but of whose writing we have no complete copy older than the thirteenth century, and no fragments older than the sixth century – fifteen centuries after the old poet died. Of the history of Herodotus there is no manuscript extant earlier than the ninth century, but this historian lived in the fifth century before the Christian era. There is no copy of Plato previous to the ninth century, and he wrote more than a thousand years before that."[1]

Today we have discovered more than 25,000 partial and complete copies of the Scriptures, and there are still many others to be discovered in monastic libraries of the East. Yes, the Holy Bible has withstood the test of time, which is another fact to substantiate God's Word.

---

1   Andrew Archibald – The Bible Verified (1890), pages 29-30.

Author	Approximate Date Written	Earliest Copy	Time Span between Original and Earliest copy	Number of Copies	Accuracy of the Copies
LUCRETIUS	Died 55 BC		100 years	2	-
PLINY	61-113 AD	850 AD	750 years	7	-
PLATO	427-347 BC	900 AD	1200 years	7	-
DEMOSTHENES	4th century BC	1100 AD	800 years	8	-
HERODOTUS	480-425 BC	900 AD	1300 years	8	-
SUETONIUS	75-160 AD	950 AD	800 years	8	-
THUCYDIDES	460-400 BC	900 AD	1300 years	8	-
EURIPIDES	480-406 BC	1100 AD	1500 years	9	-
ARISTOPHANES	450-385 BC	900 AD	1200 years	10	-
CAESAR	100- 44 BC	900 AD	900 years	10	-
LIVY	59 BC-17AD	300 AD	500 years	20	-
TACITUS	Circa 100 AD	1100 AD	1000 years	20	-
ARISTOTLE	384-322 BC	1100 AD	1400 years	49	-
SOPHOCLES	496-406 BC	1000 AD	1400 years	193	-
HOMER (ILIAD)	900 BC	1400 AD	500 years	1900	95%
THE NEW TESTAMENT	50–100 AD	130 AD	less than 100 years	5600	99.5%

Source: Manuscript Evidence for superior NT reliability – M. Slick.

The Bible verses science

We all need to feel part of a logical system making sense of our lives and the world in which we live. The worldview presented by Christianity solves this issue, because science and reason are intertwined in the Christian framework. Why? Because science emerged from a Christian approach to life. The Scientific Method used by most scientists today was invented by Christians such as Bacon, Descartes, Newton, and Galileo. In fact, Newton fused both inductive and deductive calculations into the scientific method, which became the foundation of modern science. He once said, "If I see further, it is only because I stand on the shoulders of giants." He also referred to Galileo as the father of modern science. Galileo, a strong Christian, is also credited as being the father of modern physics and astronomy.

Christians have made an enormous contribution to our understanding of the world in which we live, and the universe as a whole. Famous biologist Joshua Lederberg once said: "What is incontrovertible is that a religious impulse guides our motive in sustaining scientific inquiry."[2]

The so-called conflict raging on today between science and religion is clearly man made and designed to dilute the Word of God from our consciousness. However, when we dig below the headlines, there is ample evidence to prove the authenticity of the Bible. The famous astronomer and physicist, Robert Jastrow, once concluded with this comment:

> "For the scientist who has lived by his faith in the power of reason, the story ends like a bad dream. He has scaled the mountains of ignorance; he is about to conquer the highest peak; as he pulls himself over the final rock, he is greeted by a band of theologians who have been sitting there for centuries!"[3]

So, when you think about it seriously, you will find theology reinforces science, and science reinforces theology. So, the more we learn about science, the stronger our Christian faith becomes, and vice-versa. This, I believe, is how we should approach this hot subject.

---

2   Joshua Lederberg- Science Magazine – 8.15.1997.
3   Robert Jastrow – Perhaps his most famous quote.

What's in It for Me?

Christianity appears very strange to someone living in the shadows of life, and who has not experienced the fullness of the light of Christ. I know this only too well, because I too spent many years living in darkness before finding the light of Christ. This is the main reason why I try to reach out to people and offer my service. It is joyful for me to do so.

Many people, it seems, are reluctant to embrace Christianity based on practical and intellectual grounds, as well as in some cases just plain ignorance of how it all works. They want to know what they will get out of accepting such a faith, and how it will change their lives.

So, with these thoughts in mind, I thought it helpful to provide an insider's view of some of the many benefits available when we truly understand principles laid down in the Bible. In this way, the concept and beauty of Christianity can be fully grasped. A literal treasure trove of knowledge and wisdom becomes available to all those who convert their remaining lives to Jesus. The irony is, it is not difficult to do, yet millions take a pass. Therefore, in sharing some of the benefits mentioned below, my hope and prayer are that it might kindle renewed interest in accepting Christ as Lord and Savior, for all those who are still not sure of their own salvation. The last chapter in this book will spell out most graphically the importance of your decision, and the consequences involved.

Interestingly, making a decision now for Christ is similar to crossing a bridge to a new country. You are still alive, but the surrounding terrain appears different, as does the image of yourself, as well as other people.

Twelve helpful insights in understanding the Bible and the Christian faith

1.   Atheists continue to insist life has no meaning, because once we die it is all over. On the other hand, Christianity enlightens our soul, which energizes us with an invigorating sense of purpose for our lives. We no longer see life in black and white, but rather in color! Converts to the faith, change from gray disillusionment to a life of fascination and delight. They move from darkness into the light of Christ.

2.   The Christian faith teaches this life is not the only life to live. Christians are acutely aware of a future judgment where all earthly deeds need to be accounted for. Because of this, Christians realize it is better to suffer wrong, than to actually do wrong. In Latin it is referred to as, *sub specie aeternitatis,* or "living in the shadow of eternity." In our world today, we appear to perceive rich businessmen and celebrities as "successful," even though they may have sold their soul by lying, cheating, and doing some pretty bad things to arrive where they are today. Christians, however, are in this world, but not of this world, and as C.S. Lewis so famously put it: "All that is not eternal, is eternally useless!"

3.   We are born into this world with nothing, and we leave with nothing. This fact instills in us a sense of cosmic loneliness, whereby at the end of the day, none of us wants to ever actually experience loneliness, at least not in the long term. We are social animals that need contact with other people, but sometimes we find people in our lives who experience abject loneliness due to not having family or friends, who may have died years ago. Christians, however, are able to move beyond this existential type of loneliness because their destiny is tied to a junior partnership with God, which is eternal. A non-believer may not be able to relate to this reality, because it is

like trying to explain the idea of loving someone to a person who has never been in love. It seems strange to them. For the everyday Christian, however, this feeling is elevated, lofty, and heavenly!

4.   When people become followers of Jesus Christ, they are imbued with the Holy Spirit, which gives them access, among other things, to what Christians refer to as the Fruit of the Spirit. We are introduced, and given access to nine virtues, which have a tremendous impact on the way we treat others. Here is the list: Love, Joy, Peace, Patience, Kindness, Goodness, Faithfulness, Gentleness, and Self-Control. These virtues are a great study within themselves, and can be found in Galatians 5:22, to get you started.

5.   Christians are also given access to at least one or more of a basketful of Spiritual Gifts. They include: Wisdom, Knowledge, Teaching, Healing, Faith, Miracles, Prophecy, Discernment, Speaking in Tongues and Interpreting Tongues, Service, Exhortation, Giving, Leadership, Mercy, Helps, Apostleship, Administration, Evangelist, Pastor, Celibacy, Voluntary Poverty, Martyrdom, Missionary, and Hospitality. Some theologians also like to include other Spiritual Gifts, such as: Craftsmanship, Writing, Intercession, Deliverance, and Leading in Worship. These gifts sometimes come into a Christian's life based on circumstances, provided they are ready for them.

It has been said opportunity favors the prepared mind.

6.   Christianity helps marriages because we are inwardly driven to do better. Many of the above Fruit of the Spirit, and Spiritual Gifts, can come into play in helping us enjoy a happy marriage. Agape love is the driving force in marriage, which is a sacrificial type of love, that helps each partner to do their best in making the other one happy.

7.   We all want to be better parents, but it's all about on-the-job training without an instruction manual, unless we understand Christian principles. What better role model can parents play when they demonstrate agape love for the whole family?

8.   We want to be good citizens, and to raise the level of how we conduct our personal lives. Why do Christians want to be good? Because God stamps his virtues on their hearts, and this causes them to want to obey him, and practice his commands. Christians are good, not because they have to be, but because they want to be, thanks to Christ living in their hearts. How many of us have witnessed the conversion of a drug addict, alcoholic, or an evil criminal, in seeing them completely turn their lives around when they accept Jesus?

9.   Christians are told their body is a "temple" because Jesus Christ resides in it. Paul also refers to the body as a "tent," that encloses our spirit while we camp around earth for 70 or 80 years. Then, the tent is folded up when we die so our soul can go back to our true home with God. Paul probably used this metaphor because he was a tent maker by occupation. When we think of our body in this way, it causes us to respect and protect it. We are more sensitive to what we ingest into it, and we are more likely to take steps to ensure it continues to work properly through regular exercise. Our consciousness about our health is elevated when we realize the Bible has plenty to say about our health and sanitary awareness. We are aware our body is miraculously designed by God, which comes with many different body parts, of which some can be replaced, but others cannot. Christians are also aware of protecting their hearts and minds from the pollution of evil prevailing in the world. That is what Paul had in mind when he called for a renewing of our minds. It is good to follow Paul's admonition in Philippians 4:8, which says:

"Finally, brothers, whatever is True, whatever is Honorable, whatever is Just, whatever is Pure, whatever is Lovely, whatever is Commendable, if there is any Excellence, if there is anything worthy of Praise, think about such things!"

10. Do you have a reason for living? Do you have a reason for dying? You should have a reason for both. Christianity gives us hope whether we live or die, that we win either way, because we end up living with Jesus eternally. It has been said we have a choice:

We can either live once and die twice or live twice and die once.

This simply means if we do not accept Jesus in this life, we will live once, then die, and in the future die again when we face Jesus at the **Great White Throne Judgment** mentioned in Revelation. This is where Jesus renders final judgment on non-believers, and they end up in the lake of fire. It is a second death because it separates a person from God forever! This is like living once and dying twice. On the other hand, we can accept Jesus, which means we die to sin, and are reborn in the Spirit, so that when we die, we are able to live with Jesus forever. In other words, we live twice, but die only once.

11. Christianity has grown from a tiny mustard seed some 2,000 years ago, into the largest religion in the world today, with about 2.3 billion adherents worldwide. It started with about 100 believers at the time of Christ's death, but by the early 4th century, it had increased to some 30 million, which led to the great Roman Empire accepting Christianity as the state religion. All of this took place against forces intent to wipe the faith out altogether. In fact, as mentioned earlier, beginning with Emperor Nero (64 AD), up until the time of Diocletian (4th century), there were at least ten major persecutions against Christians, yet their numbers kept increasing despite the torture, the killings, and

the sacrifices they made in the Roman Colosseum, where they were torn apart by wild animals. As I mentioned earlier, eleven of the original twelve apostles all died violently, due to their faith in Jesus. So, why would anyone put their faith in a man branded a criminal, and hanged on a tree? Surely, cosmic forces were involved to demonstrate Christ surely was God, and the vast majority of people today, even the most skeptical, at least believe Jesus Christ was a real person.

12. Of the five major religions in the world today, Islam, Hinduism, Buddhism, Judaism, and Christianity, you will find in totality they represent the faith of about 70% of all the people in the world. Yet, the combined Judeo – Christian faith is the only one that has numerous prophecies having come true, and many more predicted to happen in the future. Try to imagine for a moment, a person predicting the exact town where a future leader would be born some 700 years before it actually happened. That is what the Prophet Micah did, in predicting Jesus would be born in Bethlehem. Or, try to imagine a man making a prediction about the death of a future leader some 900 years into the future. That is what King David did in predicting the death of Christ. These and many more examples could be given with adequate space to express them but let us discuss just eight prophecies that were scrutinized by the American Scientific Affiliation for accuracy. After careful consideration of all facts, it was determined the odds of a person fulfilling just eight prophecies about Jesus were 10^{17} or 10 with 17 zeros after it.! One professor put it in more practical terms by placing 10^{17} dollar pieces all over the State of Texas. Then a man was blindfolded and told he could travel as far as he wished across the state. All he had to do was pick up the one dollar with a special mark on it. This exercise represents just about the same chance of success the ancient prophets of the Bible would have had in fulfilling just eight of the many prophecies made about Jesus.

Although none of the other major world religions can make claim to any prophecies made hundreds of years before they happened, we find the God of Christianity has a 100 percent perfect track record of fulfilled prophecies to date. God has even gone so far as to issue a challenge to anyone who wishes to contest his record. God offers a challenge in Isaiah 41: 21-24, to any rival who claims they can actually predict the future. The basis for the challenge is only the God of the Bible can successfully predict what will happen in the future. Also, in Isaiah 42:9, it says: "Behold, the former things have come to pass, and new things I now declare; before they spring forth, I tell you of them." Can any other religion match the prophetic accomplishments of Christianity?

Whether you realize it or not, you have just completed an epic journey, scanning centuries of man's history, and his relationship with God. Man's sinful nature has caused him to rebel against God almost from the beginning, and only the Great Resets (Covenants), which God has introduced into the life of man, have kept him from annihilation many years ago. Each of God's Covenants has not only reset a way forward for us, but it has also moved us closer to the ultimate end of the story, as the Bible very clearly lays out.

However, as I stated in the Introduction, man may plan, but God determines the ultimate direction the world is going in. The World Economic Forum, along with the other elitist groups I mentioned, think they can direct the world, but this is only because they do not know God, and the plan he has for each and every one of us, as well as the world itself.

Now you have read the condensed Bible story, and hopefully placed your trust in God for your future, there is no need to be concerned, because faith crowds out fear when you place your faith in the one who is faithful and true and can always be trusted – Jesus Christ. The bottom line is, it's OK if you die broke. It's OK if you don't accomplish your life dreams. However, it is not OK to die in a pile of sin that never gets cleansed by the cross of Jesus. Remember, if you are living an empty life, the answer is simple – look to the empty tomb! The Resurrection of Jesus proves we can be reborn again and have all of our sins expunged from our life's record, thus allowing us to live the life that God wants us to live.

In the final two chapters, I will point out some important facts about what the Bible tells us to believe in, with the hope the more clarity we bring to God's message, the more we can reduce any confusion, misunderstandings, or errors, which many share in their search for life's meaning.

21

GOD'S PLAN TO SAVE US!

> The smart ones ask when they don't know, and
> sometimes even when they do!

Questions for the Ages

CHILDREN NATURALLY WONDER, "WHERE DID I COME FROM?" THEN later, as they become senior adults approaching the end of life, they often ask: "Is this life all there is? Was there a purpose for my life?" For the rest of those living in the middle of life, there is far too much busy activity, earning a living and pursuing goals and ambitions, to think too much of such an abstract subject. Yet, when we think about it, life is full of ups and downs, joys and sorrows, successes, and failures, that should cause us to think beyond the immediate moment of our life. Do any of the many life experiences we undergo, cause us to think about lasting values, directing us towards a meaningful life goal?

Life's unanswered questions have been stirring in man's mind for thousands of years, even going back to King David, who lived some 3,000 years ago. At that time, he contemplated the insignificance of human life when compared to the immensity of the night sky. In Psalm 8:3-4, he postulated: "When I look at your heavens, the work of your fingers, the moon and the stars, which you have set in place, what is man that you are mindful of him?" As a human being, David perceived how paltry man was in the overall cosmos, yet he also perceived God had a plan for all of us that was way beyond our imagination to comprehend. David went on to say: "For you have made him a little lower than the angels, and you have crowned him with glory and honor. You have made him to have dominion over the works of your hands; you have put all things under his feet, all sheep, and oxen – even the beasts of the field, the birds of the air, and the fish of the sea that pass through the paths of the seas." (v5-8). David had already figured out God had granted people the ability to manage a great part of his Creation. David also surmised there was much more to come.

In Hebrews 2:5-8, it says: For it was not to angels God subjected the world to come, of which we are speaking. It has been testified somewhere, "What is man, that you are mindful of him, or the son of man, that you care for him? You have made him a little while lower than the angels; you have crowned him with glory and honor, putting everything in subjection under his feet."

We further find in Deuteronomy, where God gave a proclamation to Moses: "that the sun, the moon, and the stars, all host of heaven . . . the Lord your God has given to all the peoples under the whole heaven as a heritage." (4:19). This is an amazing comment, because it is allowing man to share dominion with God over the creation. This could be the reason why Paul said: "What no eye has seen, nor ear heard, nor the heart of man imagined, what God has prepared for those who love him."

The above passages now make Genesis 1:26, much clearer to understand and grasp: "Let us make man in our own image, according to our likeness; let them have dominion . . ." We now see that only man, out of all the creatures on earth, was made in the image of God, and given the unique ability to rule over creation. Unfortunately, millions of people down through the centuries have failed to understand the amazing future God has in mind for all those that develop a proper relationship with him.

Notice in the above passage mentioned in Hebrews 2:5-8, where **God made man lower than the angels, but just for a little while.** The word *kingdom* is sometimes used to describe certain types of existence. For instance, there are mineral, plant, and animal kingdoms, with the human kingdom over them. Then, above the human kingdom is the spiritual kingdom, where we find the angelic kingdom, and at the very top is the Kingdom of God. So, it appears at the moment we are lower than the angels, but after death, provided we have been reborn into the Spirit of Christ, while still alive in this life, we will be above the angels in the afterlife. (1 Corinthians 6:3). Amazing to believe!

At the Beginning

In order to appreciate and fully understand God's plan for our lives, we must comprehend the beginning, because the basic key to Messianic prophecy begins in the very first book of the Bible, Genesis. It is here where we find the first of God's prophecies being given to none other than Satan himself! This is because Satan, who was created before Adam, was the first to learn about the world's deliverer, who would eventually strip Satan of his power over our world. The prophecy took place in Genesis 3:15, which represents the first of a long chain of prophecies tracing the seed of the woman down through the Bible ages to the final fulfillment of Jesus Christ coming as the Messiah of Israel.

Let's skip for a moment from the first book of the Bible to the last one, Revelation, to read what it says in 12:1-2, 4-5:

"And a great sign appeared in heaven: a woman clothed with the sun, with the moon under her feet, and on her head a crown of twelve stars. She was pregnant and was crying out in birth pains and the agony of giving birth. His tail swept down a third of the stars of Heaven. And the dragon stood before the woman who was about to give birth, so that when she bore her child, he might devour it. She gave birth to a male child, one who is to rule all the nations with a rod of iron, but her child was caught up to God and to his throne, and the woman fled into the wilderness, where she has a place prepared by God, in which she is to be nourished for 1260 days."

In the above passage, as mentioned previously, the woman represents Israel; the dragon is Satan, and the child is Jesus Christ, who is divinely named, Yeshua, which means *salvation, to rescue, to deliver*, in Hebrew. In Matthew 1:21, it says: "She will bear a son, and you shall call his name Jesus, for he will save his people from their sins." And in Isaiah 7:14, we find: "Behold, the virgin shall conceive and bear a son, and they shall call his name Immanuel."

So, Satan clearly saw Adam, the first human being, as a threat to his own power, and thus tried to destroy him. Satan caused rebellion against God by deceiving Adam's wife, Eve, into eating from the tree of the knowledge of good and evil. Adam, as the representative of humanity, followed suit by also eating the forbidden fruit. This one act brought both spiritual and physical death to both himself and all of future mankind. By proxy, Satan then became the ruler of the world (John 12:31). Satan also became "prince of the power of the air" (Ephesians 2:2). Every man, woman and child born since that time, has inherited the original sin of the first man, Adam.

We are all now in a world dominated by Satan, the devil, whom Jesus himself referred to as a "liar and the father of it."

(John 8:44). Our only escape from this life of sin and corruption is through being reborn into the Spirit of Christ. Our whole future hinges on one simple thing – faith! Faith in Jesus as our Lord and Savior is the only realistic way out for all of us.

Getting back to Genesis 3:15, for a moment, we find it is also the first gospel, which is referred to as the *Protoevangelium,* which is God's plan for his creation. God told Satan, "I will put enmity between you and the woman, and between your seed and her seed. He shall bruise your head, and you shall bruise his heel." The word *seed* in Scripture, besides being the usual explanation of physical progeny, can also refer to both moral and spiritual components of people. So, in referring to Satan's seed, it is referring to Satan's kingdom of demonic forces, which include unbelieving, nefarious, black hearted people, who live their lives under the spell of Satan. The Seed of the woman (Israel), however, refers to the Messiah being supernaturally conceived by the virgin. In referring to Satan "bruising the heel," it means Messiah would experience immense pain and torture, resulting in crucifixion. This was all part of God's plan, because Jesus was the "Lamb slain from the foundation of the world," (Rev. 13:8), and who would become the last sacrifice for man's sins.

Scripture tells us three days after the crucifixion, Jesus rose and ascended to Heaven. A bruised heel is painful, but not fatal, and we know the Resurrection of Jesus is real, which gives us the confidence and faith in knowing about our own future. Satan, meanwhile, will eventually be destroyed in the lake of fire. We have victory, because of Jesus, who came to earth to free us from slavery under Satan. Our salvation is to simply follow in the footsteps of Jesus.

God's Plan for our Future

The rebellion of the first man, Adam, had catastrophic consequences for future generations, because one trespass led to the condemnation of all men (Romans 5:18), resulting in our broken fellowship with God. Because of Adam's sin, we all died spiritually (Romans 3:1-20), and "all have sinned and fallen short of the glory of God" (Romans 3:23). Our world has subsequently been subjected to futility, chaos, corruption, immorality, and endless wars, which appear to have reached their zenith of destruction in the 20th century. Millions of people, the majority being Europeans, suddenly found their lives disrupted, resulting in economic chaos, death, and destruction, due to the atheistic ideologies of Communism, Fascism, and Naziism. Interestingly, the men who started World War I and II, were highly educated men, but they were far from God, which meant the other half of their education, the spiritual half, had never been developed, resulting in madness and mayhem for the world.

Sin gets in the way

When we look at the subject of sin and compare our attitudes today against the way people thought about sin in the not-too-distant past, it serves as a litmus test in showing us just how degenerate our society has become with our lax morals and attitudes. People believe if it feels good just do it, and don't worry about consequences. In the past, however, people bore the mark of Cain for life, due to some immoral act. The Scarlet A was placed on the back of someone who had committed adultery, and it was not uncommon to see public stocks, tongue-splitting, cheek branding, and other methods of conveying societies' displeasure with people who committed sin.

Remember, as recently as 1810, there were more than 200 capital crimes on the books in England. Previous societies did not tolerate sin as easily as we do today.

Sin, at least in a biblical context, is anything, including our thoughts, attitudes, and actions, that do not conform to the holiness of God's character as described in his moral law. The elements of sin can be described as follows:

1. Sin can be morally evil as opposed to naturally evil. Murder in the first case, and certainly terminal illnesses in the second. The Bible tells us moral evil is rebellion against God.

2. God is always involved and affected when sin happens, irrespective of its form. None of us can commit sin without God being involved.

3. Sin, of course, can be by omission when we don't do what we should, whereas sin by commission, is committing acts we should not be doing. In either case, we are breaking the law of God.

4. We make good spiritual progress when we come to accept that sin is in the very nature of who we are as human beings. Two quick Bible quotes prove this. "The heart is deceitful above all things, and desperately sick; who can understand it?" (Jeremiah 17:9). In Matthew 15:19, Jesus says: "For out of the heart comes evil thoughts, murder, adultery, sexual immorality, theft, false witness, slander."

5. It seems obvious the inculcated sin nature within us, puts us in the dock of God's judgment, due to the corruption in the hearts of people. Therefore, we are guilty under God's law, due to the pollution of our hearts and minds, leading us to work against God's law, rather than operating our lives within God's law.

This locked-in human depravity gives us no hope of experiencing an eternal life with God. However, there is one escape clause to solve our dilemma. Here is how it works:

Man's redemptive clause

For centuries, God has been able to witness man's inhumanity to man, yet his patience and grace are unending until the final story of mankind finally plays its last chapter, as mentioned previously. The sickness and depravity of the human mind could easily have caused God to prescribe his holy judgment by locking us away to eternal damnation. Thankfully, he did not. What we do find, as we study the Bible, is God enacting a plan to save us humans from slavery to our sin nature. The plan, however, would require a major sacrifice by sending his only begotten Son, Jesus, down into our world to live for a short time as a human. The purpose behind this move was for Jesus to bear the penalty for our sin, by dying on a cross in our place. This horrible act caused Jesus to die for all of our sins in accordance with Scripture (1 Corinthians 15:3).

Unlike the repeatable animal sacrifices mentioned in the Old Testament, which only temporarily satisfied sin, we learn the sacrificial blood of Jesus was a one-time event, designed to cleanse our sins forever, for all those who believe and accept Jesus as their Lord and Savior. Incidentally, the only description we have of Jesus in the Bible, happens to describe, in great detail, the ordeal of great physical torture he was subjected to leading up to his crucifixion, and untimely death. By reading the Bible text, it rams home, in a very personal way, the appalling and gruesome pain and torture, Jesus experienced for both you and for me. You can read it in Isaiah 52:13-53:12.

God's plan to free mankind from the slavery of sin, was due solely to God's mercy. By doing so, God gave us all a wonderful opportunity to be born again, while we are still living. This is done through Jesus, who paid with his own precious life, for our sins. In all the history of mankind, has there ever been a recorded act of sacrificial love that compares with the story of God allowing his only begotten Son to die on a cross in order to save a group of unregenerate sinners? This act reminds us of the New Testament passage, where it says: "For God so loved the world, he gave his only Son, that whoever believes in him should not perish but have everlasting life. For God did not send his Son into the world to condemn the world, but in order that the world might be saved through him." (John 3:16-17). As humans, it is difficult for us to wrap our heads around such a tremendous sacrifice, and act of love.

Man and creation restored

Of particular interest is a quote from Romans 8:21, which says: "the creation itself will be set free from its bondage to corruption and obtain the freedom of the glory of the children of God." We are also informed the heavens and the earth will pass away, and be radically transformed, according to 2 Peter 3:7-13, and Revelation 21:1. Also, in 22:6, it says believers will be brought into the presence of God, resulting in a life as it was originally meant to be. What you have just read indicates that when man was freed at the cross of Jesus, he also restored all of creation!

How should we all respond?

In light of everything we have now learned, what should our response be? What decision should we be making? Do we keep living in sin, without concern for the consequences? Should we act like the proverbial ostrich, who keeps his head in the sand with the hope the problem goes away? Or should we hide behind our ignorance in the hope God thinks we are good enough to be saved? After all, we are much better than those many people behind bars who have committed much more despicable sins than we have, right? We could, of course, take the position of agnostics or atheists, and simply live our lives without ever accepting God. Or, like the growing "nones," we could choose never to read the Bible or attend church, and continue living life without concern for the life after this one ends.

Of all the choices we have, I believe there is only one sensible answer. We must look to God in Christ. This means, with the help of the Holy Spirit, we can learn to control and reject sin in our lives. It is a basic truism that we cannot continue to sin and pursue progress in our relationship with God at the same time. It is important to mention, even after we accept Jesus as the Lord of our life, we are still capable of sinning, because of our inherent sin nature. Even St. Paul tells us we will still face an internal struggle when he says: "For the desires of the flesh are against the Spirit, and the desires of the Spirit are against the flesh, for these are opposed to each other, to keep you from doing the things you want to do." (Galatians 5:17). This is why Paul goes on to say: "Examine yourself to see if you are in the faith. Test yourselves." (2 Corinthians 13:5).

It is important to mention the difference between committing a sin and then asking God for forgiveness, as opposed to those who continually sin without conscience. All Christian's sin, but they are quick to ask God for forgiveness, as well as anyone who has been hurt or offended. That is the crucial difference between a believer and a non-believer.

For the above reasons, we must apply our study of Scripture on a daily basis. This simple exercise helps keep us on a path towards righteousness. We can also focus our attention on the Book of Matthew, chapters five through seven, which provides us good material in understanding how Jesus expects us to live. On a daily basis we can also impress on our minds and hearts the Fruit of the Spirit mentioned in Galatians 5:22. These nine fruits can be of great help to us as we go about interacting with people.

At this point, we must underscore the fact that when we are saved, we do not automatically become sinless. It is the wonderful gift of God's salvation, allowing us not to be sinless, and yet still be saved. For instance, it says in Romans 4:8: "blessed is the man against whom the Lord will not count his sin." Also in chapter 8:1-2, it says: "Therefore there is now no condemnation for those who are in Christ Jesus. For the law of the Spirit of life has set you free in Christ Jesus from the law of sin and death." We have learned, as part of God's plan for us, he has already planned in advance for our sin nature. Therefore, he promises us if we walk with Christ, in his light, then his blood will continue to clean us of our sin. (See 1 John 1:7). Then, when we do commit sin, we simply and sincerely confess our sin to God, and he forgives us (1 John 1:9).

The end result

At the end of Gods' story, beautifully described throughout the Bible, we know God has a plan to save his people from their sin. We can take this to the bank! This promise allows a process whereby we can be brought finally back to God himself (Matthew 1:21; 2 Timothy 2:10).

Gods' salvation plan not only has application for our present life, but also our future life and beyond. It is this plan of salvation that saves us from the penalty of sin. As Christians live out the rest of their lives during the Sanctification process, they are confident in knowing they have been saved, irrespective of what happens in their worldly future. By far, this is the greatest gift ever offered to mankind. It is very much like taking out an insurance policy, without having to pay the premium. It is truly a gift that defies comprehension in its simplicity, yet is rejected by so many. Such is the current state of man as he continues to live a life of ignorance of this gift.

JOURNAL YOUR THOUGHTS

_____

_____

_____

_____

_____

_____

_____

_____

_____

_____

_____

_____

_____

_____

_____

_____

_____

_____

_____

_____

22

THE OUTCOME FOR THE
LOST AND THE SAVED

Passport to a foreign land. Persons entering will not be permitted past the gates without having a current passport and other credentials, and having their names registered with the ruling authority. No exceptions! –(Unknown)

HAVE YOU EVER VISITED A LOST AND FOUND DEPARTMENT, AND experienced immense joy when you find out your child, jewelry, or pet had been found? This same sense of euphoria is experienced when someone finally realizes they have been saved by God to enjoy the next, eternal life with him. Unfortunately, many people today wonder if they are lost or truly saved, and so in this last chapter I will be providing some important wisdom from the Bible, regarding a place called Hell, and a place called Heaven. In this way, you will not only know for sure where you stand in your future, but you will also gain a much clearer understanding of the main differences between being saved and going to Heaven, or being lost and going to Hell. Let's see what the Bible tells us.

Identifying the lost

To start, we must realize the Bible tells us eternal punishment in Hell awaits those who refuse to accept the law of God. Hell is declared by God's reason, and demanded by his justice. Choosing a life of sin is what condemns a person, due to the free-will choices they make, rather than obeying God. The Bible clearly teaches a man reaps what he sows: "Be not deceived; God is not mocked, for whatever a man soweth, that he will also reap." (Galatians 6:7).

What does it mean to be lost?

I can think of at least seven losses, and there are probably more, that a person experiences when they live their life without God:

— A spiritual relationship with God as Father is forever lost (2 Corinthians 6:14-18). If a person is confused or lost in this present life, try to imagine life without any hope for the future. That is painfully much worse.

— There is a loss of spiritual redemption, which can only be provided by Jesus Christ to those who believe and accept him as Lord in their lives (1 Corinthians 1:30; Ephesians 1:7). Imagine going forward without an "escape clause" from this fallen world, which God offers through his Son, Jesus.

— There is also a loss in enjoying a loving relationship with God through Jesus Christ (1 John 1:3-7). By being lost, a person loses the opportunity to have God love and guide them.

— It also means losing the gift of having an eternal home in Heaven (John 14:1-6). Unless you are annihilistic, this is a really big deal, with dire consequences lasting forever.

— The lost don't realize the importance of light replacing darkness until it is too late. They will experience weeping and gnashing of teeth (Matthew 25:30). People take a lot of God's gifts for granted, and they only miss them when they are taken away. Even non-believers enjoy some form of light in this fallen world, and the complete loss of it is unimaginable to most sane people.

— It soon gets very personal when non-believers come to realize they will suffer the loss of never seeing some of their loved ones again (1 Cor. 15:12-27; Titus 2:11-14; Heb. 12:3-11; 1 John 3:2; Phil. 3:17-21). Unless a person has no family or friends, they would never want to lose out on this wonderful gift for the future.

— Scripture tells us we lose the chance of rising above the angels in our next life, and assisting God in the co-managing of creation. Our imaginations cannot comprehend the opportunities this valuable gift provides.

Still, beside all the evidence Scripture presents regarding a place called Hell, there are many who still object to the idea of Hell, and use many reasons and excuses to condemn the subject. Here are just a few of their objections:

1. "I don't believe in Hell."

2. "How could a good and loving God condemn a sinner to an eternity of torment?"

3. "I am too weak to resist sin, so how can a loving God who created me, send me to Hell?"

A 2021 survey by Christianity Today, stated the following: 73% of Americans believe in Heaven and 62% believe in Hell. One in four Americans don't believe in Hell (that's almost 90 million people!) 17% of Americans don't believe in an afterlife, and one in three believe in reincarnation! Although many Americans believe in Hell, only 2% believe they will go there![1]

---

1   Christianitytoday.com/news/2021/November/heaven-hell-survey).

In a separate Harris Poll Survey, it reported only 54% are "absolutely sure" of God's existence; 24% believe in reincarnation; 23% claim not to be religious, 25% don't believe in Hell, 26% don't believe in the devil; 29% believe in astrology, and 26% believe in witches.[2]

Many people today are perplexed by the menu of options available in exploring the meaning of their life, but appear unwilling to do the hard work to obtain the answers. Consequently, they take bumper sticker phrases, and other catchy slogans, to describe their belief system. They use many excuses to hide their ignorance of the Bible and the character of God. They take the lazy man approach by spending less time learning about Heaven and Hell than they do planning their next two-week vacation. Yet, their next trip could easily be a permanent trip to paradise, or a disastrous place of eternal torment. Why do people pay such little attention to such a serious matter? King Solomon once said, "There is a way that seems right to a man, but its end is the way of death." (Proverb 14:12). Why would anyone, with only very limited knowledge, try to second guess God who knows everything?

This whole issue of Hell can easily be put to rest with a little digging into the Bible to see what God says about this subject. It was none other than Jesus Christ himself who spoke and taught about Hell.

> One theologian referred to Jesus Christ as the theologian
> from Hell, because he knew more about Hell than
> anyone else! If Jesus believed in Hell, so should we!

There are some 264 warnings in the New Testament regarding Hell and judgment, and 70 are by Jesus Christ himself! Jesus did not come to us joyful and happy, because he was a man of sor-

---

2   Insider.com – Megan Willet-Wei. 12.17.13 (based on a Harris Poll Survey).

rows. He came to earth with a mission to warn us of the terrible end we will face if we do not repent, and do penance for our sins. Jesus was more or less telling his children they could do anything they wanted to, as long as they avoided Hell.

Some people are saddened and confused by the fact many moral evils pass by unrestricted in this life. Many injustices are not rectified here on earth, and many wrongs never get righted. If you are a person, for instance, who is the recipient of an unaddressed evil, you always know in the back of your mind, there is a divine equity that will one day balance the scales and make all things right, because God reserves revenge for himself. He says, "Vengeance is mine, and recompense for the time when their foot shall slip; for the day of their calamity is at hand, and their doom comes swiftly." (Deuteronomy 32:35).

To have doubts about Hell is to also doubt the infallible word of God; it gives an ear to the speeches of ignorant and uninformed men, rather than the sacred teachings of the church. Our life on this earth rests on faith, and it is not until our souls leave our bodies, that we are able to see with crystal clarity, that God is the only true satisfaction for our hearts. If we knew all the answers while we live, there would be no need for faith. Such is the system under which man lives. Faith in our Lord Jesus Christ is imperative to experiencing an eternal life, and when he states that Hell is a real place, we need to believe it!

Belief in Hell is good for society!

An interesting report was released some time ago, making the case that belief in Hell actually increased economic growth. What economists discovered was nations whose people had a strong belief in Hell, and fear of its consequences, actually proved to be more prosperous, and less corrupt, than nations where belief in Hell was less important. This appears to demonstrate respecting the precepts of the Bible is a good thing for society in general.[3]

Beyond comprehension and logic, the issue of going to Hell is a spiritual one as well, which is what makes a lot of people defensive when discussing the subject. Many people have come to realize Satan is not only the enemy of God, but he is also the enemy of man. He will do anything to confuse and complicate an issue.

If a person is not in the family of God, he is by default in the family of Satan!

Deuteronomy 28:66 sums up such a life quite well, "Your life shall hang in doubt before you. Night and day you shall be in dread and have no assurance of your life." However, if you are a child of God, you will find the Bible full of promises for those who are part of God's family. (Deuteronomy 25:15; 1 Kings 3:14; Proverbs 3:2; 16; 4:10; 7:1-2; 9:11; 10:27; 14:27; 19:23; 28:16; Ephesians 6:3). **Each of these Bible passages provides gifts of a full and long life for those who believe in Jesus**. This approach is far superior than any physical exercise, or good nutritional diet to extend our life, because God is promising long life just for accepting, and being faithful to Jesus Christ. This is another free gift given to believers, just for allowing Jesus to be master of their lives.

Identifying the saved

The word *saved*, unlike the word *lost*, conjures up something positive of value or sentiment that we have found or gained. From a biblical point of view, we are referring to a man's very soul. Based on the law of proportionality, we find God using the word *saved* more than 200 times in the Bible, and more than 80 times

---

3   MSNBC.com – 7.27.2004 – Federal Reserve Bank of St. Louis Survey.

in the New Testament alone. This fact should alert the reader to the seriousness God places on this simple word, for it makes the difference between ultimate life with God, or destruction in the darkness of the lake of fire. Here are three Scripture passages out of many, expressing how we can be saved:

— In Acts 16:30-31, it says: "Then he brought them out and said, "Sirs, what must I do to be saved?" And they said, "Believe in the Lord Jesus, and you will be saved, you and your household."

— Romans 10:9-10 says, "because, if you confess with your mouth that Jesus is Lord and believe in your heart that God raised him from the dead, you will be saved. For with the heart, one believes and is justified, and with the mouth one confesses and is saved."

— Ephesians 2:8-9 says: "For by grace you have been saved through faith. And this is not your own doing; it is the gift of God, not as a result of works, so that no one may boast."

In 1912 the *Titanic* left Liverpool, England, for New York. It was touted as being unsinkable, but it did, and some 1500 people lost their lives. Later, in Liverpool, two very large signs were posted outside the shipping line, which read: *Known to be Lost,* and the other said, *Known to be Saved!* Whatever you do, don't let your life sink like the *Titanic.* Grab your life-belt right now to ensure you get to the safe shore of Heaven! It is also worth mentioning, besides the many times the word *saved* is mentioned in the Bible, you will find God also expressing himself with other words describing the same thing, such as: *Purified, Redeemed, Sanctified.*

So, what does it mean to be saved?

Many people are concerned with this very important question, and to address the answer I will provide a number of blessings and benefits to be gained when a person becomes a believer in Jesus Christ, which should also fortify your own position in Christ, as to whether you feel saved or not. In Ephesians 1:3, it says: "Blessed be the God and Father of our Lord Jesus Christ, who **has blessed us in Christ with every spiritual blessing in the heavenly places...**"

Here then are ten blessings and eternal benefits you receive once you have accepted Christ:

— By being saved, it means we have a loving relationship with God the Father and Creator. It is important to place this blessing first in the order, mainly because without such a relationship we cannot be saved. We know being saved only happens with the love and grace of God. It is important to point out, however, we cannot be saved by love alone, and we cannot be saved by grace alone, mainly because the Bible does not teach these ideas. The Bible very clearly says we must believe and obey the gospel in order to be saved (Mark 16:15-16; Hebrews 5:8-9). The formula is quite simple.

— When saved, all our sins are forgiven by God. Let us pause on this statement for a moment in order to ensure it fully sinks in. Our sins are washed away; our conscience is cleared, and our accumulated sins have been wiped clean. When the word *forgiveness* is spoken with a contrite, sincere heart, it can bring us immense joy, and a feeling of relief, a feeling of comfort. It makes us more acutely aware we no longer have the burden of suffering God's wrath, at the time God stands in judgment of all those who are not forgiven (Hebrews 10:26-27). All Christians understand the principle of forgiving. We know God forgave us first, even when we were in a sin state and did not deserve it. Therefore, for us not to forgive others goes against what God expects of us.

— Being a member of a Christian church means we are saved, if we have placed our complete faith and trust in Jesus. This is based on the fact the church is part of God's plan, which provides a fulfillment of God's purpose centering around our faith in Jesus Christ (Ephesians 1:1-10, 3:1-11). The church, when you think about it more deeply, represents the reality of the prophecy focusing on Jesus. On earth, the church is the body of Christ (Colossians 1:18, Ephesians 1:22-23). Because Jesus is the Savior of the body, (Ephesians 5:23), it means he is the Savior of the church. We know, according to Acts 20:28, Jesus purchased and founded the church with his own blood, which should cause all Christians to look at the church somewhat differently than we have in the past. Remember what Jesus said in Matthew 16:18: "And I tell you, you are Peter, and on this rock, I will build my church, and the gates of hell shall not prevail against it." We are also told the people who make up the church are those whom the Lord has added. (Acts 2:47). Remember, though, that the Lord only adds those who have been saved.

— By being saved we automatically become a child of God, and it is described beautifully by Paul when he said: "For you are the children of God by faith in Christ Jesus. For as many of you who have been baptized into Christ have put on Christ." (Galatians 3:26-27). Another great passage presses home this important relationship: "See what kind of love the Father has given to us, that we should be called children of God; and so, we are. The reason why the world does not know us is that it did not know him." (1 John 3:1).

— Another important point about being saved is the fact we not only have peace in our relationship with God, we also experience greater peace while we continue to live in this world. This is due to an inner peace we develop, which surpasses our understanding. Sure, we can't necessarily experience peace with everyone, but nonetheless, as Jesus mentioned in Matthew 5:9, we should always make every attempt to be a peacemaker, thus enabling us to be called the sons of God. Paul followed up Jesus' comment by saying: "If possible, so far as it depends on you, live peacefully with all." (Romans 12:18).

— Being saved offers us a new life of holiness. We find, for instance, where it says in 1 Thessalonians 4:7: "For God has not called us for impurity, but in holiness." It is important to remember in accepting this duty, we accept certain responsibilities, which include living our lives as holy as possible, even though we are still living in our sinful body.

— Spiritually, when we are saved, we obtain security in knowing our sins have been erased from our record. This assures us our salvation is secure and complete because Christ lives within us. We are now assured God's blessings are not going to be taken away from us (John 10:27-29).

— With the gift of being saved comes our responsibility in teaching others the gospel message to lost and confused souls. All Christians have an obligation to play out their role in honoring the Great Commission mentioned in Matthew 28:19. We don't have to look very far to see sin all around us. These lost souls are doomed unless Christians get Christ's message of hope and salvation to them. Simply put, it is up to the saved to save the unsaved! The Apostle Paul stated it this way:

"How then will they call on him in whom they have not believed? And how are they to believe in him of whom they have never heard? And how are they to hear without someone preaching? And how are they to preach unless they are sent?" As it is written, "How beautiful are the feet of those who preach the good news." (Romans 10:14-15).

— When we follow Jesus, we find him making many promises to us. In 1 Corinthians 10:13, for instance, it says: "No temptation has overtaken you that is not common to man. God is faithful, and he will not let you be tempted beyond your ability, but with the temptation he will also provide the way of escape, that you may be able to endure it." Living in this world of iniquity and sin, where we are constantly exposed to corruption, theft, and immorality, it is very reassuring to realize we have the power of God on our side, who carries us through any temptations or challenges that arise.

— Finally, the greatest gift of all, which is given to all who are saved, is having the advanced knowledge of knowing we will be home in Heaven one day and live out our eternal lives with God. Once again, when we pause on this fact for a moment, it should cause us all to realize this wonderful gift is well worth sacrificing for in the remainder of the short lives we have left here on earth.

The final answers to our needs

In seeking and searching for life's meaning, modern man has many options at his disposal. They include everything from choosing any one of the other major religions besides Christianity, or the pursuit of any number of cults and isms that are available. I have had the blessing of visiting more than 100 countries on six of the seven continents, and being exposed to many people groups, their religions, and their cultures. I have taken the time to study these other religions, and made a genuine attempt to understand them. In the end, however, none of them provide the inner peace found when studying the Bible, and becoming a follower of Jesus. I must further confess, the Bible is no ordinary book, such as the latest best-selling novel. As I said at the beginning, many have read, or attempted to read the Bible, but never grasped the wisdom it provides. This happens because they did not prepare their mind for what God is trying to teach them. Here then, are some qualities we need to address in order to pull out of the Bible the rich-nuggets of knowledge and wisdom, that will help us grow in faith, which is the linchpin upon which Christianity stands. We need to be all in for Jesus as our Lord and Savior:

1.   We need a new heart (1 Corinthians 2:14). We must be born again in the Spirit, and this book has taught you what to do.

2.   We must have a hungry heart (1 Peter 2:2). Bible knowledge does not come from casual interest or occasional reading. We must study in order to unearth the wisdom it provides.

3.   We must have an obedient heart (Psalms 119: 98-100). We must be willing to obey what God shows us of his will.

4.   We must have a disciplined heart (Matthew 7:7). Once we start, we must keep on going until we discover the truth.

5.   We must have a teachable heart (Isaiah 50:4). This heart wants to learn and keep on learning. A teachable heart wants to learn from others. The more we learn, the more fulfilled we feel inside.

These five spiritual qualities are important if we really want to understand the Bible, which helps us to know God and his ways more intimately. The more we nurture them, the more we can grow and learn. If we want these spiritual qualities, however, we must ask God for them. We should always pray before we study the Bible, asking God to open up our minds and hearts to what he wants to teach us. Also, if we study the Bible with a seeking, prayerful attitude, we will be where God can teach us, which he surely will.

JOURNAL YOUR THOUGHTS

_____

_____

_____

_____

_____

_____

_____

_____

_____

_____

_____

_____

_____

_____

_____

_____

_____

_____

_____

POSTSCRIPT

CONGRATULATIONS! YOU HAVE JUST SPENT LESS THAN 12 HOURS OF your precious time reading this book, and I strongly recommend you study it carefully a second time for retention purposes. My prayer is that you gained valuable insights about God, yourself, the world in which you live, and the afterlife awaiting you. This book has provided multiple Bible passages, with explanations, that will save you many hours of independent research as you continue your spiritual development, which is ongoing for all of us.

Hopefully, you now have a better understanding of the spiritual rules that are all around us, but invisible to the naked eye. Nonetheless, these spiritual rules are even more important than the worldly rules you live by, when you consider the long-term consequences of disobeying them.

Finishing this book tells me you are serious about your relationship with God, and you have a thirst to know more about God's ways. Therefore, your next step is to start reading and studying the Bible for yourself, with help from the "roadmap" provided in this book, which should act as a tool in accelerating your learning curve. A lot of "heavy lifting" has been accomplished in this book, which should make it easier for you to grasp God's principles in the Bible itself, and help you to "connect the dots" more easily.

The Bible, as you have now learned, is inspired by God, and is the only book available that he has exclusively authored. Therefore, it is the obvious place to begin your quest for real meaning in your life. Remember, we are all ignorant, only on different things. God knows all the answers, and no matter how many earthly life-times we live, we will never learn enough until we turn our life over to God.

Living for a short time on planet earth can be a scary place considering life can be taken from us at any moment in any number of ways. We are here one moment and suddenly gone the next, unless we suffer a protracted fatal illness, which may delay the inevitable for a while. As previously mentioned, we are constantly being threatened with the possibility of chemical warfare. biological warfare, and an ever-growing world population that is outstripping our resources, and our ability to keep up with the food, medicine and shelter needed to exist. We are already witnessing certain parts of the world where hundreds of millions of our fellow human beings are on the edge of starvation. This state of affairs can easily lead to various diseases, epidemics, and environmental pollution. Superimposed over all these issues is the threat of terrorism; some 30 plus military conflicts being played out across the globe, to say nothing of a number of countries with nuclear bomb capability in the hands of people who are known enemies to us, and also enemies of other nuclear club members.

The granddaddy of all world problems, of course, besides our inherent sin nature, is the issue I raised earlier, whereby a group of very powerful men and women are intent on implementing an agenda to change our known world forever. They wish to replace our financial and economic systems, and they are clearly anti-religious. They are godless people who think they know more than our Creator God, but they are mistaken. They want to plan and supervise a Great Reset, and are willing to see millions of people suffer as a consequence. These self-centered individuals think they know more than God does, but they are deluded. Almighty God is the only one to set Great Resets, as he has done in the past, and will no doubt do so again in the future. The future is going to be enacted according to God's plan, and God's timing, not the timing of the New World Order crowd, or anyone else!

If we can all learn to take our eyes and our minds off the problems of this world for a moment, and concentrate on praying and doing everything we can to please God, then we have the very best chance of regaining lost ground in our struggle against these demonic forces. But here again, we need to realize if we pray for God's guidance, and it doesn't happen (due to his timing and not ours), then we still win as believers, because we go to a better place. If our prayers are answered, then we can look forward to more peace in this present existence, until our time comes to leave earth. So, when we think deeply about this issue, it's a win-win situation. In either case, the believers in Christ win. So, if you have not already done so, accept Christ now, so your heart will not be troubled, you will not have to worry, and you won't be anxious about anything, which is what the Bible teaches us.

Living in this visible world, and operating with our five senses, we find truth is what people say it is, and often act on their emotions. Many believe happiness is the highest good, often by the gain of wealth and fame. However, in the invisible world, we find truth is what God says it is, and our emotions are not reliable. Yes, God does want us to be happy, but most importantly, he wants us to be holy!

In conclusion, I think it important to realize there is an order to living our life with a purpose, which means accepting the fact our God is good, and he does have a desire for our happiness, and to make us holy in order to enter the next world, Heaven, where no sin is allowed. Therefore, we need to dedicate ourselves to an eternal perspective, for it is only then we begin to gain insight into our true, eternal purpose. Ultimately, this means we must be willing to suffer the loss of our temporary desires, in order to gain eternal values. Believers are aware of one very important thing about life, however. All Christians are in a sense immortal until God has finished the good work he has planned for them, which is eternal. So, if there is ever an incentive to continue with Gods' work, you now have it!

> If you have learned anything from reading this book, the concept of developing an eternal perspective, instead of a worldly one, is one of the greatest lessons for all of us to master while still in our mortal existence.

EXHIBIT "A" (Map of Old Testament Times)

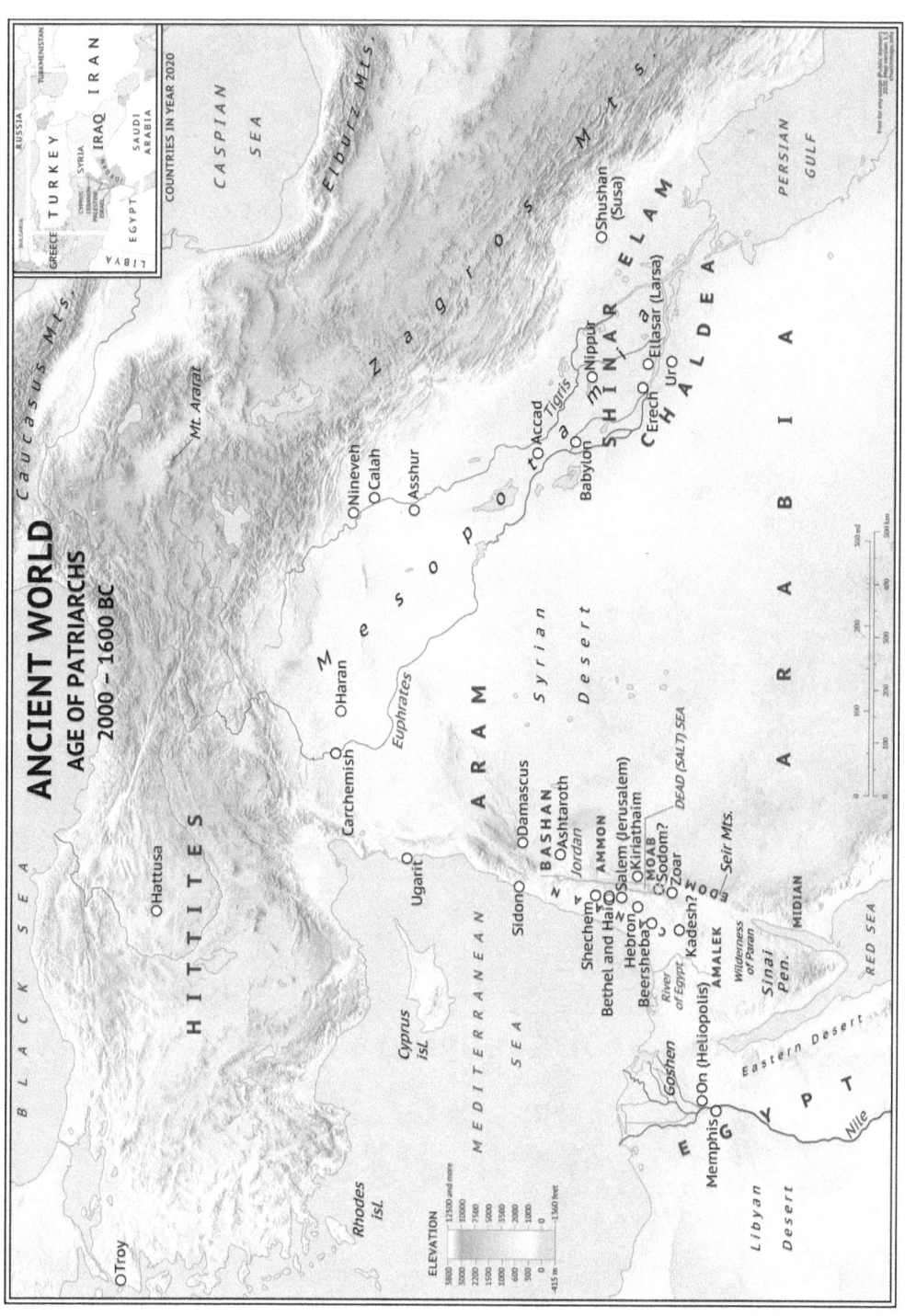

ANCIENT WORLD
AGE OF PATRIARCHS
2000 ~ 1600 BC

EXHIBIT "B" (PAUL'S MISSIONARY JOURNEYS)

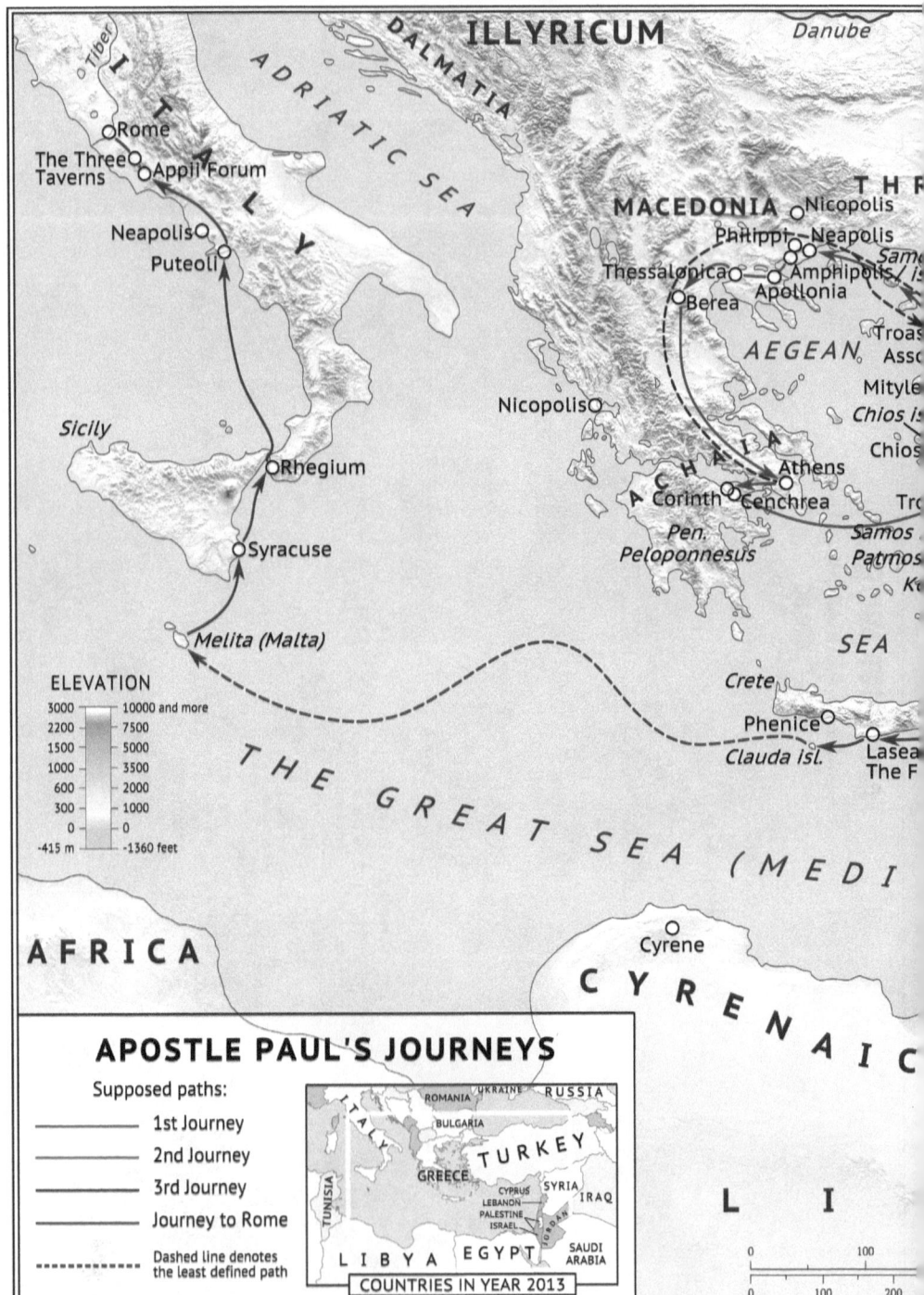

APOSTLE PAUL'S JOURNEYS

Supposed paths:

————	1st Journey
————	2nd Journey
————	3rd Journey
————	Journey to Rome
- - - - - - - -	Dashed line denotes the least defined path

COUNTRIES IN YEAR 2013

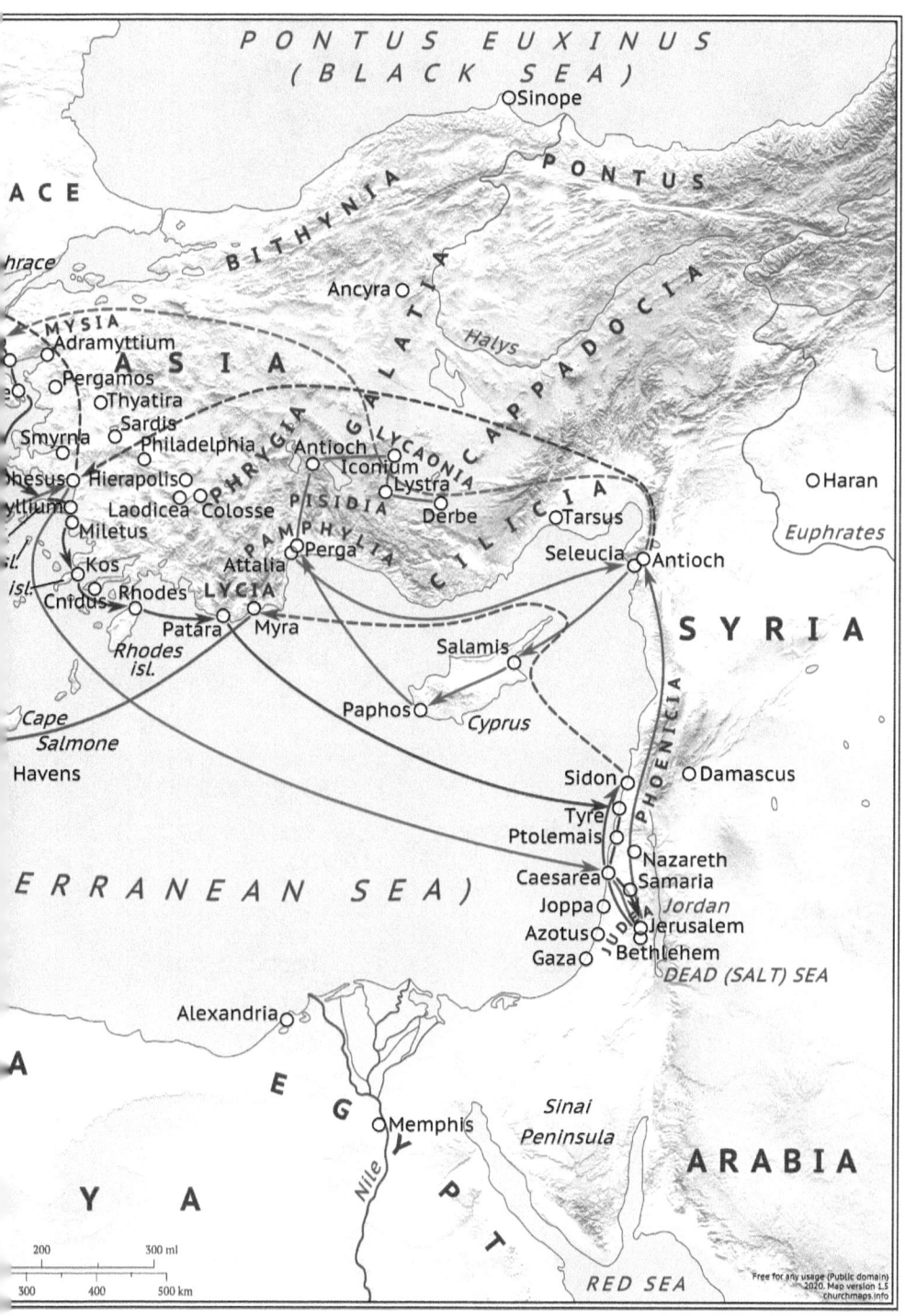

EXHIBIT "C" (BOOKS OF THE BIBLE)

Old Testament Books:

THE PENTATEUCH

Genesis	Leviticus	Deuteronomy
Exodus	Numbers	

HISTORICAL BOOKS

Joshua	2 Samuel	2 Chronicles
Judges	1 Kings	Ezra
Ruth	2 Kings	Nehemiah
1 Samuel	1 Chronicles	Esther

POETIC AND WISDOM LITERATURE

Job	Proverbs	Song of Solomon
Psalms	Ecclesiastes	

THE PROPHETIC BOOKS

Isaiah	Amos	Haggai
Jeremiah	Obadiah	Zacharia
Lamentations	Jonah	Malachi
Ezekiel	Micah	
Daniel	Nahum	
Hosea	Habakkuk	
Joel	Zephaniah	

New Testament Books:

THE GOSPELS AND ACTS:

Matthew	Luke	Acts
Mark	John	

THE EPISTLES (LETTERS): PAULINE

Romans	Philippians	2 Timothy
1 Corinthians	Colossians	Titus
2 Corinthians	1 Thessalonians	Philemon
Galatians	2 Thessalonians	
Ephesians	1 Timothy	

GENERAL LETTERS:

Hebrews James	1 John	Jude
1 Peter	2 John	Revelation
2 Peter	3 John	

EXHIBIT "D" (ANSWERS TO LIFE'S CHALLENGES)

(50) Biblical Answers to some of Life's Challenges

ABORTION: Psalm 139:13-16

ABUSE: Mark 9:42; 1 Cor. 7:2,3

ADDICTION: James 1:13-15; Prov. 14:12

ADVERSITY: Phil. 4:6, 7; 1 Peter 1:6, 7

ADULTERY: Matthew 5:27; 28, 31, 32

AFRAID: 2 Tim. 1:7; Psalm 34:4; 56:3

ANGER: Romans 12:17, 18, 21; Eph. 4:26; Prov. 15:1; 19:11

ANXIETY: Matthew 6:25; 31, 33

BEREAVEMENT: Luke 6:21b; 1 Cor. 15:20-23; 1 Thess. 4:13-18; James 5:13-16

BITTERNESS: Col. 3:19; Hebrews 12:14, 15

CRITICAL: Matthew 6: 14, 15; Rom 14:10, 13

DEATH: 1 Thess. 4:13, 14; Rev. 21:4

DEPRESSION: Psalms 3:3-5; 30:5; 40:1, 2; 42:11; 147:3

DISHONESTY: Matthew 7:2

DOUBT: Matthew 21:21; James 1:6

DRUNKENNESS: Rom. 13:13; 1 Cor. 5:11; Eph. 5:18

DISASTER: Psalm 55:16, 17, 22; 91:1, 2; 118:5, 6

DISCOURAGED: 2 Cor. 4:8, 16; Phil. 4:6, 7; Psalm 23:1, 4

FEAR: 2 Tim. 1:7; Psalm 31:24; 91:10; 121:1, 2

FORGIVENESS: John 3:16; 1 John 1:9

FRIENDS FAIL: Luke 17:3, 4; 2 Tim. 4:16-18; Prov. 18:24

FUTURE: Matthew 6:25, 33, 34; James 4:13-15

GOSSIP: Matt.12:36; Eph. 4:29; James 3:1, 2; Ps. 19:14, 101:5, 141:3, Prov. 20:19

GREED: Matt. 6:19-21; Luke 12:15, 34; 1 Tim. 6:10; Prov. 11:24, 25, 15:27, 23:4

GUILT: Hebrews 10:17; Psalm 32:5; Prov. 28:13

GAMBLING: Matt. 6:29, 30; 1 Tim. 6:10; Heb. 13:5

HOPELESSNESS: Hebrews 10:23

INSECURITY: John 10:27, 28

LAZINESS: 2 Thess. 3:10-13; Prov. 6:6-11; 13:4

LONELINESS: Psalm 23, 27:1, 143:8; Heb. 13:5; 1 Peter 5:7

PEACE: John 14:1-4; 14:27, 16:33; Rom. 5:1-5; Phil. 4:6, 7

PEER PRESSURE: 1 Cor. 15:33; Psalm 1:1, 2; Prov. 1:10-15

QUESTIONING GOD: John 1:1-4; John 14:6; Col. 1:15-17

RELATIONSHIPS: 1 Cor. 15:33; Prov. 13:20, 17:17, 18:24

REVENGE: Matthew 5:44; 1 Thess. 5:15

SELF-RIGHTEOUSNESS: Luke 18:11, 12

SEX: Matthew 5:27, 28; Rom. 1:26, 27; 1 Cor. 6:18-20; 2 Tim. 2:22

Sickness/Pain: 2 Cor. 12:9, 10; James 5:14, 15

Sin: John 8:34, 36; Rom. 3:23

Sorrow (Grief): 2 Cor. 1:3, 4; Psalm 23, 34:18, 147:3

Stealing: Eph. 4:28; 1 Peter 4:15; Prov. 29:24

Stress: Matthew 11:28; Phil 4:11-13; Psalms 9:9, 27:5, 34:4, 37:7, 8, 56:3

Suicide: Psalm 143:7-11

Swearing: Eph. 4:29; Col. 3:8

Temptation: Matt. 26:41; 1 Cor. 10:13; James 4:7; 2 Peter 2:9; Psalm 119:11

Trouble: Psalm 20:1, 2; 23; 71:1, 2

War: Phil. 4:6, 7; Psalm 37:3-7

Weary: Matt. 11:28-30; Galatians 6:9

Wisdom: Psalm 111:10; Prov. 1:5, 2:6, 7, 15:22

Worried: Matt. 6:19-34; 1 Peter 5:6, 7

OTHER BOOKS BY AUTHOR
ALAN W. HAYDEN

Your Last Chance to get it Right
(A Journey from Darkness into Light)

BORN IN ENGLAND DURING WORLD WAR II, THE AUTHOR GREW UP WITHOUT knowing God, and learned first-hand a life of ignorance and darkness in not knowing God's Word. After serving in British Special Forces in the Middle East, the author has since traveled to more than 100 countries, where his experiences exposed him to people in their indigenous environment of poverty and squalor. He witnessed idol worship, talismans, and amulets to ward off enemy spirits, and people constantly living in fear. The degradation and hopelessness of so many people living with only darkness in their lives, not just in the darkest corners of our planet, but also in educated Europe, all helped the author towards the light of Jesus Christ, as the only true way forward. Non-believers still have a chance to get it right with God, but they need to do it before this life ends, as it surely will one day.

Managing Your Money Spiritually
(Secrets of the Ages Revealed)

GOD PROVIDES MUCH WISDOM IN HOW TO MANAGE OUR PERSONAL MONEY responsibilities. He mentions the importance of this subject more than 2300 times in the Bible, which is a good indicator of the special importance he places on this issue, due to the great harm that debt can cause us. Unfortunately, millions of families are not following God's advice, and it is wrecking their marriages, and their future. There are solutions to this dilemma, however, which the author demonstrates in this book. He provides valuable and practical guidance into how to use certain investments to grow your wealth, as well as methods for getting out of debt, and creating a budget that works. All this while working towards a dignified retirement.

The Mystery of the Jews
(Exposing the Truth to the World)

JEWS MAKE UP ABOUT ONE-FIFTH OF ONE-PERCENT OF THE WORLD'S POPULA-tion, yet their contributions to the advancement of mankind is nothing short of amazing. Yet, notwithstanding their achievements, that we all have benefited from, they continue to be the most vilified and hated people on the planet! The voting record of the United Nations, the European Union, and the Arab League, have consistently voted against the State of Israel. Even mainstream American churches are part of the BDS (Boycott, Divestment and Sanctions) movement, who refuse to transact any business with the State of Israel. The mystery of the Jews, and why they have been so maligned and persecuted over the centuries, makes for a fascinating story. So, if you want to learn more about the Jews, realizing Jesus was a Jew, his apostles were Jews, all the Old Testament writers were Jews, and all the New Testament writers were Jews, with the exception of Luke, you now have a book that covers all the controversies and accomplishments of the Jewish population.

For prayers and free counseling, contact:
AlanHayden007@Yahoo.com